Mediterranean Spain

Costas del Sol & Blanca

RCC PILOTAGE FOUNDATION

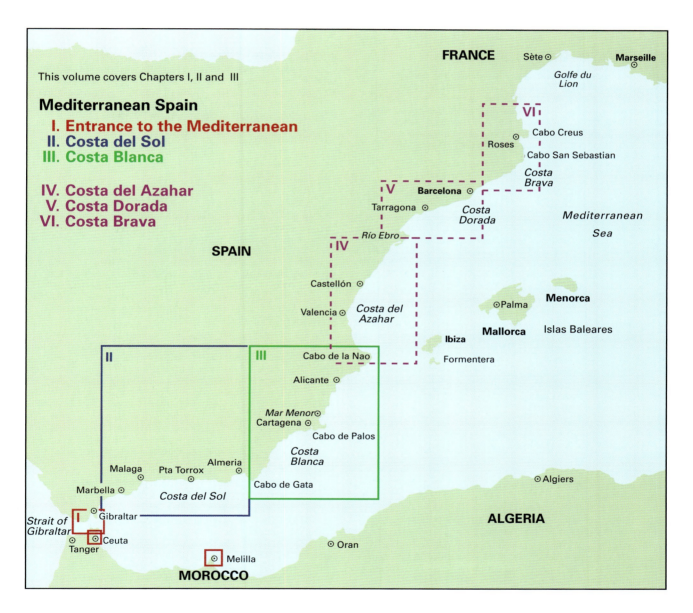

This volume covers Chapters I, II and III

Mediterranean Spain
I. Entrance to the Mediterranean
II. Costa del Sol
III. Costa Blanca

IV. Costa del Azahar
V. Costa Dorada
VI. Costa Brava

FRANCE — Sète ⊙ — **Marseille** ⊙

Golfe du Lion

VI

⊙ Cabo Creus

Roses | — Cabo San Sebastian

Costa Brava

V — **Barcelona** ⊙

Tarragona ⊙ — *Costa Dorada*

Río Ebro — IV

SPAIN

Castellón ⊙

Valencia ⊙ — *Costa del Azahar*

Cabo de la Nao

Alicante ⊙

Mar Menor ⊙
Cartagena ⊙

Cabo de Palos

Costa Blanca

Cabo de Gata

Malaga ⊙ — Pta Torrox — Almeria ⊙

Marbella ⊙ — *Costa del Sol*

I — ⊙ Gibraltar

Strait of Gibraltar — ⊙ Ceuta

Tanger ⊙

⊙ Melilla

MOROCCO

Mediterranean Sea

⊙ Palma — **Menorca**

Ibiza — **Mallorca** — Islas Baleares

Formentera

⊙ Algiers

ALGERIA

⊙ Oran

Imray Laurie Norie & Wilson

Published by
Imray Laurie Norie & Wilson Ltd
Wych House The Broadway
St Ives Cambridgeshire PE27 5BT England
www.imray.com
2009

1st edition 1989
2nd edition 1995
3rd edition 1998
4th edition 2001
5th edition 2005
6th edition 2009

ISBN 978 184623 183 4

British Library Cataloguing in Publication Data.
A catalogue record for this title is available from the British
Library.

This work, based on surveys over a period of many years, has
been corrected to July 2008 from land-based visits to the ports
and harbours of the coast, from contributions by visiting
yachtsmen and from official notices. The majority of the aerial
photographs were taken during September 2004.

Printed in Singapore by Star Standard Industries Pte

CORRECTIONAL SUPPLEMENTS

This pilot book may be amended at intervals by the issue of
correctional supplements. These are published on the internet
at our web site www.imray.com (and also via www.rccpf.org.uk)
and may be downloaded free of charge. Printed copies are also
available on request from the publishers at the above address.
Like this pilot, supplements are selective. Navigators requiring
the latest definitive information are advised to refer to official
hydrographic office data.

ADDITIONAL INFORMATION

Additional information may be found under the Publications
page at www.rccpf.org.uk. This includes a downloadable
waypoint list, links to Google maps, additional photographs and
mid season updates when appropriate. Passage planning
information may also be found on that website.

CAUTION

Whilst the RCC Pilotage Foundation, the author and the publishers
have used reasonable endeavours to ensure the accuracy of the
content of this book, it contains selected information and thus is not
definitive. It does not contain all known information on the subject in
hand and should not be relied on alone for navigational use: it should
only be used in conjunction with official hydrographic data. This is
particularly relevant to the plans, which should not be used for
navigation.

The RCC Pilotage Foundation, the author and the publishers believe
that the information which they have included is a useful aid to prudent
navigation, but the safety of a vessel depends ultimately on the
judgment of the skipper, who should assess all information, published
or unpublished.

The information provided in this pilot book may be out of date and
may be changed or updated without notice. The RCC Pilotage
Foundation cannot accept arty liability for arty error, omission or
failure to update such information.

To the extent permitted by law, the RCC Pilotage Foundation, the
author(s) and the publishers do not accept liability for any loss and/or
damage howsoever caused that may arise from reliance on information
contained in these pages.

POSITIONS

All positions in the text have been derived from C-Map electronic
charts at WGS 84 datum.

Positions given in the text and on plans are intended purely as an aid
to locating the place in question on the chart. A WGS 84 position
check was carried out at each harbour in 2007.

Over the past few years the Spanish Authorities have been updating
their charts/documents to WGS 84 datum although many charts in
current use will be to European 1950 datum or other. The differences
are usually only ±0´.1 (that is 200 yards or 180 metres) but, as
always, care must be exercised to work to the datum of the chart in
use.

WAYPOINTS

This edition of the Mediterranean Spain pilot includes the
introduction of waypoints. The RCC Pilotage Foundation consider a
waypoint to be a position likely to be helpful for navigation if entered
into some form of electronic navigation system for use in
conjunction with GPS. In this pilot they have been derived from
electronic charts. They must be used with caution. All waypoints
are given to datum WGS 84 and every effort has been made to
ensure their accuracy. Nevertheless, for each individual vessel, the
standard of onboard equipment, aerial position, datum setting,
correct entry of data and operator skill all play a part in their
effectiveness. In particular it is vital for the navigator to note the
datum of the chart in use and apply the necessary correction if
plotting a GPS position on the chart.

Our use of the term 'waypoint' does not imply that all vessels can
safely sail directly over those positions at all times. Some – as in
this pilot – may be linked to form recommended routes under
appropriate conditions. However, skippers should be aware of the
risk of collision with another vessel, which is plying the exact
reciprocal course. Verification by observation, or use of radar to
check the accuracy of a waypoint, may sometimes be advisable
and reassuring.

We emphasise that we regard waypoints as an aid to navigation
for use as the navigator or skipper decides. We hope that the
waypoints in this pilot will help ease that navigational load.

PLANS

The plans in this guide are not to be used for navigation – they are
designed to support the text and should always be used together
with navigational charts.

It should be borne in mind that the characteristics of lights may be
changed during the life of the book, and that in any case
notification of such changes is unlikely to be reported
immediately. Each light is identified in both the text and where
possible on the plans (where it appears in magenta) by its
international index number, as used in the *Admiralty List of
Lights*, from which the book may be updated.

All bearings are given from seaward and refer to true north.
Symbols are based on those used by the British Admiralty – users
are referred to *Symbols and Abbreviations (NP 5011)*.

Contents

THE RCC PILOTAGE FOUNDATION

In 1976 an American member of the Royal Cruising Club, Dr Fred Ellis, indicated that he wished to make a gift to the Club in memory of his father, the late Robert E Ellis, of his friends Peter Pye and John Ives and as a mark of esteem for Roger Pinckney. An independent charity known as the RCC Pilotage Foundation was formed and Dr Ellis added his house to his already generous gift of money to form the Foundation's permanent endowment. The Foundation's charitable objective is 'to advance the education of the public in the science and practice of navigation', which is at present achieved through the writing and updating of pilot books covering many diffent parts of the world.

The Foundation is extremely grateful and privileged to have been given the copyrights to books written by a number of distinguished authors and yachtsmen including the late Adlard Coles, Robin Brandon and Malcolm Robson. In return the Foundation has willingly accepted the task of keeping the original books up to date and many yachtsmen and women have helped (and are helping) the Foundation fulfil this commitment. In addition to the titles donated to the Foundation, several new books have been created and developed under the auspices of the Foundation. The Foundation works in close collaboration with three publishers – Imray Laurie Norie and Wilson, Adlard Coles Nautical and On Board Publications – and in addition publishes in its own name short run guides and pilot books for areas where limited demand does not justify large print runs. Several of the Foundation's books have been translated into French, German and Italian.

The Foundation runs its own website at www.rccpf.org.uk which not only lists all the publications, and provides additional information to support the Pilot books, but also contains free downloadable web pilots and Passage Planning Guides.

The overall management of the Foundation is entrusted to trustees appointed by the Royal Cruising Club, with day-to-day operations being controlled by the Director. These appointments are unpaid. In line with its charitable status, the Foundation distributes no profits; any surpluses are used to finance new books and developments and to subsidise those covering areas of low demand.

PUBLICATIONS OF THE RCC PILOTAGE FOUNDATION

Imray
Norway
Faroe, Iceland and
 Greenland
Norway
The Baltic Sea
Channel Islands
North Brittany and
 the Channel Islands
Isles of Scilly
North Biscay
South Biscay
Atlantic Islands
Atlantic Spain & Portugal
Mediterranean Spain
 Costas del Sol and Blanca
Costas del Azahar,
 Dorada & Brava
Islas Baleares
Corsica and North
 Sardinia

Adlard Coles Nautical
Atlantic Crossing Guide
Pacific Crossing Guide

On Board Publications
South Atlantic Circuit
Havens and Anchorages
 for the South American
 Coast

The RCC Pilotage Foundation
Supplement to Falkland
 Island Shores
Guide to West Africa

RCCPF Website
www.rccpf.org.uk
Supplements
Support files for books
Passage Planning Guides
Web Pilots

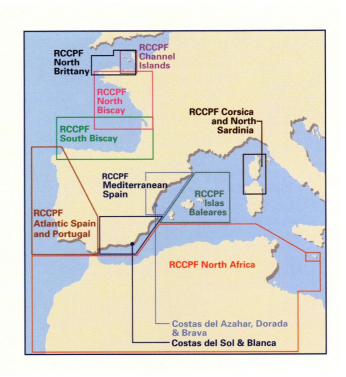

Preface

FOREWORD TO THE SIXTH EDITION

The origins of this book go back to the late Robin Brandon's *East Spain Pilot*, first produced in 1975. It is one of a family of three – the others being *Mediterranean Spain Costas del Azahar, Dorada and Brava* and *Islas Baleares*. The RCCPF titles in the Western Mediterranean also include *North Africa and Corsica* and *North Sardinia*.

Despite being crowded in the high season, this coast remains popular with yachtsmen whether they are passing through or cruising in slow time. It is a good place to keep a yacht in the sun or to overwinter with easy access by land or air.

Since 1975 regular updates and revisions have been made to keep up with the constant development along this Spanish coast. The major work of the 1990s by Oz Robinson, Claire James and Anne Hammick has been continued in this decade by John Marchment. He has followed his extensive revisions of 2001 and 2004 with yearly supplements and a further recent visit.

The harbours along this coast were all revisited in 2007 to prepare for this addition – by Graham Hutt (Chapter I), John Marchment (Chapter II) and Peter Taylor and Robin Rundle (north of Mar Menor and Chapter III).

Chapter I has been extended to take note of the reduction in facilities at Gibraltar and the expanding Spanish facilities close to the Strait. The book proper finishes at Cabo de la Nao where yachtsmen bound northwest may switch to the Mediterranean companion pilot covering Costas del Azahar, Dorada and Brava (Ports Javeaand Denia have been included for convenience) and those heading east will find our 'Islas Baleares' provides the necessary information.

This pilot is prepared by yachtsmen for yachtsmen. The Pilotage Foundation warmly thanks John Marchment for his continuing work and also all those who have alerted us to changes. We welcome feedback – as text or photographs, email or hard copy – from those currently sailing this coast so that we can continue to update this book when practicable. Readers should note that, in addition to yearly supplements, additional information, including downloadable waypoint lists, a link to Google maps, and mid season text or photo updates are available on the Pilotage Foundation website:www.rccpf.org.uk. This site also includes detailed passage planning information which those visiting the Mediterranean for the first time may find useful.

Martin Walker
Hon Director
RCC Pilotage Foundation
March 2009

ACKNOWLEDGEMENTS

This edition has been fully revised with several personal visits (the last in November 2007) and many inputs from the internet. Thanks must go to Martin Walker for his detailed work on the initial draft and Peter Taylor and Robin Rundle for their painstaking survey of the northern part of the coast in late 2007. The aerial photos are mainly by Patrick Roach and the rest are attributed to the persons that took the shot.

The injection of money into the northern part coast does not seem to have happened to this southern part of the Spanish coast. There have been a few improvements, however, and although a number of ports appeared closed due to silting, the immense backlog of people awaiting berths reported in the last edition does appear to have eased slightly.

My thanks must also go to Dr Sloma, editor of the *Gibraltar Yacht Scene*, for her permission to use her Straits tidal information and Graham Hutt for his inputs on the African coast ports and his recent inputs on Gibraltar.

Once again Imray have worked very hard on updating the harbour plans and restructuring the entire volume and my thanks goes to all who had a hand in this work.

John Marchment
March 2009

Introduction

Overview of the region

This pilot, with its companion, covers from the western entrance to the Mediterranean and along the six hundred miles Spanish coastline to the French border. Millions of tourists are drawn regularly to the area and the effect is clear to see – high rise and densely packed resorts, strip development along the coast line, packed beaches and the noise of bars, restaurants and discos. However, there are still areas that the developers have yet to reach and much more to Spain than this popular image. The yachtsman has plenty to choose from – both afloat and ashore. The area offers a clear climate, good food, great scenery, modern marinas and many anchorages as well as the cultural heritage of the Moors and Christians.

Mediterranean Spain Costas del Azahar, Dorada and Brava covers Chapters IV to VI. This book covers Chapters I to III.

Chapter I includes the Straits, Algeciras Bay and Gibraltar and also the two Spanish enclaves of Ceuta and Melilla. Yachtsmen heading along the North African coast should consult Imray/RCCPF pilot book *North Africa* by Graham Hutt.

Chapter II Costa del Sol. This sun coast stretches for east of Gibraltar to Cabo de Gata. West lie the sherry bodegas of Jerez. North is the dramatic ravine town of Rhonda and the white rural villages of Andalucia. Further east is Grenada and the wonders of the Alambra Palace – and easy access to the skiing mountains of the Sierra Nevada. Coastal villages offer the chance to anchor for a swim or a paella lunch ashore.

Chapter III Costa Blanca. The white coast provides anchorages to the north of Cabo de Gata before giving way to the sports grounds of La Manga and the tourist resorts stretching up to Cabo de la Nao.

Chapter IV Costa Azahar. The high cliffs in the south rapidly give way to long sandy beaches running up to the Ebro Delta. Azahar means blossom and reflects the huge groves of orange and lemon trees. The Amerca's Cup of 2007 has led to much recent development around Valencia.

Chapter V Costa del Dorada. This area runs between the rivers Ebro and Tordera. The major ports of Tarrogona and Barcelona break the run of golden beaches which give this coast its name.

Chapter VI Costa Brava. The rocky savage coast, with few marinas but many deep calas, heads towards the Pyrénées and the border with France.

In the Mediterranean, yachts are usually in commission from May to October, the north European holiday season. Whilst there is little chance of a gale in summer, there are few days when there is a good sailing breeze. In winter, whilst it is true that off-shore the Mediterranean can be horrid, there are many days with a good sailing breeze and the weather is warmer and sunnier than the usual summer in the English Channel. Storms and heavy rain do occur but it is feasible to dodge bad weather and slip along shore from harbour to harbour as they are not far apart. In general the climate is mild and, particularly from January to March, very pleasant. A great advantage is that there are no crowds and the local shops and services are freer to serve the winter visitor. Many Clubs Náutico, which have to turn people away in summer, welcome visitors. Local inhabitants can be met, places of interest enjoyed and the empty beaches and coves used in privacy.

History

There are many traces of prehistoric inhabitants but recorded history starts with a group of unknown origin, the Ligurians, who came from N Africa and established themselves in southern Spain in about the 6th century BC; with the Carthaginians at Málaga and the Phoenicians who had been trading in the area since the 12th century BC and living in various small colonies dotted along the coast.

In 242 BC a force of Carthaginians under Hamilcar Barca, who had previously been driven from Sicily by the Romans, captured and held the south of Spain until 219 BC when the Romans took over occupation, which lasted until the Barbarian invasion in the 5th century AD. This period was one of development and construction when many of the towns were first established. The Barbarians – the Suevi, Vandals and Alans – were, in turn, overrun by the Visigoths who held the area from the 5th to the 8th century AD.

In 711 AD a huge force of Moors and Berbers under Tarik-ibn-Zeyab crossed the Strait of Gibraltar and captured the whole of Spain except for a small enclave in the N. The Moors took over the S and the Berbers the N. By the 10th century AD huge strides had been made in education and development

Opposite. Images of Andalucia by Graham Hutt. From top left clockwise: The Alhambra in Granada, Almoraima - Costa del Sol, Malaga, oranges on the Costa del Sol, Andalucia village scene.

and Cordoba which had become independent was renowned throughout Europe as a seat of learning.

By the 13th century, the Moors and Berbers had been driven out of the country by a long series of wars undertaken by numerous Spanish forces who were supported by the armies of the nobles of France. Granada alone remained under the Moors until 1491 when they were finally driven out by Isabella of Castile and Ferdinand of Aragon who united Spain under one crown.

Then followed a period of world-wide expansion and, when the crown went to the house of Hapsburg in the 16th century, of interference in the affairs of Europe which continued when the house of Bourbon took over in the 18th century.

Over the years the country has been in constant turmoil. Wars and rebellions, victories and defeats, sieges and conquests were common occurrences but none were quite as terrible as the Civil War which started in 1936 and lasted for two-and-a-half years, leaving nearly a million dead. Since then the country has moved away from a dictatorship into the different turmoils of democracy and the European Union, but the Civil War has not been forgotten. Though the country is governed centrally from Madrid, provinces have considerable local autonomy.

Local economy

Along all the coasts tourism is of course a significant factor in the economy but this coastal development is, in a manner of speaking, skin-deep. Inland, agricultural patterns remain though some of them have been drastically developed, for instance by the introduction of hydroponics supported by kilometres of plastic greenhouses. Fishing fleets, inshore and mid-range, work out of many ports and they, together with a supporting boat building industry, help provide the skills on which marinas depend.

Language

The Castilian spoken in Andalucía sounds different to that spoken further north, principally in that the cedilla is not lisped. In Catalunya, Catalan is actively promoted. Though close to Spanish, there are Catalan alternatives for Castilian Spanish, some of which have French overtones, such as: *bondia* – good morning (rather than *buenos días*), *bon tarde* – good afternoon (*buenos tardes*), *s'es plau* – please (*por favor*).

Many local people speak English or German, often learnt from tourists, and French is taught as a second language at school.

Place names appear in the Spanish (i.e. Castilian) form where possible – the spelling normally used on British Admiralty charts – with local alternatives, including Catalan, in brackets.

Currency

The unit of currency is the Euro. Major credit cards are widely accepted, as are Eurocheques. Bank hours are normally 0830 to 1400, Monday to Friday, with a few also open 0830 to 1300 on Saturday. Most banks have automatic telling machines (ATM).

Time zone

Spain keeps Standard European Time (UT+1), advanced one hour in summer to UT+2 hours. Changeover dates are now standardised with the rest of the EU as the last weekends in March and October respectively.

Unless stated otherwise, times quoted are UT.

National holidays and fiestas

There are numerous official and local holidays, the latter often celebrating the local saint's day or some historical event. They usually comprise a religious procession, sometimes by boat, followed by a fiesta in the evening. The Fiesta del Virgen de la Carmen is celebrated in many harbours during mid-July. Official holidays include:

1 January	*Año Nuevo* (New Year's Day)
6 January	*Reyes Magos* (Epiphany)
19 March	*San José* (St Joseph's Day)
	Viernes Santo (Good Friday)
	Easter Monday
1 May	*Día del Trabajo* (Labour Day)
early/mid-June	*Corpus Christi*
24 June	*Día de San Juan* (St John's Day, the King's name-day)
29 June	*San Pedro y San Pablo* (Sts Peter and Paul)
25 July	*Día de Santiago* (St James' Day)
15 August	*Día del Asunción* (Feast of the Assumption)
11 September	Catalan National Day
12 October	*Día de la Hispanidad* (Day of the Spanish Nation)
1 November	*Todos los Santos* (All Saints)
6 December	*Día de la Constitución* (Constitution Day)
8 December	*Inmaculada Concepción* (Immaculate Conception)
25 December	*Navidad* (Christmas Day)

When a national holiday falls on a Sunday it may be celebrated the following day.

Practicalities

OFFICIAL ADDRESSES

See Appendix VIII

USEFUL WEB PAGES

Spanish Tourist Office www.tourspain.co.uk
British Airways www.britishairways.com
Iberia Airlines www.iberia.com
Andalucía www.andalucia.org
Murcia www.murciaturistica.es
Valencia www.comunidadvalenciana.com
Weather websites on page 16
Port websites at each port

VAT

Note Value Added Tax (VAT) is called *Impuesto de Valor Agregado* (IVA) and the standard rate is 16%.

Documentation

Spain is a member of the European Union. Other EU nationals may visit the country for up to 90 days with a passport but no visa, as may US citizens. EU citizens wishing to remain in Spain may apply for a *permiso de residencia* once in the country; non-EU nationals can apply for a single 90-day extension, or otherwise obtain a long-term visa from a Spanish embassy or consulate before leaving home.

In practice the requirement to apply for a *permiso de residencia* does not appear to be enforced in the case of cruising yachtsmen, living aboard rather than ashore and frequently on the move. Many yachtsmen have cruised Spanish waters for extended periods with no documentation beyond that normally carried in the UK. If in doubt, check with the authorities before departure.

Under EU regulations, EU registered boats are not required to fly the Q flag on first arrival unless they have non-EU nationals or dutiable goods aboard. Nevertheless, clearance should be sought either through a visit to or from officials or through the offices of the larger marinas or yacht clubs. Passports and the ship's registration papers will be required. A Certificate of Competence (or equivalent) and evidence of VAT status may also be requested. Other documents sometimes requested are a crew list with passport details, the radio licence and evidence of insurance. Subsequently, at other ports, clearance need not be sought but the *Guarda Civil* may wish to see papers, particularly passports. Marina officials often ask to see yacht registration documents the skipper's passport, and sometimes evidence of insurance.

Marine insurance is compulsory in most countries around the Mediterranean and it is essential that territorial cruising limits are extended to cover the planned voyage. The minimum third party insurance required in Spain is €1,000,000 and the insurers should provide a letter to this effect written in Spanish. This is usually provided free of cost and should be requested from the insurers if not sent out with the policy.

Temporary import and laying up

A VAT paid or exempt yacht should apply for a *permiso aduanero* on arrival in Spanish waters. This is valid for twelve months and renewable annually, allowing for an almost indefinite stay. Possession of a *permiso aduanero* establishes the status of a vessel and is helpful when importing equipment and spares from other EU countries.

A boat registered outside the EU fiscal area on which VAT has not been paid may be temporarily imported into the EU for a period not exceeding six months in any twelve before VAT is payable. This period may sometimes be extended by prior agreement with the local customs authorities (for instance, some do not count time laid up as part of the six months). While in EU waters the vessel may only be used by its owner, and may not be chartered or even lent to another person, on pain of paying VAT (*see Appendix VIII for further details*). If kept in the EU longer than six months the vessel normally becomes liable for VAT. There are marked differences in the way the rules are applied from one harbour to the next, let alone in different countries – check the local situation on arrival.

Chartering

There is a blanket restriction on foreign-owned and/or skippered vessels based in Spain engaging in charter work. See Appendix VII for details.

Light dues

A charge known as *Tarifa G5* is supposedly levied on all vessels. Locally-based pleasure craft (the status of a charter yacht is not clear) pay at the rate of €5 per square metre per year, area being calculated as LOA x beam. Visiting pleasure craft pay at one tenth of that sum and are not charged again for ten days. Boats of less than 7m LOA and with engines of less than 25hp make a single payment of €30 per year. In practice this levy appears to be added to the marina or mooring charges on a daily basis.

Charts

See Appendix II. Current British Admiralty information is largely obtained from Spanish sources. The Spanish Hydrographic Office re-issues and corrects its charts periodically, and issues weekly Notices to Mariners. Corrections are repeated by the British Admiralty, generally some months later.

Pilot books

Details of principal harbours and some interesting background information appear in the British Admiralty Hydrographic Office's *Mediterranean Pilot Vol 1 (NP 45)*. *NP 291, Maritime Communications* will be found useful. Harbour descriptions are also to be found in *Guía del Navigante – La Costa de España y el Algarve* (PubliNáutic Rilnvest SL) written in colloquial English with a Spanish translation. Published annually, it carries many potentially useful advertisements for marine-related businesses.

For French speakers, *Votre Livre de Bord – Méditerranée* (Bloc Marine) may be helpful. In German there are *Spanische Gewässer, Lissabon bis Golfe du Lion* (Delius Klasing). See also Appendix II.

Positions and Waypoints

All positions in this pilot are to WGS 84 and have been derived from C-Map electronic charts. If plotting onto paper charts then the navigator is reminded that some source charts of this area remain at European 1950 datum (ED50) and appropriate use of offsets may be necessary.

This pilot includes waypoints: note the caution on page ii. A full list is given in Appendix I and may be downloaded from rccpf.org.uk.

Coastal waypoints are indicated there in bold and are shown on the plans at the beginning of each chapter. They form a series with which one is able to steer from off Cabo San Antonio to French border. However, it is essential to keep a good look out at all times while making a coastal passage in this area.

Waypoints which are not listed in bold, have been selected as close approach waypoints for all but the most minor harbours. The detail is shown in the data section at the beginning of each port and on the associated harbour plan. They have not been proven at sea and should be used with caution. Where scale permits they have been plotted on the harbour plan. The track line from waypoint to harbour mouth may be given on these plans to help orientation. Where the waypoint has been positioned more than 0·1M from the harbour the bearing and distance from waypoint to harbour is given with the port data.

The numerical sequence of the waypoint list does not indicate that port waypoints may be grouped together to form a route from one harbour to another. The navigator will need to plot them on a chart in order to plan a hazard-free route.

Magnetic variation

Magnetic variation is noted in the introduction to the coastal sections.

Traffic zones

There are traffic separation zones in the Straits of Gibraltar, off Cabo de Gata, Cabo de Palos and Cabo de la Nao.

Navigation aids

Lights

The four-figure international numbering system has been used to identify lights in the text and on plans – the Mediterranean falls in Group E. As each light has its own four figure number, correcting from *Notices to Mariners* or the annual *List of Lights and Fog Signals*, whether in Spanish or English, is straightforward. Certain minor lights and all buoys with a five figure number are listed in the Spanish *Faros y Señales de Niebla Part II* but are not included in the international system.

Harbour lights follow the IALA A system and are normally listed in the order in which they become relevant upon approach and entry, working from Gibraltar towards France.

It should be noted that, whilst every effort has been taken to check the lights agree with the documents mentioned above, the responsibility for maintaining the lights appears to rest with the local *capitanía* and, depending on their efficiency, this can mean some lights may be defective or different from the stated characteristics at times.

Buoyage

Buoys follow the IALA A system, based on the direction of the main flood tide. Yellow topped black or red rusty buoys 500m offshore mark raw sewage outlets. Many minor harbours, however, maintain their own buoys to their own systems. Generally, yellow buoys in line mark the seaward side of areas reserved for swimming. Narrow lanes for water-skiing and sailboarding lead out from the shore and are also buoyed.

Hazards

Restricted areas

Restricted areas are outlined in the coastal sections.

Night approaches

Approaches in darkness are often made difficult by the plethora of background lights – fixed, flashing, occulting, interrupted – of all colours. Though there may be exceptions, this applies to nearly all harbours backed by a town of any size. Powerful shore lights make weaker navigation lights difficult to identify and mask unlit features such as exposed rocks or the line of a jetty. If at all possible, avoid closing an unknown harbour in darkness.

Skylines

Individual buildings on the coast – particularly prominent hotel blocks – are built, demolished, duplicated, change colour, change shape, all with amazing rapidity. They are not nearly as reliable as landmarks as might be thought. If a particular building on a chart or in a photograph can be positively identified on the ground, well and good. If not, take care.

Tunny nets and fish farms

During summer and autumn these nets, anchored to the sea bed and up to six miles long, are normally laid inshore across the current in depths of 15–40m but may be placed as far as 10 miles offshore. They may be laid in parallel lines. The outer end of a line should be marked by a float or a boat carrying a white flag with an 'A' (in black) by day, and two red or red and white lights by night. There should also be markers along the line of the net.

These nets are capable of stopping a small freighter but should you by accident, and successfully, sail over one, look out for a second within a few hundred metres. If seen, the best action may be to sail parallel to the nets until one end is reached.

The Pilotage Foundation is not aware of nets being laid off the Costas Azahar, Dorada and Brava.

However, many *calas* and bays had fish farms proliferating. These latter are often lit with flashing yellow lights but great care should be taken when entering small *calas* at night.

The positions of some fish farms are indicated on the latest charts but be aware these farms change position frequently. Fish farming is developing along this coast and navigators must be prepared to encounter ones not shown on plans and charts.

Commercial fishing boats

Commercial fishing boats should be given a wide berth. They may be:
- Trawling singly or in pairs with a net between the boats.
- Laying a long net, the top of which is supported by floats.
- Picking up or laying pots either singly or in groups or lines.
- Trolling with one or more lines out astern.
- Drifting, trailing nets to windward.

Do not assume they know, or will observe, the law of the sea – keep well clear on principle.

Small fishing boats

Small fishing boats, including the traditional double-ended *llauds*, either use nets or troll with lines astern and should be avoided as far as possible. At night many *lámparas* put to sea and, using powerful electric or gas lights, attract fish to the surface.

When seen from a distance these lights appear to flash as the boat moves up and down in the waves and can at first be mistaken for a lighthouse.

Speed boats etc

Para-gliding, water-skiing, speedboats and jet-skis are all popular, and are sometimes operated by unskilled and thoughtless drivers with small regard to collision risks. In theory they are not allowed to exceed five knots within 100m of the coast or within 250m of bathing beaches. Water-skiing is restricted to buoyed areas.

Scuba divers and swimmers

A good watch should be kept for scuba divers and swimmers, with or without snorkel equipment, particularly around harbour entrances. If accompanied by a boat, the presence of divers may be indicated either by International Code Flag A or by a square red flag with a single yellow diagonal, as commonly seen in north America and the Caribbean.

Preparation

THE CREW

Clothing

Summer sunburn is an even more serious hazard at sea, where light is reflected, than on land. Lightweight, patterned cotton clothing is handy in this context – it washes and dries easily and the pattern camouflages the creases! Non-absorbent, heat retaining synthetic materials are best avoided. When swimming wear a T-shirt against the sun and shoes if there are sea-urchins around.

Some kind of headgear, preferably with a wide brim, is essential. A genuine Panama Hat, a *Montecristi*, can be rolled up, shoved in a pocket and doesn't mind getting wet (they come from Ecuador, not Panama, which has hi-jacked the name). A retaining string for the hat, tied either to clothing or around the neck, is a wise precaution whilst on the water.

Footwear at sea is a contentious subject. Many experienced cruisers habitually sail barefoot but while this may be acceptable on a familiar vessel, it would be courting injury on a less intimately known deck and around mid-day bare soles may get burnt. Proper sailing shoes should always be worn for harbour work and anchor handling. Ashore, if wearing sandals the upper part of the foot is the first area to get sunburn.

At the other end of the year, winter weather may be wet and cold. Foul weather gear as well as warm sweaters etc. will be needed.

Shoregoing clothes should be on a par with what one might wear in the UK – beachwear is not often acceptable in restaurants and certainly not on more formal occasions in yacht clubs.

Medical

No inoculations are required. Minor ailments may best be treated by consulting a *farmacia* (often able to dispense drugs which in most other countries would be on prescription), or by contact with an English-speaking doctor (recommended by the *farmacia*, marina staff, a tourist office, the police or possibly a hotel). Specifically prescribed or branded drugs should be bought before setting out in sufficient quantity to cover the duration of the cruise. Medicines are expensive in Spain and often have different brand names from those used abroad.

Apart from precautions against the well recognised hazards of sunburn (high factor sun cream is recommended) and stomach upsets, heat exhaustion (or heat stroke) is most likely to affect newly joined crew not yet acclimatised to Mediterranean temperatures. Carry something such as *Dioralyte* to counteract dehydration. Insect repellents, including mosquito coils, can be obtained locally.

UK citizens should carry a European Health Insurance Card (EHIC) application for which can be obtained at a Post Office or online at www.ehic.org.uk. This provides for free medical treatment under a reciprocal agreement with the National Health Service. Private medical treatment is likely to be expensive and it may be worth taking out medical insurance (which should also provide for an attended flight home should the need arise).

THE YACHT

A yacht properly equipped for cruising in northern waters should need little extra gear, but the following items are worth considering if not already on board.

Radio equipment

In order to receive weather forecasts and navigational warnings from Coast Radio Stations, a radio capable of receiving short and medium wave Single Sideband (SSB) transmissions will be needed. Do not make the mistake of buying a radio capable only of receiving the AM transmissions broadcast by national radio stations, or assume that SSB is only applicable to transmitting radios (transceivers).

Most SSB receivers are capable of receiving either Upper Side Band (USB) or Lower Side Band (LSB) at the flick of a switch. The UK Maritime Mobile Net covering the Eastern Atlantic and Mediterranean uses USB, and again it is not necessary to have either a transceiver or a transmitting licence to listen in, just a receiver. All Coast Radio Stations broadcast on SSB – whether on USB or LSB should be easy to determine by trial and error.

Digital tuning is very desirable, and the radio should be capable of tuning to a minimum of 1kHz and preferably to 0·1kHz.

Ventilation

Modern yachts are, as a rule, better ventilated than their older sisters though seldom better insulated. Consider adding an opening hatch in the main cabin, if not already fitted, and ideally another over the galley. Wind scoops over hatches can be a major benefit.

Awnings

An awning covering at least the cockpit provides much relief for the crew, while an even better combination is a bimini which can be kept rigged whilst sailing, plus a larger 'harbour' awning, preferably at boom height or above and extending forward to the mast.

Fans

Harbours can be hot and windless. The use of 12V fans for all cabins can have a dramatic effect on comfort.

Cockpit tables

It is pleasant to eat civilised meals in the cockpit, particularly while at anchor. If nothing else can be arranged, a small folding table might do.

Refrigerator/ice-box/freezer

If a refrigerator or freezer is not fitted it may be possible to build in an ice-box (a plastic picnic coolbox is a poor substitute), but this will be useless without adequate insulation. An ice-box designed for northern climes will almost certainly benefit from extra insulation, if this can be fitted – 100mm (4in) is a desirable minimum, 150mm (6in) even better. A drain is also essential.

If a refrigerator/freezer is fitted but electricity precious, placing ice inside will help minimise battery drain.

Hose

Carry at least 25 metres. Standpipes tend to have bayonet couplings of a type unavailable in the UK – purchase them on arrival. Plenty of five or 10 litre plastic carriers will also be useful.

Deck shower

If no shower is fitted below, a black-backed plastic bag plus rose heats very quickly when hung in the rigging. (At least one proprietary model is available widely).

Mosquito nets

Some advocate fitting screens to all openings leading below. Others find this inconvenient, relying instead on mosquito coils and other insecticides and repellents. For some reason mosquitoes generally seem to bother new arrivals more than old hands, while anchoring well out will often decrease the problem.

Harbours, marinas and anchorages

In spite of the growth in both the number and size of marinas and yacht harbours there is still a chronic shortage of berths. A recent expansion of many marinas has eased the situation. One must check in advance whether a berth is available and note that mobile phones are replacing VHF for this function.

Harbour organisation

At local level, the ultimate authority for the workings of a harbour is the *capitán de puerto* whose office is the *capitanía*. In fishing ports there may also be a *guarda de puerto*; in this case the *capitán* looks after the waters of the harbour and delegates berthing arrangements to the *guarda*.

At ports where there is an organised yachting presence, there is almost always a *club náutico*, a marina or both, and arrangements for handling yachts are delegated to them. For the visiting yacht, the first point of reference is the marina if there is one; and if not, the *club náutico*.

Harbour charges

All harbours and marinas charge, at a scale which varies from season to season and usually increases from year to year. May to September are normally 'high season' with charges that are normally nearly double that of the 'low season'. Longer term contracts may work out up to a third cheaper than the daily rate. Some marinas include water, electricity, harbour and light dues, while others charge separately. Published rates rarely include the IVA (at 16%) and sometimes the published information does not always specify all the charges. One should take great care in checking what exactly one is paying for if one is to avoid problems when finally settling up.

With the shortage of berths, mentioned above, costs have risen drastically and, with a few exceptions, are now fairly similar along the entire stretch of coast covered by this volume. Charges for a 12 metre craft average around €30 a night (€25 with water and electricity etc. charged separately) in high season and around €20 a night (€15 with water and electricity charged separately) in low season. Departures from these average figures are sometimes great. A further complication is that the newer marinas are beginning to charge by beam times length (or sometimes beam alone). It is not practical either to generalize further on harbour dues or to give detailed charges, let alone give an opinion on value for money but the foregoing may provide some guidance for financial planning. Where a relatively expensive or cheap rate has been found this is noted in the text. *El Mercado Náutico* – the Boat Market, which generally appears every other month during the summer, carries tariffs and is probably the most up-to-date guide to be found.

Berthing

Due to the vast numbers of yachts and limited space available, berthing stern-to the quays and pontoons is normal.

For greater privacy berth bows-to. This has the added advantages of keeping the rudder away from possible underwater obstructions near the quay and making the approach a much easier manoeuvre. An anchor may occasionally be needed, but more often

a bow (or stern) line will be provided, usually via a lazyline to the pontoon though sometimes buoyed. This line may be both heavy and dirty and gloves will be useful. Either way, have plenty of fenders out and lines ready.

Most cruising skippers will have acquired some expertise at this manoeuvre but if taking over a chartered or otherwise unfamiliar yacht it would be wise both to check handling characteristics and talk the sequence through with the crew before attempting to enter a narrow berth.

Detailed instructions regarding Mediterranean mooring techniques will be found in *Mediterranean Cruising Handbook* by Rod Heikell.

Mooring lines – surge in harbours is common and mooring lines must be both long and strong. It is useful to have an eye made up at the shore end with a loop of chain plus shackles to slip over bollards or through rings. Carry plenty of mooring lines, especially if the boat is to be left unattended for any length of time.

Gangplanks – if a gangplank is not already part of the boat's equipment, a builder's scaffolding plank, with holes drilled at either end to take lines, serves well. As it is cheap and easily replaced it can also be used outside fenders to deal with an awkward lie or ward off an oily quay. A short ladder, possibly the bathing ladder if it can be adapted, is useful if berthing bows-to.

Moorings

Virtually all moorings are privately owned and if one is used it will have to be vacated should the owner return. There are generally no markings to give any indication as to the weight and strength of moorings so they should be used with caution. Lobster pot toggles have been mistaken for moorings.

Laying up

Laying up either afloat or ashore is possible at most marinas, though a few have no hardstanding. Facilities and services provided vary considerably, as does the cost, and it is worth seeking local advice as to the quality of the services and the security of the berth or hardstanding concerned.

In the north of the area, the northwesterly *tramontana* (*maestral*) can be frequent and severe in winter and early spring, and this should be borne in mind when selecting the area and site to lay up. Yachts with wooden decks and varnished brightwork will benefit with protection from the winter sun.

The paperwork associated with temporary import and laying up is detailed on page 3.

Yacht clubs

Most harbours of any size support at least one *club náutico*. However the grander ones in particular are basically social clubs – often with tennis courts, swimming pools and other facilities – and may not welcome the crews of visiting yachts. Often there is both a marina and a club, and unless there are special circumstances the normal first option for a visitor is the marina. That said, many *club náuticos* have pleasant bars and excellent restaurants which appear to be open to all, while a few are notably helpful and friendly to visitors. The standard of dress and behaviour often appears to be somewhat more formal than that expected in a similar club in Britain.

General regulations

Harbour restrictions

All harbours have a speed limit, usually three knots. The limits are not noted in the text and none are known which is less than three knots. There is a five knot speed limit within 100m of coast, extending to 250m off bathing beaches.

In most harbours anchoring is forbidden except in emergency or for a short period while sorting out a berth.

Harbour traffic signals

Traffic signals are rare, and in any case are designed for commercial traffic and seldom apply to yachts.

Storm signals

The signal stations at major ports and harbours may show storm signals, but equally they may not. With minor exceptions they are similar to the International System of Visual Storm Warnings.

Flag etiquette

A yacht in commission in foreign waters is legally required to fly her national maritime flag; for a British registered yacht, this is commonly the Red Ensign. If a special club ensign is worn it must be accompanied by the correct burgee. The courtesy flag of the country visited, which normally is the national maritime flag, should be flown from the starboard signal halliard. The flag for Spain is similar to the Spanish national flag but without the crest in the centre.

Insurance

Many marinas require evidence of insurance cover, though third party only may be sufficient. Many UK companies are willing to extend home waters cover for the Mediterranean, excluding certain areas.

Garbage

It is an international offence to dump garbage at sea and, while the arrangements of local authorities may not be perfect, garbage on land should be dumped in the proper containers. Marinas require the use of their onshore toilet facilities or holding tanks.

Large yachts

Many harbours are too small, or too shallow, for a large yacht, which must anchor outside whilst its crew visit the harbour by tender. It is essential that the skipper of such a yacht wishing to enter a small harbour telephones or radios the harbour authorities well in advance to reserve a berth (if available) and receive necessary instructions.

Scuba diving

Inshore scuba diving is strictly controlled and a licence is required from the *Militar de Marina*. This involves a certificate of competence, a medical certificate, two passport photographs, the passport itself (for inspection), knowledge of the relevant laws and a declaration that they will be obeyed. The simplest approach is to enquire through marina staff. Any attempt to remove archaeological material from the seabed will result in serious trouble.

Spearfishing

Spearfishing while scuba diving or using a snorkel is controlled and, in some places, prohibited.

Water-skiing

There has been a big increase in the use of high powered outboards for water-skiing over the past decade, accompanied by a significant increase in accidents. In most of the main ports and at some beaches it is now controlled and enquiries should be made before skiing. It is essential to have third party insurance and, if possible, a bail bond. If bathing and water-skiing areas are buoyed, yachts are excluded.

Security

Crime afloat is not a major problem in most areas and regrettably much of the theft which does occur can be laid at the door of other yachtsmen. Take sensible precautions – lock up before leaving the yacht, padlock the outboard to the dinghy, and secure the dinghy (particularly if an inflatable) with chain or wire rather than line. Folding bicycles are particularly vulnerable to theft, and should be chained up if left on deck.

Ashore, the situation in the big towns is no worse than in the UK and providing common sense is applied to such matters as how handbags are carried, where not to go after the bars close etc., there should be no problem.

The officials most likely to be seen are the *guardia civil*, who wear grey uniforms and deal with immigration as well as more ordinary police work, the *Aduana* (customs) in navy blue uniforms, and the *Policía*, also in blue uniforms, who deal with traffic rather than criminal matters.

Anchorages

There are a large number of attractive anchorages in *calas* and off beaches, even though many have massive buildings in the background and crowds in the foreground. Where known, particular hazards are mentioned but an absence of comment in the text or on the sketch charts does not mean there are no hazards. There are always hazards approaching and anchoring off the shoreline. The plans are derived from limited observation and not from a professional survey; depths, shapes, distances etc. are approximate. Any approach must be made with due care. Skippers are advised that anchorages near hotels and towns may be cordoned off, by small floating buoys, to protect swimmers and therefore not be suitable. It cannot be assumed that anchorages listed in this book are always available for use by cruising yachtsmen.

The weather can change and deteriorate at short notice. During the day the sea breeze can be strong, especially if there is a valley at the head of an anchorage. Similarly a strong land breeze can flow down a valley in the early hours of the morning. If anchored near the head of a *cala* backed by a river valley, should there be a thunderstorm or heavy downpour in the hills above take precautions against the flood of water and debris which will descend into the *cala*.

Many *cala* anchorages suffer from swell even when not open to its off-shore direction. Swell tends to curl round all but the most prominent headlands. Wash from boats entering and leaving, as well as from larger vessels passing outside, may add to the discomfort. If considering a second anchor or a line ashore in order to hold the yacht into the swell, take into account the swinging room required by yachts on single anchors should the wind change.

In a high-sided *cala* winds are often fluky and a sudden blow, even from the land, may make departure difficult. This type of anchorage should only be used in settled calm weather and left in good time if swell or wind rise.

Whatever the type of *cala*, have ready a plan for clearing out quickly, possibly in darkness. It is unwise to leave an anchored yacht unattended for any length of time.

Choice of anchor

Many popular anchorages are thoroughly ploughed up each year by the hundreds of anchors dropped and weighed. At others the bottom is weed-covered compacted sand. Not without good reason is the four-pronged grab the favourite anchor of local fishermen, though difficult to stow. A conventional fisherman-type anchor is easier to stow and a useful ally. If using a patent anchor – Danforth, CQR, Bruce, Fortress etc. – an anchor weight (or chum) is a worthwhile investment and will encourage the pull to remain horizontal.

Anchoring

Once in a suitable depth of water, if clarity permits look for a weed-free patch to drop the anchor. In rocky or otherwise suspect areas – including those likely to contain wrecks, old chains etc. – use a sinking trip line with a float (an inviting buoy may be picked up by another yacht). Chain scope should be at least four times the maximum depth of water and nylon scope double that. It is always worth setting the anchor by reversing slowly until it holds, but on a hard or compacted bottom this must be done very gently in order to give the anchor a chance to bite – over enthusiasm with the throttle will cause it to skip without digging in.

Supplies and services

Fresh water

In many places drinking water (*agua potable*) is scarce. Expect to pay for it, particularly if supplied by hose, and do not wash sails and decks before checking that it is acceptable to do so. In those harbours where a piped supply is not available for yachts, a public tap can often be found – a good supply of five or 10 litre plastic cans will be useful.

Water quality is generally good. However it varies from place to place and year to year. Always check verbally and taste for salinity or over-chlorinating before topping up tanks. If caught out, bottled water is readily available in bars and supermarkets.

Ice

Block ice for an ice-box is widely obtainable – use the largest blocks that will fit; chemical ice is sometimes available in blocks measuring 100 x 20 x 20cms. The latter must not be used in drinks, the former only after inquiring of those who have tried the product. Cube or 'small' ice is obtainable and generally of drinks quality, particularly if bought in a sealed bag.

Fuel

Diesel (*gasoleo, gasoil* or simply *diesel*) is sold in two forms throughout Spain, *Gasoleo B* which attracts a lower tax and is only available to fishing craft, and *Gasoleo A* which is available to yachts. Not all harbours sell *Gasoleo A*, particularly the smaller fishing harbours. A more limited number also have a pump for petrol (*gasolina*). *Petróleo* is paraffin (kerosene). Credit cards are widely, but not universally, accepted – if in doubt, check first.

Bottled gas

Camping Gaz is widely available from marinas, supermarkets or *ferreterias* (ironmongers), in the 1.9kg bottles identical to those in the UK.

As of 2002 REPSOL/CAMPSOL depots will no longer fill any UK (or any other countries') Calor Gas bottles even with a current test certificate. It is therefore essential to carry the appropriate regulator and fittings to permit the use of Camping Gas bottles. Yachts fitted with propane systems should consult the Calor Gas Customer service agent (☎ 0800 626 626).

Electricity

The marina standard is 220 volt, 50Hz, generally via a two-pin socket for which an adapter will be needed, though some marinas provide 380 volt supplies to berths for yachts over 20–25m. If using 110 volt 60Hz equipment seek advice – frequency may be a greater problem than voltage. Even if the yacht is not wired for mains, a 25m length of cable and a trickle charger may be useful.

Food and drink

There are many well stocked stores, supermarkets and hypermarkets in the larger towns and cities and it may be worth doing the occasional major stock-up by taxi. As a rule, availability and choice varies with the size of the town. Most older settlements (though not all tourist resorts) have a market with local produce at reasonable prices. Alcohol is cheap by UK standards with, unsurprisingly, good value Spanish wines. Spanish gin and vodka are also good value; Scotch whisky can only come from Scotland but the genuine article is often lower in price than in the U.K. Shop prices generally are noticeably lower away from tourist resorts.

Most shops, other than the largest supermarkets, close for *siesta* between 1400 and 1700 and remain closed on Sunday though some smaller food shops do open on Sunday mornings. In larger towns the produce market may operate from 0800 to 1400, Monday to Saturday; in smaller towns it is more often a weekly affair. An excellent way to sample unfamiliar delicacies in small portions is in the form of bar snacks, *tapas* or the larger *raciónes*. Tapas once came on the house but are now almost invariably charged – sometimes heavily.

Repairs and chandlery

There are many marinas equipped to handle all aspects of yacht maintenance from laying up to changing a washer. Nearly all have travel-hoists and the larger have specialist facilities – GRP work, electronics, sailmaking, stainless welding and so forth. Charges may differ – widely so – if practicable, shop around.

The best equipped chandleries will be found near the larger marinas. Smaller harbours or marinas are often without a chandlery, though something may be found in the associated town. Basic items can sometimes be found in *ferreterias* (ironmongers).

Telephones and Fax

Telephone kiosks are common, both local and *teléfono internacional*, and most carry instructions in English. Both coins and phonecards, available from tobacconists (*estancos*), are used. If no kiosk is available marina offices have telephones and many have faxes. Most bars and hotels have metered telephones and the latter usually have faxes, though these are seldom metered. Wi-Fi is widely available.

- When calling from within Spain, dial the whole code (beginning with the figure 9) whether or not the number you are calling has the same code. In some areas the number of digits to be dialled is nine, in others eight. To make an international call, dial 00 followed by the relevant country code (44 for the UK). If calling the UK do not dial the first figure of the number if it is 0.

- To reach the international operator dial 025. A telephone number beginning with the figure 6 indicates a mobile telephone which will have no area code and its own code for calling its international operator. The number for information is 1003 and the land based emergency services can be contacted by this route.

- To call Spain from abroad, dial the international access code (00 in the UK) followed by the code for Spain (34), then the area code (which begins with 9 except for mobile phones) followed by the individual number.

Warning Apart from a major re-organisation of area codes, individual numbers in Spain change surprisingly often.

Mail

Letters may be sent *poste restante* to any post office (*oficina de corréos*). They should be addressed with the surname (only) of the recipient followed by *Lista de Corréos* and the town. Do not enter the addressee's initials or title: that is likely to cause misfiling. Collection is a fairly cumbersome procedure and a passport is likely to be needed. Alternatively, most marinas and some *club náuticos* will hold mail for yachts, but it is always wise to check in advance if possible. Uncollected letters are seldom returned.

Mail to and from the UK should be marked 'air mail' (*por avión*) but even so may take up to ten days, so if speed is important communicate by fax or Email. Post boxes are yellow; stamps are available from tobacconists (*estancos*), not from post offices though the latter will accept and frank mail. Almost every town has a Post Office; ask – *donde esta el Correo?*

Tourist offices

There is at least one tourist office in every major town or resort. Their locations vary from year to year – ask at the port or marina office.

Transport and travel

Every community has some form of public transport, if only one *autobús* a day and many of the coastal towns are served by rail as well.

Taxis are easily found in the tourist resorts though less common outside them, but can always be ordered by telephone. Car hire is simple, but either a full national or international driving licence must be shown and many companies will not lease a car to a driver over 70 years old.

Air – Alicante, Barcelona and Valencia have year round international flights and seasonal charter flights; Gibraltar has year round connections with the UK. Other airports, Málaga, Murcia, Alicante and Tarragona, have international scheduled and charter flights in summer and year round connections within Spain.

Western Mediterranean weather

The weather pattern in the basin of the western Mediterranean is affected by many different systems. It is largely unpredictable, quick to change and often very different at places only a short distance apart. See Appendix III for Spanish meteorological terms.

WINDS

Winds most frequently blow from the west, northwest, north and east but are considerably altered by the effects of local topography. The Mediterranean is an area of calms and gales and the old saying that in summer there are nine days of light winds followed by a gale is very close to reality. Close to the coast, normal sea and land breezes are experienced on calm days. Along the Costa Brava, northwest, north and northeast winds are most common, especially in winter, though winds from other directions frequently occur. This area is particularly influenced by the weather in the Golfo de León and is in the direct path of the northwesterly *tramontana* (see below), making it particularly important to listen to regular weather forecasts.

The winds in the Mediterranean have been given special names dependent on their direction and characteristics. Those that affect this coast are detailed below.

Northwest – *tramontana*

This wind, also known as the *maestral* near Río Ebro and the *mistral* in France, is a strong, dry wind, cold in winter, which can be dangerous. It is caused by a secondary depression forming in the Golfo de León or the Golfo de Génova on the cold front of a major depression crossing France. The northwesterly airflow generated is compressed between the Alps and the Pyrenees and flows into the Mediterranean basin. In Spain it chiefly affects the coast to the north of Barcelona, the Islas Baleares, and is strongest at the northern end of the Costa Brava.

The *tramontana* can be dangerous in that it can arrive and reach gale force in as little as fifteen minutes on a calm sunny day with virtually no warning. Signs to watch for are brilliant visibility, clear sky – sometimes with cigar-shaped clouds – very dry air and a steady or slightly rising barometer. On rare occasions the sky may be cloudy when the wind first arrives although it clears later. Sometimes the barometer will plunge in normal fashion, rising quickly after the gale has passed. If at sea and some way from land, a line of white on the horizon and a developing swell give a few minutes' warning. The only effective warning that can be obtained is by radio – Marseille (in French) and Monaco (in French and English) are probably the best bet. *See page 13 for transmission details.*

The *tramontana* normally blows for at least three days but may last for a week or longer. It is frequent in the winter months, blowing for a third of the time and can reach Force 10 (50 knots) or more. In summer it is neither as strong nor as frequent.

West – *vendaval*

A depression crossing Spain or southern France creates a strong southwest to west wind, the *vendaval* or *poniente*, which funnels through the Strait of Gibraltar and along the south coast of Spain. Though normally confined to the south and southeast coasts, it occasionally blows in the

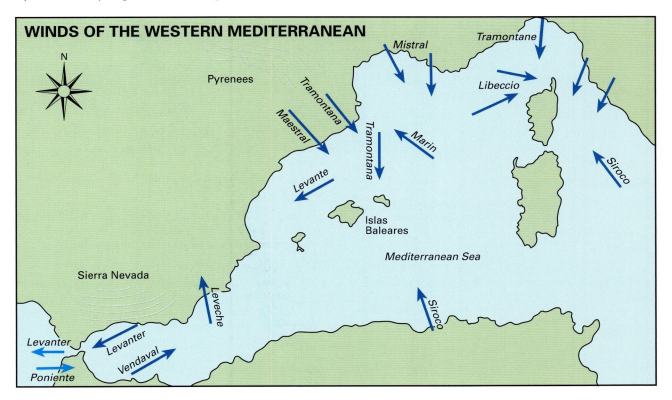

WINDS OF THE WESTERN MEDITERRANEAN

northeast of the area. It is usually short-lived and at its strongest from late autumn to early spring.

East – *levante*

Encountered from Gibraltar to Valencia and beyond, the *levante*, sometimes called the *llevantade* when it blows at gale force, is caused by a depression located between the Islas Baleares and the North African coast. It is preceded by a heavy swell (*las tascas*), cold damp air, poor visibility and low cloud which forms first around the higher hills. Heavy and prolonged rainfall is more likely in spring and autumn than summer. A *levante* may last for three or four days.

South – *siroco*

The hot wind from the south is created by a depression moving east along or just south of the North African coast. By the time this dry wind reaches Spain it can be very humid, with haze and cloud. If strong it carries dust, and should it rain when the cold front comes through, the water may be red or brown and the dust will set like cement. This wind is sometimes called the *leveche* in southeast Spain. It occurs most frequently in summer, seldom lasting more than one or two days.

Clouds

Cloud cover of between ⅘ and ⅝ in the winter months is about double the summer average of ⅖. Barcelona, however, seems to manage a year round average of ⅜ to ⅝. The cloud is normally cumulus and high level. In strong winds with a southerly component, complete cloud cover can be expected.

Precipitation

Annual rainfall is moderate and decreases towards the north from about 760mm at Gibraltar to 560mm at Barcelona. The rainy seasons predominantly in autumn and winter and in most areas the summer months are virtually dry. The Costa Brava however usually manages about 25mm of rain during each summer month. Most of the rain falls in very heavy showers of 1–2 hours.

Thunderstorms

Thunderstorms are most frequent in the autumn at up to four or five each month, and can be accompanied by hail.

Water spouts

Water spouts occur in the Strait of Gibraltar in winter and spring, usually associated with thunderstorms.

Snow

Snow at sea level is very rare but it falls and remains on the higher mountain ranges inland. Snow on the Sierra Nevada is particularly noticeable from the sea.

Visibility

Fog occurs about four days a month in summer along the Costa de Sol but elsewhere is very rare.

Occasionally dust carried by the southerly *siroco* reduces visibility and industrial areas such as Valencia and Barcelona produce haze.

Temperature

Winter temperatures at Gibraltar average 10–15°C, rising steadily after March to average 20–29°C in July and August. Afternoon (maximum) temperatures may reach 30–33°C in these months. At Barcelona, summer temperatures are much the same as at Gibraltar but winter temperatures are lower, 6–13°C.

Humidity

The relative humidity is moderate at around 60% to 80%. With winds from the west, northwest or north, low humidity can be expected; with winds off the sea, high humidity is normal. The relative humidity increases throughout the night and falls by day.

Local variations

In the northeastern area, the common winds blow between northwest and northeast. Gales may be experienced for 10% of the time during the winter, dropping to 2% in July and August, sometimes arriving with little warning and rapidly building to gale force.

The sea

Currents

There is a constant E-going surface current of one to two knots, passing in to the Mediterranean through the Strait of Gibraltar between the Costa del Sol and the African coast to replace water lost by evaporation. Northeast of Cabo de Gata up to the border with France, a significant inshore counter-eddy runs roughly SSW at one to 1½ knots. The shape of the coast produces variations in both direction and strength, especially around promontories.

Tides

Tides should be taken into account at the west end of the Costa del Sol and are noted in the introduction to that section. From Alicante to the border with France, the tide is hardly appreciable.

Swell

Winds between NE and SE can produce a dangerous swell on the E coast. Swell has a nasty capability of going round corners and getting into *calas*.

Scouring and silting

Many harbours and anchorages are located in sandy areas where depths can change dramatically in the course of a storm or a season. Dredging is a common feature but there is no certainty that depths will be maintained. Charts and drawings give no sure guide. When approaching or entering such areas, it is of great importance to sound carefully and to act on the information received.

Sea temperature

Sea temperatures in February are around 14°C on the Costa del Sol and 12°C on the Costa Brava. In summer, along the Costa Blanca it can rise to 20°C. Winds from the south and east tend to raise the temperature and those from the west and north to lower them.

Radio and weather forecasts

Details of coast radio stations, weather forecasts, weatherfax (radio facsimile) Navtex and Inmarsat-C coverage follow. See individual harbour details for port and marina radio information. All times quoted are in UT (universal time) unless otherwise specified. France Inter on LW, 163kHz, France Info on MW and Monaco 3AC on 4363kHz all use local time. Details of frequencies, channel and times are to be found in ALRS Vol 3 (1), RYA Booklet G5 and on the Internet.

Coast radio stations

VHF/MF

Coast radio stations are controlled from Malaga or Valencia – see diagram page 14. Full details will be found in the Admiralty *List of Radio Signals Vol 1 Part 1 (NP281/1)*.

On receipt of traffic, Spanish coast radio stations will call vessels once on Ch 16; after that the vessel's call sign will be included in scheduled MF traffic lists.

Malaga lighthouse

Weather forecasts

Marine VHF and MF

Inshore waters and Sea area forecasts are broadcast in Spanish and English on marine VHF all round Mediterranean Spain and the Balearic Islands. There are also broadcasts of Inshore waters forecasts and actual weather in Spanish only. *For details see the tables on page 14.*

For local area FM broadcast near Gibraltar *see page 25* for details of BFBS and Gibraltar BC.

Sea area forecasts can also be heard in English and Spanish on MF radio (*Table page 14*).

Non-radio weather forecasts

A recorded marine forecast in Spanish is available by ☎ (906) 36 53 71. The 'High Seas' bulletin includes the Islas Baleares.

Spanish television shows a useful synoptic chart with its land weather forecast every evening after the news at approximately 2120 weekdays, 1520 Saturday and 2020 Sunday. Most national and local newspapers also carry some form of forecast.

Nearly all marinas and yacht harbours display a synoptic chart and forecast, generally updated daily (though often posted rather late to be of use).

Rescue and emergency services

In addition to VHF Ch 16 (MAYDAY or PAN PAN as appropriate) the marine emergency services can be contacted by telephone at all times on ☎ 900 202 202.

The National Centre for Sea Rescue is based in Madrid but has a string of communications towers. On the spot responsibility for co-ordinating rescues lies with the Capitanías Marítimas with support from the Spanish Navy, customs, guardia civil etc. Lifeboats are stationed at some of the larger harbours but the majority do not appear to be all-weather boats.

The other emergency services can be contacted by dialling 003 for the operator and asking for policía (police), bomberos (fire service) or Cruz Roja (Red Cross). Alternatively the police can be contacted direct on 091.

Radio fax and teleprinter

Northwood (RN) broadcasts a full set of UK Met Office charts out to five days ahead on 2618.5, 4610, 8040 and 11086.5kHz. (Schedule at 0236, surface analysis at three hourly intervals from 0300 to 2100 and 2300.) Deutscher Wetterdienst broadcasts German weather charts on 3855, 7880 and 13882.5kHz. (Schedule at 1111, surface analysis at 0430, 1050, 1600, 2200.)

DWD broadcasts forecasts using RTTY on 4583, 7646 and 10001.8kHz (in English at 0415 and 1610), 11039 and 14467.3kHz (in German at 0535). Note that the 4583 and 14467.3kHz may not be useable in the Mediterranean. The most useful

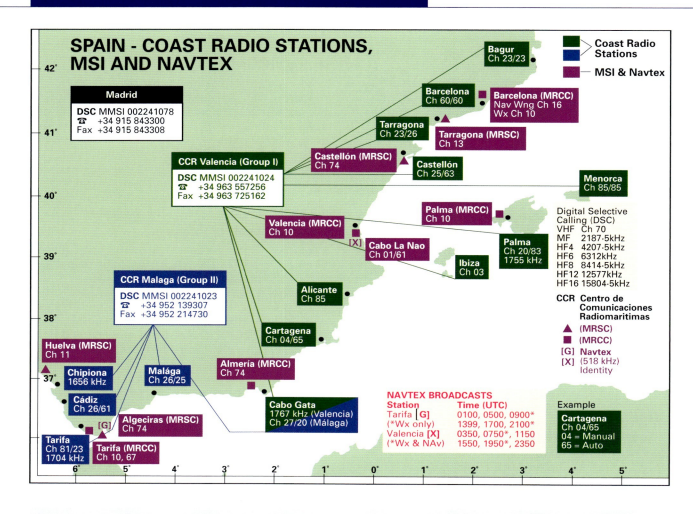

SPAIN - COAST RADIO STATIONS, MSI AND NAVTEX

Legend:
- ■ Coast Radio Stations (green)
- ■ MSI & Navtex (blue)

Madrid
DSC MMSI 002241078
☎ +34 915 843300
Fax +34 915 843308

CCR Valencia (Group I)
DSC MMSI 002241024
☎ +34 963 557256
Fax +34 963 725162

CCR Malaga (Group II)
DSC MMSI 002241023
☎ +34 952 139307
Fax +34 952 214730

Stations on map:
- Bagur Ch 23/23
- Barcelona Ch 60/60
- Barcelona (MRCC) Nav Wng Ch 16 Wx Ch 10
- Tarragona Ch 23/26
- Tarragona (MRSC) Ch 13
- Castellón (MRSC) Ch 74
- Castellón Ch 25/63
- Menorca Ch 85/85
- Palma (MRCC) Ch 10
- Palma Ch 20/83 1755 kHz
- Valencia (MRCC) Ch 10
- [X] Cabo La Nao Ch 01/61
- Ibiza Ch 03
- Alicante Ch 85
- Cartagena Ch 04/65
- Huelva (MRSC) Ch 11
- Chipiona 1656 kHz
- Málaga Ch 26/25
- Almería (MRCC) Ch 74
- Cádiz Ch 26/61
- Algeciras (MRSC) Ch 74
- Cabo Gata 1767 kHz (Valencia) Ch 27/20 (Málaga)
- Tarifa Ch 81/23 1704 kHz
- Tarifa (MRCC) Ch 10, 67
- [G]

Digital Selective Calling (DSC)
VHF Ch 70
MF 2187·5kHz
HF4 4207·5kHz
HF6 6312kHz
HF8 8414·5kHz
HF12 12577kHz
HF16 15804·5kHz

CCR Centro de Comunicaciones Radiomaritimas
▲ (MRSC)
■ (MRCC)
[G] Navtex
[X] (518 kHz) Identity

NAVTEX BROADCASTS

Station	Time (UTC)
Tarifa [G]	0100, 0500, 0900*
(*Wx only)	1399, 1700, 2100*
Valencia [X]	0350, 0750*, 1150
(*Wx & NAv)	1550, 1950*, 2350

Example:
Cartagena
Ch 04/65
04 = Manual
65 = Auto

Inshore waters forecasts and reports of actual weather are broadcast in English and Spanish as follows.

MRCC	VHF Ch	Time UT
CZCS Tarifa	10, 67, 73	H2+15
CLCS Algeciras	74	0315, 0515, 0715, 1115, 1515, 1915, 2315
CRCS Almería	10, 67, 73	H1+15
CRCS Barcelona	10	0600, 0900, 1500, 2000
CRCS Valencia	10, 67	H2+15
CLCS Tarragona	13	0533, 0933, 1533, 2033
CRCS Palma	10	0735, 1035, 1535, 2035

H1 = odd hours. H2 = even hours

Sea area forecasts are broadcast in English and Spanish as follows

Station	kHz	Time UT
Chipiona	1656kHz	0733, 1233, 1933
Tarifa	1704kHz	0733, 1233, 1933
Cabo de Gata	1767kHz	0750, 1303, 1950
Palma	1755kHz	0750, 1303, 1950

Sea area and inshore waters forecasts are broadcast in Spanish as follows

MRCC Málaga	VHF Ch	Times UT
Cádiz	26	
Tarifa	81	0833, 1133, 2003
Málaga	26	
Cabo Gata	27	

MRCC Valencia	VHF Ch	Times UT
Cartagena	4	
Alicante	85	
Cabo La Nao	2	
Castellón	25	
Tarragona	23	0910, 1410, 2110
Barcelona	60	
Bagur	23	
Menorca	85	
Palma	20	
Ibiza	3	

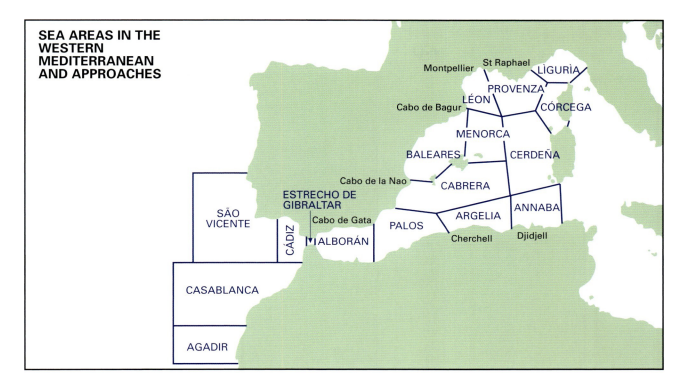

SEA AREAS IN THE WESTERN MEDITERRANEAN AND APPROACHES

The Spanish and French use a common set of sea areas and use the same names although spelling and pronunciation differ at times. The French names for the Mediterranean Sea areas are Alboran, Palos, Alger, Cabrera, Baléares, Minorque, Lion, Provence, Ligure, Corse, Sardaigne, and Annaba. In the approaches to the Mediterranean the French names are identical to the Spanish.

products are forecasts up to five days ahead at 12 hourly intervals and up to two days ahead at six hour intervals. Alternatively, a dedicated receiver 'Weatherman' will record automatically: see www.nasamarine.com.

UK Marine Mobile Net

The Net covering the Eastern Atlantic and the Mediterranean, can be heard daily on 14303kHz USB at 0800 and 1800 UT. On Saturday morning the broadcast sometimes contains a longer period outlook. Forecasts will be a rehash of what the Net leader has gleaned from various sources. No licence is required if a receive-only HF radio is used.

Monaco 3AC

Monaco 3AC broadcasts on 8728 and 8806kHz USB at 0715 and 1830 in French and English. The texts are those broadcast by INMARSAT-C for the western part of METAREA III. Monaco also broadcasts on 4363kHz at 0903 and 1915 LT in French and English and at 1403 in French only. Texts are as the latest Toulon NAVTEX broadcast.

NAVTEX AND INMARSAT-C

NAVTEX and INMARSAT-C are the primary GMDSS modes for transmission of all Marine Safety Information. Broadcast times for weather are as follows

Transmitter	Times (UTC)
Tarifa – G (518kHz)	0900 and 2100
Cabo la Nao – X (Valencia) (518kHz)	0750 and 1950
La Garde – W (Toulon) (518kHz)	1140 and 2340
La Garde – S (Toulon) (490kHz)	0700 and 1900
INMARSAT-C METAREA III	1000 and 2200

Internet

Many sites provide weather information and most, even the official sites, do change from time to time. For a good starting point, the RCCPF recommends Frank Singleton's site www.franksingleton.clara.net Also see www.rccpf.org.uk under technical matters. Skippers are urged to use the Internet as a supplementary source of information and to ensure that CMDSS forecasts can be obtained on board.

GRIB coded forecasts

This service enables arrow diagram forecasts for up to five days ahead, and other information to be obtained in email form (or by marine HF and HAM radio). The data is highly compressed so that a great deal of information can be acquired quickly, even using a mobile phone connected to a laptop. See websites under Internet. There is no charge for this service.

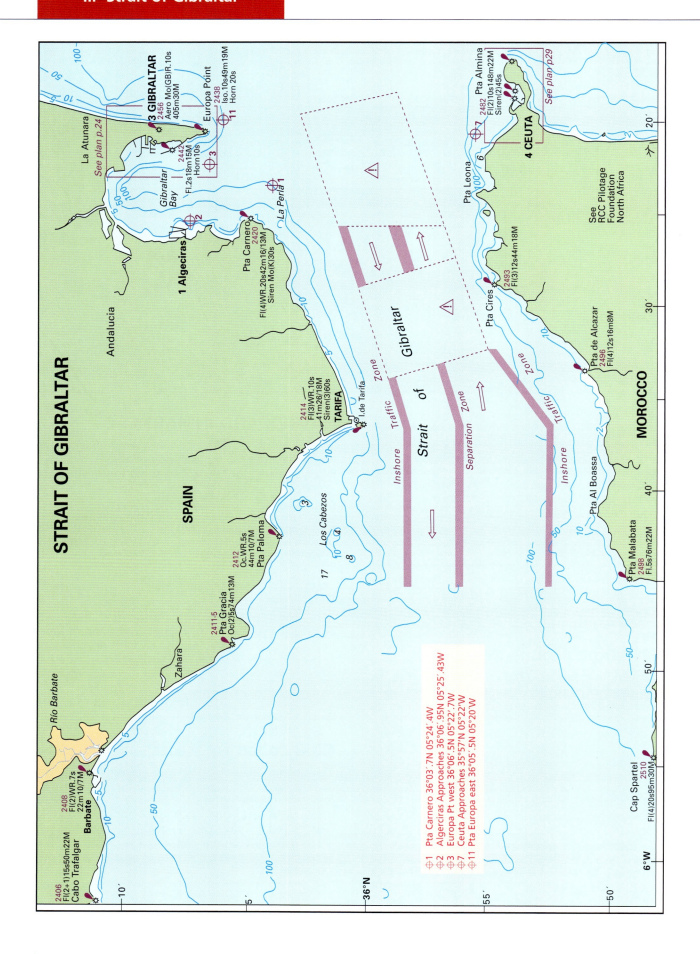

STRAIT OF GIBRALTAR

3 GIBRALTAR

2456 Aero Mo(GB)R.10s
405m30M

Europa Point
2438 Iso.10s49m19M
Horn 20s

11

2442 Fl.2s18m15M
Horn 10s

3

La Atunara
See plan p.24

Gibraltar Bay

1 Algeciras

Pta Carnero
2420
Fl(4)WR.20s42m16/13M
Siren Mo(K)30s

La Perla **1**

2

1

Andalucia

SPAIN

Zahara

2411.5
Pta Gracia
Oc(2)5s74m13M

2412
Oc.WR.5s
44m10/7M
Pta Paloma

Los Cabezos

17   8   4   3
10

2414
Fl(3)WR.10s
41m26/18M
Siren(3)60s

TARIFA

I.de Tarifa

Inshore Traffic Zone

Strait of Gibraltar

Separation Zone

⚠

⚠

Río Barbate

Barbate
2408
Fl(2)WR.7s
22m10/7M

2406
Fl(2+1)15s50m22M
Cabo Trafalgar

Cap Spartel
2510
Fl(4)20s95m30M

Pta Leona

Pta Almina
2482 Fl(2)10s148m22M
Siren(2)45s

4 CEUTA
See plan p.29

7

Pta Cires

2493
Fl(3)12s44m18M

Inshore Traffic Zone

See
RCC Pilotage
Foundation
North Africa

Pta de Alcazar
2496
Fl(4)12s16m8M

MOROCCO

Pta Al Boassa

Pta Malabata
2498
Fl.5s76m22M

⊕1   Pta Carnero 36°03′.7N 05°24′.4W
⊕2   Algeciras Approaches 36°06′.95N 05°25′.43W
⊕3   Europa Pt west 36°06′.5N 05°22′.7W
⊕7   Ceuta Approaches 35°57′N 05°22′W
⊕11 Pta Europa east 36°05′.5N 05°20′W

6°W   10′   5′   55′   50′

36°N   20′   30′   40′   50′

I. ENTRANCE TO THE MEDITERRANEAN

I.i Strait of Gibraltar

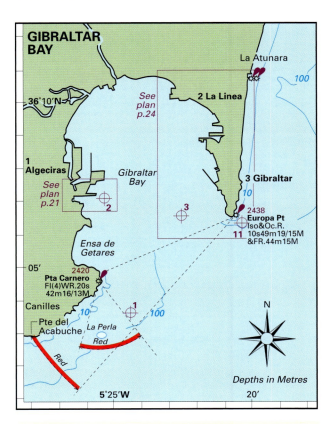

Waypoints

⊕1 Pta Camero 36°03'.7N 05°24'.4W
⊕2 Algerciras Approach 36°06'.95N 05°25'.43W
⊕3 Europa Pt W. 36°06'.5N 05°22'.7W
⊕4 South Mole 36°08'N 05°22'.3W
⊕5 North Mole 36°09'N 05°22'.35W
⊕6 La Linea Approach 36°09'.5N 05°22'.2W
⊕7 Ceuta Approach 35°57'N 05°22'W
⊕8 Ceuta Hbr 35°54'N 05°18'.5W
⊕9 Cabo Tres Forcas 35°27'.5N 02°55'W
⊕10 Melilla Hbr 35°17'.5N 02°55'W
⊕11 Europa Pt E 36°05'.5N 05°20'W

PORTS

1. **Algeciras**
2. **La Linea**
3. **Gibraltar**
4. **Ceuta (Sebta)**
5. **Melilla**

Introduction

This chapter covers the Strait of Gibraltar, Algeciras Bay, Gibraltar and the two North African Spanish enclaves of Ceuta and Melilla.

Reference books for the approach from the RCC Pilotage Foundation:

From the Atlantic
Atlantic Crossing Guide 2003
Atlantic Islands 2004

From the north
Atlantic Spain and Portugal 2006

From the south
North Africa 2005

Around Gibraltar, weather usually conforms to the local area forecast, (unlike further E where local forecasting is notoriously difficult). A full gale can be blowing in Tarifa, while a short distance away E of the Strait, winds are light. Winds in excess of 30 knots are said to blow at Tarifa for 300 days of the year. There is almost always some wind in the Strait and can be expected to be either E (*Levante*) or W (*poniente*). The E winds bring a large cloud which hangs over the W side of the rock, often for several days, producing high humidity and miserable conditions. On rare occasions, as low pressure and associated fronts move N from the Canaries in winter, strong SW winds bring rain and squally conditions. These winds often mean the airport is closed. The general summer wind pattern is light overnight, rising to Force 3 or 4 during the afternoon and going down at sunset.

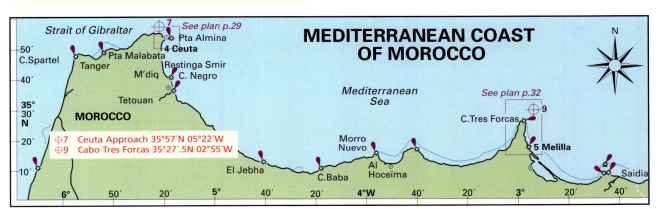

Traffic Separation Zone

There is a Traffic Separation Zone in the Strait of Gibraltar between 5°25'.5W and 5°45'W – see plan on page 16. The Inshore Traffic Zone to the north is nowhere less than 1.7M wide (off the Isla de Tarifa) and generally more than 2M. Tarifa Traffic monitors VHF Ch 16 and 10 and vessels are advised to maintain a listening watch whilst in the area. Weather and visibility information for an area including the Traffic Separation Zone is broadcast on VHF Ch 10 and 67.

PRINCIPAL LIGHTS

Europe

2406 Cabo Trafalgar Fl(2+1)15s51m22M
    White conical tower and building 34m
2411.5 Punta de Gracia (Punta Camarinal)
    Oc(2)5s75m13M Masonry tower 20m
2412 Punta Paloma Oc.WR.5s45m10/7M
    010°-W-340°-R-010° (over Bajo de Los Cabezos)
    Two-storey building 5m
2414 Tarifa Fl(3)WR.10s41m26/18M
    089°-R-1130-W-089° (over Bajo de Los Cabezos)
Racon Mo 'C'(-") 20M White tower 33m
    Siren (3)60s Masonry structure 10m
2420 Punta Carnero Fl(4)WR.20s42m16/13M
    018°-W -325°-R-018° (Red sector covers La Perla
    and Las Bajas shoals) Siren Mo(K)30s
    Round tower and white building 19m
2438 Europa Point, Gibraltar
    Iso.IOs49m19M 197°-W-042°-R-067°-W-125°
    Oc.R.IOsISM and F.R.15M 042°-vis-067° (Red sector
    covers La Perla and Las Bajas shoals) Horn 20s
    White tower, red band 19m

Africa

2510 Cabo Espartel Fl(4)20s95m30M
    Yellow square stone tower 24m
2498 Pta Malabata Fl.5s77m22M
    Brown square tower on dwelling 18m
2496 Ksar es Srhir Fl(4)12s16m8M
    Column on metal tower 11m
2493 Pta Cires Fl(3)12s44m18M
    Brown tower 8m
2482 Pta Almina Fl(2)10s148m22M
    White tower and building 16m

Gibraltar from the south

Transiting the Straits of Gibraltar

Many yachts use Gibraltar as their departure point for trips to the east, west or south. Many elements combine to produce a complex system of tides and current in the Straits, an appreciation of which will greatly help yachtsman, especially when heading west as it is possible to spend many fruitless hours trying to make a passage through the Straits. The paragraphs below are included to assist the yachtsman transiting the Straits.

Eight miles separate Europe from Africa at its narrowest point in the Straits. The water at the western end of the 30 mile stretch is some 2–3m higher than at the eastern end, thus causing a constant surface flow into the Mediterranean. This is partially due to evaporation in the Mediterranean, which is three times faster than the rate at which the combined waters from rivers flow into it; and the fact that the Atlantic is tidal with a predominantly westerly swell, whereas the land-locked Mediterranean, is virtually non tidal. This produces a standing E-going surface current of between one and two knots.

Differences in salinity between the Atlantic and the Mediterranean force the heavier water down, causing a sub surface current in the opposite direction.

Wind also creates a surface current, depending whether it is E (levante) or W (poniente), which confuses the equation still further.

Then there are the tides, which are well documented in Admiralty tide tables. At the eastern end of the Straits the range is only half a metre and negligible once a few miles into the Mediterranean, whereas at Tanger, Morocco, the spring range is 3m. Barometric pressure differences also affect the height of water.

On the N side of the Western Straits is Tarifa. Winds in excess of 30 knots are said to blow there for 300 days of the year, whereas at the same time, winds at the eastern end may be negligible, resulting in conditions at one end of the Strait being very different from those at the other.

Currents also vary in different parts of the Straits, and even run in opposite directions at the same time, as shown on the tidal charts. From these conflicting and confusing parameters some guidelines can be extracted.

Eastbound vessels

For yachts entering the straits from the W there is no real problem going eastwards, unless there is a strong easterly wind, in which case the passage will be rough, especially around Tarifa, where winds often reach 40 knots. If strong winds are forecast, stay in Tanger or Barbate until it drops, or anchor in the lee of Tarifa if strong E winds are encountered once on passage.

During periods of light easterly winds, sea mist or fog may be persistent in the Straits, especially during the morning.

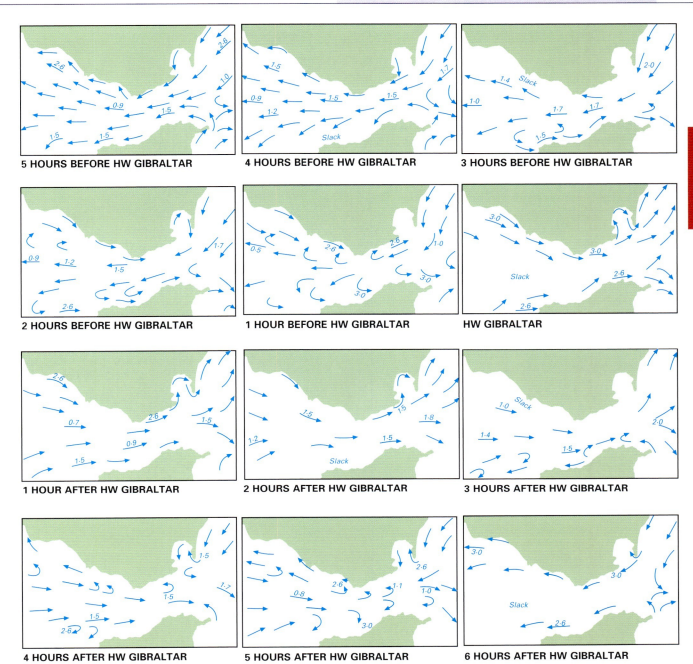

5 HOURS BEFORE HW GIBRALTAR

4 HOURS BEFORE HW GIBRALTAR

3 HOURS BEFORE HW GIBRALTAR

2 HOURS BEFORE HW GIBRALTAR

1 HOUR BEFORE HW GIBRALTAR

HW GIBRALTAR

1 HOUR AFTER HW GIBRALTAR

2 HOURS AFTER HW GIBRALTAR

3 HOURS AFTER HW GIBRALTAR

4 HOURS AFTER HW GIBRALTAR

5 HOURS AFTER HW GIBRALTAR

6 HOURS AFTER HW GIBRALTAR

These diagrams are published with the kind permission of Dr M Sloma, editor of *Yacht Scene*. Under no circumstances will *Yacht Scene* or the Pilotage Foundation be liable for any accident or injury, which may occur to vessels or persons whilst using the above current predictions

The best time to depart for the trip east is soon after LW. From Tanger, keeping close inshore, the light and increasing E-going current off Punta Malabata will be useful. If going to Gibraltar, most vessels cross to Tarifa from Punta Malabata, or from Punta Ciris, 12 miles further E.

Westbound vessels

In strong westerlies it is almost impossible to make headway W, due to the combined E-going current that can, with unfavourable tide, reach six knots or more, with heavy steep swell and overfalls off Ceuta Point, Tarifa and Punta Malabata.

In good conditions, to make use of the favourable current, set off from Gibraltar two hours after HW. Keeping close inshore, a foul current of around a knot will be experienced off Punta Carnero.

A favourable W-going current four hours after HW will assist passage during springs, although this is weak and E-going at neaps.

Crossing from Tarifa to Tanger it is usually wise to use the engine to make a fast passage, to combat the increasing E-going current, or anchor in the sheltered W side of Tarifa and wait for the next favourable tide, around LW to make the crossing. It is possible, using the engine, to make a fast passage

I. ENTRANCE TO THE MEDITERRANEAN

from Gibraltar without encountering heavy adverse currents.

From Ceuta, the timing is similar: set off two hours after HW, keeping close inshore to make use of the counter current.

Gibraltar to Ceuta

Crossing from N to S and vice versa can normally be undertaken at any state of tide, since winds through the Straits are predominantly E or W, although it is important to leave enough sea room to counter the tide and currents.

Remember, in general, a combined current of 1–2 knots is usually E-going, in addition to tidal effects. Beware of rough over-falls and stronger currents around Europa Point and Ceuta Point. Entering Ceuta harbour, this is particularly noticeable one mile NE, off the entrance.

The above information is based on several articles regarding tides, current and wind effects in the Straits of Gibraltar, as well as many hours testing out the theories in over 50 journeys transiting them.

The currents in the Straits are still full of surprises and for sailing purists who do not want a motor-assisted transit, this can be very challenging.

The Dársena del Saladillo at Algeciras, seen from east-southeast. Although the Real Club Náutico de Algeciras, the Club Náutico Saladillo and the Club Deportivo El Pargo all have pontoons in the harbour, none currently accept visitors

1 Algeciras

Waypoints
⊕1 Punta Carnero 36°03'.7N 05°24'.4W
(1.3M SE of point)
⊕2 Marina entrance 36°06'.95N 05°25'.43W

Tides
Standard port – Gibraltar
Mean time differences HW -0010, LW -0010
Heights in metres

MHWS	MHWN	MLWN	MLWS
1.1	0.9	0.4	0.2

Charts	Approach	Harbour
Admiralty	91, 773, 142, 3578, 1448	1455
Imray	C19, C50	
Spanish	44C, 45A, 105, 445, 445A	4451

Principal lights

Commercial harbour
2425 **NE breakwater** Fl.R.5s11m7M Red tower 8m
Work is still going on refilling SE of Isla Verde and there are now 2 breakwaters that have nearly joined just N of the yacht basin. There are lights at the ends of the breakwaters but yachts should keep well clear of the ongoing work.
East pier (under construction)
20163-b(S) E head Fl(4)Y.12s4m3M Yellow post with X top
20164(S) S head VQ(6)+LFl.10s4m3M S cardinal post .
Darsena del Saladillo (yacht basin)
2423 **Dique de Abrigo head** Fl(3)R.9s4m3M Red post 1m.

Night entry is not advised since all three marinas in the darsena are private and anchoring is forbidden.

Coast Radio Station
Algeciras Digital Selective Calling
MMSI 002241001 VHF Ch16, 74
Weather bulletins in Spanish & English VHF Ch 74 at 0315, 0515, 0715, 1115, 1515, 1915, 2315 UTC
Navigational warnings in Spanish & English on request.

Harbour Communications
Port Authority ☎ 956 585400/585431
Fax 956 585443/585431
Email comercial@apba.es www.apba.es
VHF Ch 8, 13, 16, 74 (call Algeciras trafico)
Real Club Nautico de Algeciras VHF Ch 9, 16
☎ 956 600666 *Fax* 956 601402

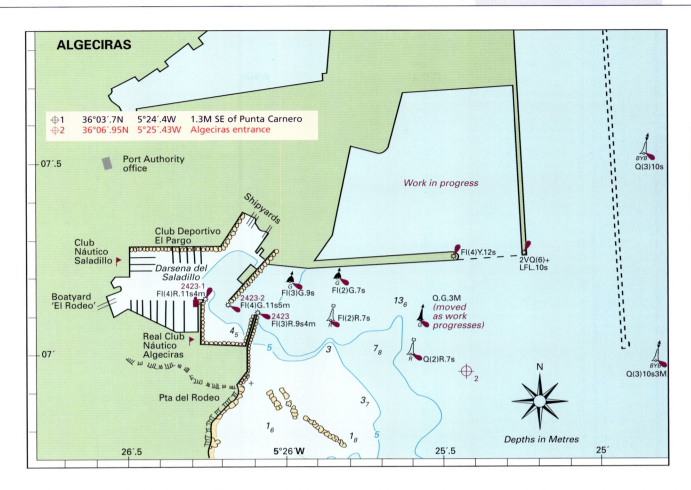

I. ENTRANCE TO THE MEDITERRANEAN

Major commercial harbour, with three private marinas in a separate basin

Algeciras is primarily an industrial and ferry port, through which passes many of the guest-workers returning to Africa with roof racks bending under their loads.

Yachts have their own basin – the Darsena del Saladillo – south of the main harbour, where three separate clubs run three separate marinas. Sadly none welcome visiting yachts (see Berthing, below). The following approach and entrance instructions are given for the Darsena del Saladillo in the hope that this situation may one day change.

Approach

The approaches to Algeciras are extremely busy with commercial traffic of all sizes. In particular, a sharp watch needs to be kept for the many high-speed ferries, including hydrofoils, which run between Algeciras and Morocco. These are notorious for maintaining their course and speed at all times, presumably adhering to the 'might is right' principle.

Coming from the west, there are dangers up to 1M offshore between Punta de Gala Arenas and Punta Carnero. On rounding this headland the city and harbour will be seen some 3M to the north behind a mile-long breakwater terminating with a light. Various ledges run out from the headlands between Punta Carnero and the entrance to the Darsena del Saladillo (also lit).

If approaching from Gibraltar or other points east, the entrance to the Darsena del Saladillo should be easily seen south of the oil tanks on the commercial quay and it can be approached directly.

If approaching from the south, possibly from Ceuta or elsewhere in Morocco, WP1 lies in clear water southeast of Punta Carnero, a course of 346° for 3.4M leading to WP2 in the approaches to the Darsena del Saladillo, passing close to a spherical yellow ODAS buoy off Punta Calero en route.

Yachts can safely cut inside the east cardinal buoy placed nearly a mile offshore, though an offing of at least 0.5M should be maintained. Further ledges lie both north and south of the entrance, and the three buoys marking the approach should under no circumstances be ignored. In 2008 major infilling work was taking place to the north of the Saladillo entrance (see plan) outside of which a new breakwater is under construction, marked by additional E cardinal light buoys. Keep well clear.

Entrance

The dogleg entrance to the Darsena del Saladillo has been very well designed, such that when visited in a 30 knot easterly wind no swell at all was entering. As noted above, three buoys mark the final approach, after which the entrance itself is straightforward.

Berthing

As stated above none of the three marinas in the Darsena del Saladillo accept visitors. Taken clockwise on entry these are the Real Club Nautico de Algeciras, which previously had premises in the main harbour, the Club Nautico Saladillo and the Club Deportivo El Pargo. The first (southern) marina is also the largest by a considerable margin, and would undoubtedly be the best one to try in an emergency. It is also the club where some English is most likely to be spoken, and visitors are also welcome to dine in the Real Club Nautico's restaurant.

Facilities

The Real Club Nautico Marina is provided with all the usual facilities, including a fuel berth at the end of the breakwater which forms its eastern limit.

The city offers all normal facilities. Trains run to many destinations, including Madrid, and buses to La Línea from which it is a short walk to the airport at Gibraltar.

Spanish charts may be obtained either from SUISCA SL ☎ 902 220 007 or from Valnáutica ☎ 956 570677.

La Linea Marina under construction

Below are a model and photo of the new 800 berth marina at La Linea under construction in March 2009 for opening early 2010. La Linea old private marina in foreground, Gibraltar airport runway beyond.
Marina ☎ 956 791 000 *Fax*: 956 791 045
www.alcaidesa.com

2. La Linea

⊕6 36° 09'.5N 05° 22'.2W

Charts
Admiralty 1455
Imray C19, C50
Spanish 4451

Lights
2436.8 Dique de Abrigo head Fl(2)G.7s8m3M. Green tower 3m
2436.81 Puerto Chico Jetty head Q.R.5m3M Red tower 3m
Note: Three starboard hand buoys form an approach channel for the RoRo ferries.

Communications
Club Maritimo Linense ☎ 956 176 506 *Fax* 956 176 479

New marina construction

With the difficulties of finding room to anchor in Gibraltar it was, until recently, possible to anchor north of the La Linea breakwater. However, as of early September 2008 all anchored craft were asked to vacate the area as a company, Alcaidesa Group ☎ 956 791 000 *Fax* 956 791 045, had started to construct a huge marina in the southeast part of the anchorage area. An artist's impression of the marina can be seen on www.puertodeportivoalcaidesa.es/es/.

The present club and Puerto Chico jetty will remain with its 11 pontoons but it is strictly private with no space for visitors. One is allowed to use the restaurant in the club.

Facilities

At present there are only limited facilities for the yachtsman here but there is good shopping, including a large supermarket and an excellent produce market in the town. Gibraltar is well within walking distance but note it is necessary to show one's passport to cross the border.

It has been reported (September 2007) that there is a spate of dinghy stealing going on at La Linea. It is recommended that dinghies be hoisted aboard during the night and to carefully lock dinghy and all oars, motors etc. when leaving it ashore.

⊕6 La Linea Approach 36°09'.5N 05°22'.2W

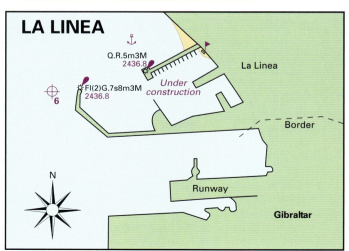

I.ii Gibraltar

3. Gibraltar

36°09'N 5°22'W

Tides

Gibraltar is a standard port.
Heights in metres

MHWS	MHWN	MLWN	MLWS
1.0	0.7	0.3	0.1

Charts

	Approach	Harbour
British Admiralty	*91, 142*	*145*
	773, 3578	*144*
Spanish	*445, 445A*	*4452*
French	*7042, 7300*	*7026*
Imray	*M11, C19*	*M11*
	C50	*C50*

Lights
Approach

2414 **Tarifa** 36°00'.IN 05°36'.6W
Fl(3)WR.10s41m26/18M White tower
33m 113°-W-089°-R-113°

2420 **Punta Camero** 36°04'.6N
05°25'.6W Fl(4)WR20s42m16/13M
018°-W-325°-R-018° Siren Mo(K)30s
Round tower and white building 19m

2456 **Gibraltar Aeromarine** 36°08'.6N
05°20'.6W Mo(GB)RI0s405m30M
Obscured on westerly bearings within
2M

2438 **Europa Point** 36°06'.6N 05°20'.7W
Iso.10s49m 19M OcR 10s15M and F.R
15M 042°-vis-067° Horn 20s White
round tower, red band 19m

Harbour

2442 **South breakwater, north end (A
head)** Fl.2s18m15M Horn 10s White
tower 15m

2445 **Detached breakwater, south end
(B head)** Q.R.9m5M Metal structure
on concrete building 11m

2446 **Detached breakwater, north end
(C head)** Q.G.10m5M Metal structure
on concrete building 11m

2448 **North breakwater, southwest arm
(D head)** Q.R.18m5M Round tower
17m

2449.2 **North breakwater, northwest
elbow (E head)** F.R.28m5M Tower
Plus other lights in the interior of the
harbour and to the north

Port communications
Radio

Gibraltar Port Control VHF Ch 16,
6,12,13,14 (24 hours)
Lloyds radio VHF Ch 8,12,14,16
(24 hours)

Queens Harbourmaster VHF Ch 8
(0800–1600 Monday to Friday) All
marinas VHF Ch 71 (0830–2030, later in
summer)

Telephone and email
Port Captain ☎ 200772 54
Port Operations Room ☎ 20078134/
20077004
Queensway Quay ☎ 20044700
Fax 20044699
Email qqmarina@gibnet.gi
Marina Bay Office ☎ 20073300
Fax 20042656
Email pieroffice@marinabay.gi
www.marinabay.gi
Sheppards Marina Repair facilities
☎ 200768 95, Chandlery ☎ 200771 83
Ocean Village ☎ 20040048
Email info@oceanvillage.gi
www.oceanvillage.gi

I. ENTRANCE TO THE MEDITERRANEAN

Gibraltar: Rounding
Europa point. Note
the mosque behind
the light
Graham Hutt

Major commercial port with good facilities

Gibraltar's location on the southern tip of the Iberian peninsula, its proximity to North Africa and its small population (30,000) predominantly English speaking community, makes 'The Rock' invaluable to yachtsmen. It has an airport with daily flights to the UK and Madrid and is an ideal place to take on supplies, fuel, carry out repairs and explore Spain. It offers a safe place to maintain ship, with many facilities available with European and US agencies represented for servicing and chandlery. Due to

many changes taking place affecting mooring availability, space is currently limited, These changes have also downgraded the services and supplies available from local chandleries, as reported by several yachtsmen based in the area.

There are two marinas, both on the western side of the Rock, in the Bay of Gibraltar (known as the Bay of Algeciras to the Spanish). A third is currently under construction next to Marina Bay. This 'Ocean Village' complex will be combined with Marina Bay to enlarge the yacht mooring facilities.

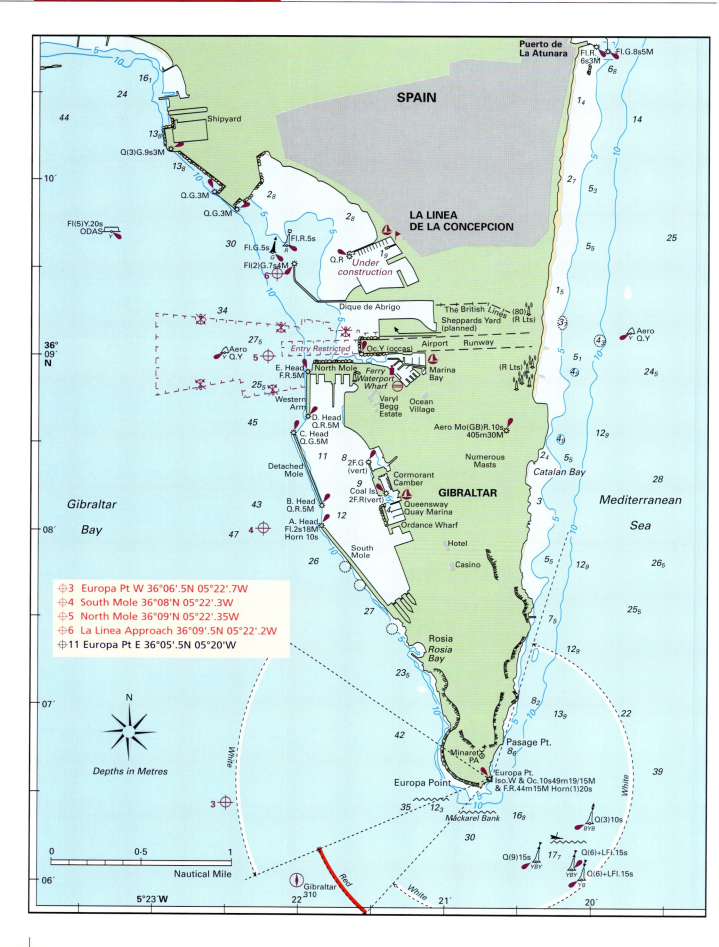

Puerto de La Atunara

Fl.R. 6s3M Fl.G.8s5M

6₈

1₄

14

SPAIN

24

16₁

44

Shipyard

13₈

Q(3)G.9s3M

13₈

Q.G.3M

Q.G.3M

2₈

2₇

5₃

25

2₈

LA LINEA DE LA CONCEPCION

Fl(5)Y.20s ODAS

30

Fl.G.5s Fl.R.5s

Fl(2)G.7s4M

6

Q.R

1₉

Under construction

5₅

34

Dique de Abrigo

The British Sheppards Yard (planned)

Lines (80) (R Lts)

1₅

27₅

Aero Y Q.Y

5

Entry Restricted

Airport   Runway

Aero Y Q.Y

3

5₁

4₉

24₅

E. Head F.R.5M

North Mole

Oc.Y (occas)

(R Lts)

36° 09' N

25₅

Western Arm

Ferry Waterport Wharf

Marina Bay

Varyl Begg Estate

Ocean Village

Aero Mo(GB)R.10s 405m30M

4₉

12₉

D. Head Q.R.5M

45

C. Head Q.G.5M

Numerous Masts

2₄

5₅

28

11

8 2F.G (vert)

Detached Mole

9 Coal Is 2F.R(vert)

Cormorant Camber

GIBRALTAR

3

Catalan Bay

Gibraltar

43

B. Head Q.R.5M

Queensway Quay Marina

Mediterranean

Bay

12

A. Head Fl.2s18M Horn 10s

47 4

26

South Mole

Ordance Wharf

Hotel

Casino

5₅

12₉

Sea

26₅

27

25₅

Rosia Rosia Bay

23₅

7₅

12₉

22

N

42

8₂

13₉

Depths in Metres

Minaret PA

Pasage Pt.

8₆

39

White

Europa Point

Europa Pt. Iso.W & Oc.10s49m19/15M & F.R.44m15M Horn(1)20s

3

35   12₃

Mackarel Bank

16₈

Q(3)10s BYB

30

Q(9)15s YBY

17₇

Q(6)+LFl.15s YBY

Q(6)+LFl.15s YB

White

White

Red

0   0.5   1

Nautical Mile

Gibraltar 310

22

5°23'W

21'

20'

36° 10'

08'

07'

06'

⊕3 Europa Pt W 36°06'.5N 05°22'.7W
⊕4 South Mole 36°08'N 05°22'.3W
⊕5 North Mole 36°09'N 05°22'.35W
⊕6 La Linea Approach 36°09'.5N 05°22'.2W
⊕11 Europa Pt E 36°05'.5N 05°20'W

Note: Until Ocean village marina developments have been completed, available moorings for visiting yachts are extremely limited so it is essential to book ahead.

Approach

By day

Gibraltar Rock, rising to 406m, is clearly visible except in fog, which is rare, though more frequent in summer, It is safe to enter the Bay of Gibraltar (Algeciras Bay) in almost any conditions but beware of squalls near the Rock once in the bay, particularly during strong easterlies, when strong downdraughts occur off the Rock From the Sand E, Europa point is prominent, with its lighthouse at the end. A short distance further up the point, the minaret of a new mosque will be observed, Strong currents and overfalls occur around the tip of the point when wind is against tide. From the W, Pt Carenero light lies at the SW entrance to the bay, near an old whaling station. The coast is fringed with wrecks from all eras, many popular as dive sites – any vessel flying International Code Flag A (white with a blue swallowtail) should be given a generous clearance, Yachts must also give way to naval and commercial vessels at all times.

By night

The W side of the Rock is well illuminated by the town; and to the E by the bright red lights marking the radio antennas on the N face; which is itself illuminated by spotlights. This can be confusing even in good visibility and makes lights difficult to identify. The most conspicuous are likely to be those on the S mole's A head and N moles D head. To the S is the lighthouse on Europa point, easily seen from NNE through to NNW, with a small red sector indicating the dangerous rocky shoreline to the W between Pta del Acebuche and Pta Carnero, which must be given a wide berth. If approaching in poor visibility beware the amount of traffic in the vicinity. From WP3 in the SE part of the Bay a course of 012° for 15M leads to WP4 for approach to Queensway Quay, or 007° for 25M to WP5 for approach to Marina Bay.

GPS Waypoints

WP3 gives clearance rounding Europa Point, WP1 clears the dangers coming from the W around Pta Carenero. WP4 is off the detached mole leading to Queensway Quay Marina and WP5 is off the N mole leading to Nfarina bay.

Entry formalities

Whereas in the past all yachts calling at Gibraltar first proceeded to the customs and immigration offices opposite Marina Bay, this no longer applies. Proceed to any marina where paper formalities are part of the check-in process carried out by marina staff.

Gibraltar, like the UK, is not party to the Shengen agreement, which has different visa requirements to Spain. Check for latest information from the Gibraltar government web site www.gibraltar.gov,gi or contact the immigration department ☎ 20046411 *Email* rgpimm@gibynex.gi.

Gibraltar weather forecasts

Radio Gibraltar (GBC) and British Forces Radio (BFBS) broadcast local weather forecasts (see table below). The marinas post weather faxes on their notice boards daily. See also www.bbc.co.uk/weather/coast/pressure/ and http://meteonet.nl/aktueel/brackall.htm for five day forecasts. Sites www.sto-p.com/atol and www.accuweather.com give complete hour-by-hour predictions over 16 hours and general forecasts up to 15 days.

Tarifa Radio broadcasts area weather on Channel 16 at regular intervals, in Spanish and English.

Gibraltar weather forecasts

LT	BFBS 1			BFBS2	Gibraltar BC		
	Mon-Fri	Sat	Sun	Mon-Fri	Mon-Fri	Sat	Sun
0530					X	X	
0630					X	X	X
0730					X	X	X
0745	X						
0845	X	X	X				
0945		X	X				
1005	X						
1030					X		
1200				X			
1202		X	X				
1230					X	X	X
1602		X					
1605	X						

Also storm warnings on receipt			1438 AM
	93.5 FM	89.4 FM	91.3 FM
	97.8 FM	99.5 FM	92.6 FM
Includes high and low water times			100.5 FM

Crew intending to remain ashore, or obtain work in Gibraltar should inform Immigration Authorities of their intention and supply an address.

Anchoring in the Bay

Anchorage is possible (although not encouraged) N of the runway in 4–6m sand, with good holding. As this area is British territory it is first necessary to clear Customs and Immigration, which may create a problem now that these are handled only by the marinas (see above). For safety reasons yachts are prohibited from anchoring close to the runway or on the flight path anywhere W of the runway, Closer to the Spanish shore of La Linea is a newly completed long jetty, The anchorage has been considerably reduced by the placing of buoys in the area, Some surging can be expected during S winds. A better anchorage is NNW, near the La Linea harbour mole.

Queensway Quay Marina

Location 36°08'.1N 05°21'.3W

The Marina

This is the closest marina to Europa Point. The marina was reconstructed during 2005/2006 due to initial design faults which allowed unacceptable surging, with resulting damage to yachts, The entry point moved to the NW and construction is still in progress on the new breakwater (early 2008). The marina entrance was moved from west to north with a new 'island' created between marina and harbour. Queensway Quay Development will include luxury apartments, a restaurant and many business enterprises around the marina.

Queensway Quay Marina has the advantage of being some distance from the airport, with all noise, and is close to the largest supermarket, Morrisons, and Main Street, which is also within walking distance. It provides 150 berths. Some will be allocated to the owners of the houses being built on the new island.

Entry formalities

Both marina and entry formalitles are now completed at the marina office.

Approach

The marina is approached through the main harbour via either of the two entrances, continuing towards the gap between Coaling Island and the new island which forms the W side of Queensway Quay (soon to be colonized by sizeable apartments). On passing through this gap the entrance lies immediately to starboard. The buildings overlookmg the marina are floodlit.

Berthing

Visitors' berths are few and it's best to call ahead on VHF Ch71 to ask if one is available. Mooring is stern – or bows-to floating pontoons. A limited number of deepwater berths varying from 3–7m in depth at LWS, with power points, and water are available along the southern wall of the marina. Berth at the reception pontoon on the E side of the new entrance on first arrival. The marina office is to be relocated to overlook the area but in the meantime is situated near the root of the N mole. Hours are 0830–2200 daily in summer. 0830–2100 in winter. During the renovations the marina was dredged to 4m throughout.

Charges

High season April–October: Day £15. Low season November–April: Day £10.65. Multihulls: +50%. Plus metered electricity and water. Full information available on the web or by contacting the marina on email at the address given.

Facilities

Every berth has access to a Service Module, with electricity, water, intercom and telephone. Access to the floating pontoons is by coded lockable gates and security is excellent. Car park by the Marina Control Centre (MCC), Office facilities available from the MCC include fax and photocopying, book swap and restaurant, showers and laundry.
Repairs Only available at Sheppard's ☎ 20076895 *Fax* 20071780.
Showers and WC Situated in the MCC. Facilities available for the disabled. Bath available for £3.50. These amenities close 30 minutes earlier than the rest of the establishment. Toilets for after-hours use can be found along the Main Quayside to the rear of the large anchor. Lock code available from Reception.
Laundry Incorporating a dry cleaners. Others in the town.
Security Access to pontoons (after-hours) is by a coded digital lock.

Weather Daily reports are posted in the office. A weather station is on view at the MCC.
Transport Local buses from the bus station. No. 3 bus to the frontier from Line Wall Road near the Museum.

Ocean Village Marina

A new marina complex is being constructed on the site of Sheppard's old piers, just south of Marina Bay and now apparently combining with Marina Bay. With a draft of 4.5m and over 200 berths Ocean Bay Marina can accommodate most vessels including super yachts. Each berth has new facility points for water, power, telephone, fax and satellite TV. New shower and toilet facilities, including disabled, are available at the pier office. Ocean Village is a vibrant new waterfront area with a variety of international stores and a range of restaurants and bars to suit all tastes. The Leisure Island complex will feature a casino, nightclub, champagne bar and much more. An artist's impression of the development can be seen on www.oceanvillage.gi/map.html.

Marina Bay

Location 36°08'.9N 05°21'.4W

The Marina

Just S of the runway, Marina Bay is an excellent location from which to visit Gibraltar or Spain. The ground tackle which fell into disrepair has been replaced and facilities are excellent. The marina can take over 200 yachts up to 70m or 4.5m draught. The nearby bars and restaurants along the quay and in Neptune House provide excellent food and a good social atmosphere, as well as providing protection form the E winds.

Approach

The marina is 0.5M E of the N mole. and is approached by rounding the N Mole's E head. At night a row of red lights at the end of the airport runway mark the N side of the channel. Note that yachts **may not move in the vicinity** while the runway lights are flashing, There is also a height restriction of 23m.

Berthing

Call the marina office on Ch 71 for berth allocation. Note: Depths in the marina are around 25m but some areas are less. Make sure the berthing master knows your draft to ensure the correct location in the marina. If staff are not around, berth alongside the office, towards the outer end of the main pier or find an empty mooring. Hours are 0820–2200 daily in summer, 0830–2030 in winter. Berthing is Mediterranean-style – bow or stern-to with a buoy and lazy-line provided to the pontoon.

Charges for a 12m Yacht

High season May–October: Day £14.
Low season November–April: Day £8.50. Multihulls +50%. Plus electricity and water. Cash discounts l0%, 6 months 20%, Annual 25%. Full information

Looking west over Queensway Quay *Graham Hutt*

available on the web or by contacting the marina on email at the address given.

Facilities

Water Available at every berth charged at 1p per litre.
Electricity Available at every berth charged at 15p/Kwh.
Repairs Mechanics can be brought to the yacht.
Showers and WC On ground floor under Pier Office building. Facilities for the handicapped.
Launderette In the marina.
Dentist Mr C. Linale, Neptune House Marina Bay.
Security Security guards 24hr ☎ 20040477.
Weather Daily bulletins are posted at the Pier Office, BFBS Radio ☎ 20053416.
Eating out Enjoy the relaxed atmosphere of the waterfront restaurants within the marina complexes or the many restaurants, pubs and fastfood houses in the town, particularly in Main Street. A full list may be obtained from the tourist board.
Transport The No. 9 bus from the frontier to the bus station stops in Winston Churchill Avenue in front of the tower blocks at the northern end of Glacis Road, but it is only a 10 minute walk to the bus station and city centre.

General facilities

Gas Available from New Harbours ☎ 2007026. All bottled gas is imported from Spain by Rumagas and sold through outlets including the Shell office at the fuel berth and most filling stations.
Fuel Diesel (and water) is obtainable at the Shell or BP stations opposite Marina Bay. Shell ☎ 20048232, BP ☎ 20072261.
Provisions Morrisons supennarket is a short walk from Queensway Quay and not far from Marina Bay. It is on the No. 4 and 10 bus route (see below), fresh fruit and vegetables are best obtained from La Linea market, just

across the border in Spain, on Wednesday mornings, Duty-free stores are available via Albor Ltd ☎/*Fax* 20073283, at Marina Bay – which doubles as a newsagent, bookshop and cybercafe – where almost anything in almost any quantity for a yacht in transit can be purchased.
Charts Available from the Gibraltar Chart Agency, Irish Town ☎ 20076293.
Chandlery Most items available at Sheppard's (temporarily at the old marina site ☎ 20077183 *Fax* 20042535 www.sheppard.gi which has the best range of yacht chandlery here. **However**, do be aware that with all the changes – including a move of the Sheppard's chandlery shop – several yachtsmen have complained that availability of 'just about anything' no longer applies. There are also smaller chandlers located at Marina Bay.
Repair facilities Sheppard's boatyard and repair facilities are currently reduced because of the closure of the yard for the Ocean Village development and move to new premises. However, they are operating a 40-ton travel-hoist and crane and engineering facilities from temporary premises near Queensway Quay, (Coaling Island) ☎ 20076895.
Engineers Sheppard's can handle light engineering, welding, engine servicing and repairs to most makes and are Volvo Penta agents. Also-Marine Maintenance Ltd ☎ 20078954 *Fax* 20074754 *Email* fred@gibnet.gi (Perkins and Yanmar) at Manna Bav, and Medmarine Ltd ☎ 20048888 *Fax* 20048889, (Yamaha) at Queensway Quay, Tempco Marine Engineering ☎ 20074657 *Fax* 2007617, specialise in refrigeration and radio repairs Sheppard's workshops (as above) or ElectroMed ☎ 20077077 *Fax* 20072051 *Email* mail@electro-med.com www.eletro-med.com at Queensway Quay, who can supply and repair equipment from most major manufacturers.

Marina Bay

Sailmaker/sail repairs Sail makers, ☎ 20041469 in South Pavilion Road, who also handle general canvaswork and upholstery. Alternatively Magnusson Sails ☎ 952 791241 *Fax* 952791241, about 35 miles away in Estepona, who may be willing to deliver/collect. Canvas work and sprayhood (but not true sailmaking) is also undertaken by ME Balloqui & Sons ☎ 20078105 *Fax* 20042510, at 3941 City Mill Lane.
Rigging Sheppard's workshops, as above.
Liferaft servicing GV Undery & Son ☎ 200731 07 *Fax* 20046489 *Email* compass@gibtelecom.net (who are also compass adjusters). Note: Currently with the old Sheppard's boatyard and repair facilities in a temporary location, facilities in Gibraltar are limited. A crane can lift yachts, which are then placed on the hard and moved by travel lift. The process is expensive and not suited to larger displacement yachts. The plan to move the boatyard and haul-out facility to the N side of the runway has been abandoned. The nearest boatyard and travel hoist is currently Sotogrande Marina, 10M N of Gibraltar. Other possibilities for larger vessels are the old Naval shipyards S of Queensway quay.

Money The UK Pound Sterling is legal tender, along with the Gibraltar pound and of equal value, but only in Gibraltar. Beware of trying to exchange excess Gibraltar currency in the UK, as it is worth very little there. Euros can also be used in most shops but not in the Post Office where only sterling is accepted. There are several Bureaux de Change agencies in Main Street. Visa, Switch, American Express, Mastercard etc, are accepted almost everywhere, though not the post office and some government offices. ATMs at Barclays Bank in Main Street and Morrisons supermarket.

Banks Gibraltar has well established banking services for both offshore and local customers with a full range of international banks, including several UK institutions, Banking hours are generally between 0900–1530 Monday to Friday.

Crossing the Border Crossing the border into Spain is quick and easy on foot but another matter by car. In both cases a passport must be carried. By car, it is normal to queue in either direction, but while the queue to come into Gibraltar seldom exceeds ten minutes, it is not unusual to queue for up to an hour to leave during rush hour. Long queues also result when planes take off and land, There is a very reasonably priced airport carpark opposite the airport, near the border which charges about 50p an hour short term and £4 for 24 hour parking.

International travel Gibraltar airport is located close to the frontier for daily flights to the UK and onward connections ☎ 20073026. Málaga airport is a little an over an hour's drive up the coast (A7 or AP7 *peaje* toll road) for more destinations. Taxis are expensive- about €100 or £62.

La Línea   Marina Bay   Ocean Village Site

Gibraltar: The northern anchorage and entrance to Marina Bay

I.iii Spanish enclaves

4. Ceuta (Sebta)

A marina in the Spanish enclave of Ceuta, 13M due S of
Europa Point, (Gibraltar) and 27M E of Tanger. Tetouan is
nearby across the land border.

Location 35°54'.0N 05°18'.6W

Tides

MHWS	MHWN	MLWN	MLWS
1m	0.8m	0.4m	0.2m

Charts

	Approach	Port
Admiralty	92,142,773, 3578	2742
French	7042, 7300	7503
Spanish	44C, 105, 445, 451	4511
US	52039	52048

Lights

Approach

2482 **Punta Almina** 35°54'N 05°16'.8W Fl(2)10s148m22M
White tower on house 16m

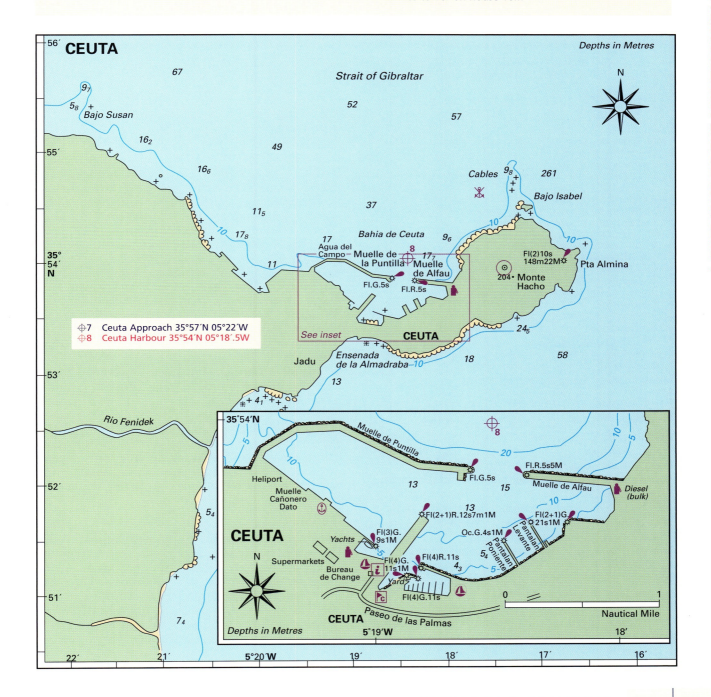

I. ENTRANCE TO THE MEDITERRANEAN

Hercules Marina distant far left, behind the ancient tower and wall. Ceuta's unmistakable glass tower on the right. *Graham Hutt (2008)*

Harbour

2486 **Dique de Poniente** Fl.G.5s13m5M Siren 15s Conical green tower 6m
F.R on Tank Farm 1.3m W
2484 **Dique de Levante** Fl.R.5s13m5M Conical red tower 7m
2487 **Spur E corner** Fl(2)G.8s7m1M Green post 4m
2488 **Muelle de Espana head W corner** Fl(2+1)R.12s7m3M Red post green band 4m
2490 **Nuevo Porto Deportivo breakwater head** Fl(4)R.11s8m1M Red mast 6m
2490.5 **Elbow** Fl(4)G.11s6m1M Green post 4m
2490.7 **Head** Fl(4)G.11s5m1M Green mast 3m
2492 **Muelle de Ribera W head** Fl.G.4s7m1M Green mast 3m
2492.2 **E head** Fl(2+1)G.12s7m1M Green mast, red band 3m.

Communications

Port Authority ☎ 956 527000
VHF Ch 16,12, 13, 14, 15 (24 hrs)
Hercules Marina Office ☎/*Fax* 956 525001
Email info@mahersa.es www.mahersa.es

Hercules marina

In the past Ceuta had a reputation of being a smuggling base with no secure place for yachts. This has changed and it now has a splendid and clean marina away from the main harbour, fenced around its entire perimeter. An enormous amount of money has been spent on developing the marina and the area around it.

Because of its small size and excellent facilities it is usually quite full, though room can be found along the N wall if not on a pontoon. It is an excellent place to stock up – probably the best and cheapest in the western Mediterranean and a rival to Gibraltar.

The marina has now been privatized and the restrictions placed on the number of visits has been abolished.

Approach

By day
The hills on the W side of Ceuta are high (850m) and very steep. To the E is a conspicuous lighthouse on the S face of Punta Almina. Ceuta town itself is low-lying though the harbour is easily seen. There are low-lying rocks to the E of the entrance, N of Monte Hacho. The final approach has to be made from the N quadrant so care must be taken with the set and tide in the straits, especially in strong westerly winds. Ferries and hydrofoils from Algeciras will be seen entering and leaving the harbour throughout the day and until around midnight.

Once through the outer moles, continue SW where a large futuristic glass tower situated on the outer end of the harbour's central mole will be observed. An ancient limestone observation tower will also be seen on the SE mole. Rounding this to port enters the marina.

By night
The port is well lit and lights reliable. The lighthouse NE of the port on Punta Almina is the most conspicuous light, followed by the entry lights, Fl.G.5s and Fl.R.5s. The marina entry light Fl(4)R is sited by the old round tower protecting the marina to the N.

Berthing

Minimum depths in the entrance of the marina are 5m, with around 2.5m once inside. Finger pontoons will be seen once round the breakwater with moorings available for up to 200 boats. The outer pontoons nearest the tower have depths of around 4m and the E end is principally for visitors. When full, some yachts have been directed to use the N wall, where bollards and services are also located.

If there is no room in the marina, an alternative, especially for larger yachts, is alongside on the W side of the central jetty of the main harbour or further in behind the short mole running SE. This area is usually oily and uncomfortable because of the ferries arriving and turning in the port.

Anchoring is usually prohibited anywhere in the harbour.

Charges

Marina charges are approximately €15 per day for a 12 metre yacht.

However, charges do change!

Formalities

As in Spain, there are technically no formalities required for a yacht coming from Spain or Gibraltar, though customs and immigration authorities may call at the yacht and check that papers are in order. More checks are done here than in Spanish ports because of the incidence of smuggling drugs and illegal immigrants.

The marina is now under the management of a private company 'Marina Hercules'.

All paperwork is completed in the marina office when checking in.

Facilities

Water and electricity At each berth on the quay and on the N wall.

Fuel There is now a fuel station in the marina itself, located on the S side of the rectangular end of the marina mole.

Showers & toilets A security key to the pontoons and toilets is avaiable from the office.

Provisions Two large supermarkets are close to the marina and both have a wide range of articles especially suited for provisioning yachts. These include powdered milk, canned butter, meat, dried hams, fruits, vegetables, beer, wine and spirits at lower prices than the Spanish hipermercados. Other shops sell everything from food to diving equipment, fishing tackle, electronics etc. These are very much cheaper than in Gibraltar or on the Spanish mainland.

Gas Available in town or by arrangement with the marina office. If you have an odd fitting ask a taxi driver for the gas plant, Butano SA. You can wait while your bottles are being filled. All types of bottles can be filled, including Calor gas butane bottles with snap-on fittings and propane bottles.

Post Office and banks In the centre of town – there are change shops around the ferry terminal but check their exchange rates and commission.

Repairs A light hoist (8 tons) is located in the marina. Most emergency repairs can be taken care of and a wide range of nautical chandlery is available here.

I. ENTRANCE TO THE MEDITERRANEAN

Ceuta, looking north with Gibraltar behind city

5. Melilla

A Spanish enclave 36M from the Algerian border, excellent yacht facilities in a safe marina and port of entry for Spain.

⊕10 35°17′.5N 02°55′W

Tides

MHWS	MHWN	MLWN	MLWS
0.6m	0.5m	0.3m	0.2m

Charts

	Approach	Port
Admiralty	773, 2437	580
French	6570	5864
Spanish	432	4331
US	52040	52047

Lights

Approach

6778 **Cabo Tres Forcas** 35°26′.3N 02°57′.8W
Fl(3+1)20s112m19M Grey square tower18m
083°-viz-307° Siren (3+1)60s

6776 **Los Farallones** 35°25′.7N 02°56′.4W Iso.Y.2s21m6M
White and grey tower 5m.

6758 **Melilla LtHo** 35°17′.7N 02°55′.9W Oc(2).6s40m14M
Brown tower 12m.

Harbour

6762 **Dique Nordeste E head** Fl.G.4s32m7M Grey tower, green lantern 28m

6763 **Dique Nordeste W head** Fl.G.4s7m5M Green tower 5m

6764 **Pier 1 elbow** Fl(2)G.7s7m3M Green tower 5m

6770 **Muelle de Ribera** SE Fl(2+1)G.12s8m3M Green tower, red band 5m.

6773 **Muelle de Ribera** W Fl(4)G.11s7m1M Green tower 5m

6774 **Fish basin W head** Fl(4)R.11s8m1M Red structure 4m

6765 **Marina dique** Fl.R.5s4m5M Red post 2m

6766 **Dique corner** Q(3)10s4m3M Cardinal E post BYB 2m

6767 **Marina espigon** Fl.G.4s3m1M Green post 1m.

6768 **Ore loading pier head** Fl(2+1)R.12s8m3M Red tower, green band 5m.

Port communications

Port authority VHF Ch 9 ☎ 952 673600 Fax 952 674838
Email info@puertodemelilla.es www.puertodemelilla.es

The Port

Another of the peculiar Spanish possessions on the Moroccan coast, Melilla used to be of commercial importance during the time of the Spanish Protectorate but declined after Moroccan independence. The outer entrance is shared with the Moroccan port of Nador which has taken over the mineral trade. The ferry terminal is the most important activity today along with fishing and, to a lesser extent than in the past, smuggling.

The new and well protected marina built on the south side of the old jetty, Cargedero de Minerales, has only recently been completed and facilities installed. A friendly yacht club is located in the S corner of the Darsena Pesquera. Security was a problem in the past but this new facility seems to have solved this.

By Moroccan standards supplies are abundant, but they pale in comparison to Ceuta. There is a good mercado (covered market) with fresh produce and the two supermarkets, mentioned in the facilities, have a good supply of staples, beer, wine and spirits etc.

Melilla is quite useful as a base to explore northern Morocco and now a safe place to leave a yacht.

Approach

By day

The headland of Cabo Tres Forcas is an unmistakable landmark and makes the approach to Melilla easy from any direction, although care should be exercised when coming from the west to avoid the Los Farallones bank SE of the Tres Forcas lighthouse. The starboard entrance and the port side is part of the Moroccan port of Nador, hence the unique peculiarity of the entrance.

Minimum depths of over 7m are found in the outer basin and the new marina entrance has been dredged to 9m.

⊕9   Cabo Tres Forcas 35°27′.5N 02°55′W
⊕10 Melilla Harbour 35°17′.5N 02°55′W

By night

Cabo Tres Forcas light (35°26'.3N 02°57'.8W) 6778 Fl(3+1)20s112m19M is usually reliable and the best landfall, It can be seen at about 15M. Closer in both Spanish and Moroccan harbours are equipped with the usual lights for night entry, but these are obscured by the bright lights on the quays until quite close.

Note: The Nador breakwater light (35°17'.1N 2°55'.1W) 6757.6 Fl(2)R.6s8m5M is rarely functioning.

By GPS

Having arrived at WP9 steer due south for 10 miles to WP10. The entrance is then some 500m away on a WSW course.

Berthing

Once inside the outer basin, head W to the outer mole of the new marina. Depths inside the marina are from 3.3m near the entrance to 2.1m at the end of the quays. Marineros are in attendance 24 hours a day but visitors are often directed to the main quay, rather than the projecting pontoons, except for longer stays. There is less security at the main pier, but the area is patrolled.

Harbour charges

A new scale of charges is being prepared but is currently unavailable. Until now rates have been based on LOA x Beam x €0.2/day. This results in a comfortable €10 or less for a 12m yacht (note water and electricity are charged separately).

Formalities

Formalities are now more relaxed than previously. If coming from Spain, no formalities are technically necessary, but a visit to the capitania is advisable and officials may want to check papers.

Facilities

Water and electricity Laid on at each berth on the pontoons.

Fuel From a pump on the S mole at very cheap prices.

Provisions The covered mercado has a wide assortment of Spanish products. It is 200m past the end of the main street, Avenida del Generalisimo, about 20 minutes walk from the port. Just before the market there is a well stocked Moroccan owned supermercado, Hakin. Moroccans also operate many of the stands at the market. All shops sell duty-free electronic equipment, cheap alcoholic beverages and cigarettes. A new supermarket has opened 200m S of the marina with another large one further S.

Showers Excellent facilities near the pontoons (a long walk if on the quay).

Post Office & telephone On the N side of Avenida del Generalisimo.

Banks In the ferry terminal and on the main street. Many money changers on the street corners but be careful of their rates and commission.

Repairs Most engine repairs can be carried out.

Travel-lift A 65-ton travel hoist is available.

Chandleries There are now two in the harbour.

Internet café Several opened in the town near the tourist office and the Darsena Pesquera.

Eating out Several bars and restaurants in the marina complex and the yacht club serve excellent tapas.

Transport In summer daily ferries run to Malaga, Benalmedena and Almeria. Buses to the border leave from Plaza de España.

I. ENTRANCE TO THE MEDITERRANEAN

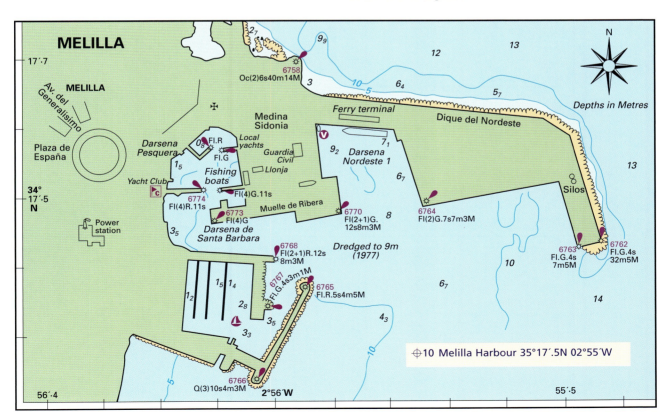

II. COSTA DEL SOL

Introduction

GENERAL DESCRIPTION

The coast between Gibraltar and Cabo de Gata some 155M to the E is called the Costa del Sol (the Sun Coast). It lives up to its name in that sunshine averages 300 days a year. The three main ports, Gibraltar, Málaga and Almería, are large and can be entered under most conditions; there are 16 smaller harbours.

The section starts with the singular mass of the Rock of Gibraltar which stands high and island-like and can be seen for miles. Behind the Rock is a low, flat and sandy coast backed by high mountain ranges which stretches to Málaga. Beyond Málaga, behind the coastal mountains are the even higher snow-covered ranges of the Sierra Nevada. In many places the mountains reach the sea and form high rocky cliffs and promontories.

The development of the coast for tourism has resulted in many sections supporting rows of tower blocks or flats and hotels. The latest tourists to arrive are the Russians who came with suitcases of dollars to buy up property. The general problem of plastic pollution is compounded by the 100m sheets of polythene discarded from kilometres of greenhouses established on any land suitable for hydroponic cultivation.

Many harbours, now improved by the construction of breakwaters, are based on small fishing harbours originally established in bays where some protection from the winds is available.

COASTAL WAYPOINT LIST

The waypoints listed form a series with which one is able to steer from off Gibraltar to Cabo de Gata. The waypoints are all at WGS 84 datum and although the track avoids the main fish farm areas these farms come and go, seemingly overnight sometimes, and a good lookout must be kept at all times. There are over 50 'official' farms along this section of coast, which are lit and reported in the light lists – however inshore and in various *calas* there are many more farms and these are usually unlit. It is therefore essential to keep a lookout at all times while making a coastal passage in this area.

⊕1	Pta. Carnero	36°03′.7N	05°24′.4W
⊕3	Pta Europa west	36°05′.5N	05°22′.7W
⊕11	Pta Europa east	36°05′.5N	05°20′W
⊕14	SE of Pta de la Doncella	36°22′.5N	05°08′W
⊕20	Pta de Calaburras	36°29′N	04°38′W
⊕24	Puerto del Candado	36°41′N	04°20′.5W
⊕27	Pta Torrox	36°42′N	03°57′.4W
⊕28	Pta de la Concepción	36°42′.5N	03°44′W
⊕31	Cabo Sacratif	36°41′N	03°28′W
⊕34	SSE of Pta de las Entinas	36°37′.5N	02°46′W
⊕38	S of Pta del Río	36°46′.5N	02°25′.5W
⊕39	Cabo de Gata	36°41′N	02°10′W

At most places the shore may be approached to 100m; headlands with cliffs, for instance Cabo de Gata, may have off-shore rocks or shoals. There are many small river courses, called ramblas, that are dry for most of the year but run in spate when the rare rains fall. Extensive deltas are found at their mouths which are often steep-to.

GALES – HARBOURS OF REFUGE

In the event of onshore gales and heavy seas, Gibraltar, Málaga and Almería are the safest to enter. No attempt should be made to enter small harbours until the seas have subsided.

VISITS INLAND

In addition to the places to visit in the immediate vicinity of each harbour, there are many fascinating places lying some distance inland. Among the many interesting places are the following:

Sevilla, capital of Andalucía and of ancient origin with a wealth of interesting old buildings. In April a famous fair is held here; book very early.

Cordoba, the cordwainers city, developed by the Moors. The cathedral was the second largest mosque in the world, and the site of the oldest synagogue in Spain is in the city.

Granada, with the extraordinary Alhambra, one of the outstanding sites of Europe.

Ronda, a town in a spectacular setting with Roman remains and caves nearby.

Jérez de la Frontera, an intriguing town and centre for the sherry trade which retains strong British connections.

Cádiz, well known to the British since Elizabethan times, retains its seawards fortifications within which the old town plan is largely undisturbed. The Hydrographic Office, where charts may be bought, is just outside the town walls, above the railway line.

Medina Sidonia, an example of the 'white towns' of Andalucia and in a splendid position, was part of the estate of the ill-starred Commander of the Spanish Armada and served as a leading mark into the distant Bay of Cádiz.

If the reader is at the western end of the Costa del Sol, the last three might be combined in a long day's expedition.

Pilotage and navigation

TIDES

The standard port is Gibraltar; secondary ports are Málaga and Almería. From Alicante to the north-east the tide is hardly appreciable. The figures are:

		Heights			Mean
	MHWS	MHWN	MLWS	MLWN	Level
Gibraltar	1.0	0.7	0.3	0.1	0.50
Differences					
	HW	LW			
Málaga					
+0005	−0005	−0.3	−0.1	0.0	+0.1	0.45
Almería					
+0010	−0010	−0.5	−0.3	0.0	+0.2	0.40

CURRENTS

There is usually an east going current along the coast. It can be as much as 2–3 knots at the western end and slackens towards the east. It has to be reckoned with when planning a passage and when entering or leaving a harbour.

SOUNDINGS

In most harbours sand builds up at or near the entrance, particularly after a blow, and is periodically dredged. Reported depths are not necessarily accurate and care should be taken to sound whilst approaching and entering harbour.

MAGNETIC VARIATION

Costa del Sol (Malaga) 02°30′W (2008) decreasing 8′ annually.

RESTRICTED AREAS

Anchoring is not permitted in the following areas which should be avoided if possible:
- W and E of the Rock of Gibraltar
- The prolongation of the airstrip at Gibraltar
- An area 2M to E of Estepona
- An area 2M to SW of Málaga
- An area 1M to S of Málaga where passage is also forbidden.

TUNNY NETS

During the summer months, tunny nets may be set between February and October in the following localities:
- Off La Línea
- Off the coast N of Fuerte de Santa Barbara
- Near Marbella
- Near Adra
- Off Punta del Sabinal
- To W of Cabo de Gata.

FISH HAVENS

There are extensive fish havens along this coast.

LANDINGS

The beaches are regularly patrolled by *guardia civil* with a brief to intercept smugglers and drug traffickers. If you wish to land do not be surreptitious.

PLASTIC SHEETS

Gales can dump polythene sheets from the greenhouses into the sea. They may be up to 100m long.

PLANNING GUIDE AND DISTANCE TABLES

See page 36.

II.i Europa Point to Pta del Torrox

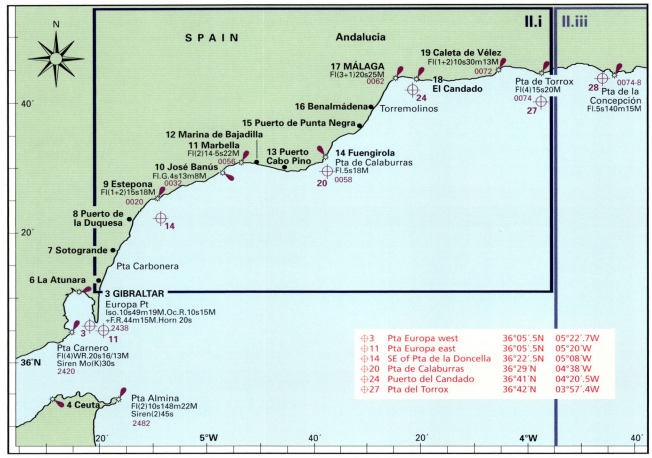

Within the map:

N

SPAIN   **Andalucia**

II.i   II.iii

19 Caleta de Vélez
Fl(1+2)10s30m13M
0072

17 MÁLAGA
Fl(3+1)20s25M
0062

18
El Candado
24

Pta de Torrox
Fl(4)15s20M
0074

28 Pta de la
Concepción
Fl.5s140m15M
0074·8

40′

Torremolinos   **27**

16 Benalmádena

15 Puerto de Punta Negra

12 Marina de Bajadilla
11 Marbella
Fl(2)14·5s22M
0056

**13 Puerto
Cabo Pino**

14 Fuengirola
Pta de Calaburras
Fl.5s18M
20   0058

10 José Banús
Fl.G.4s13m8M
0032

9 Estepona
Fl(1+2)15s18M
0020

**8 Puerto de
la Duquesa**   **14**

20′

7 Sotogrande

Pta Carbonera

6 La Atunara

3 GIBRALTAR
Europa Pt
Iso.10s49m19M.Oc.R.10s15M
+F.R.44m15M.Horn 20s
2438

3   **11**

Pta Carnero
Fl(4)WR.20s16/13M
Siren Mo(K)30s
2420

36°N

4 Ceuta   Pta Almina
Fl(2)10s148m22M
Siren(2)45s
2482

20′   5°W   40′   20′   4°W   40′

⊕			
⊕3	Pta Europa west	36°05′.5N	05°22′.7W
⊕11	Pta Europa east	36°05′.5N	05°20′W
⊕14	SE of Pta de la Doncella	36°22′.5N	05°08′W
⊕20	Pta de Calaburras	36°29′N	04°38′W
⊕24	Puerto del Candado	36°41′N	04°20′.5W
⊕27	Pta del Torrox	36°42′N	03°57′.4W

Planning guide and distances

⌁ Anchorage

Miles	Harbours, anchorages & headlands
	3. **Gibraltar** (page 23)
	Europa Point
8M	6. **La Atunara** (page 37)
7M	⌁ Río Guadiaro
	7. **Puerto de Sotogrande** (page 37)
5M	⌁ Cala Sardina
	Punta de la Chullera,
	Punta de la Salo de la Mora
	8. **Puerto de la Duquesa** (page 39)
5M	⌁ Fondeadero de la Sabinilla
	9. **Puerto de Estepona** (page 40)
11M	
	10. **Puerto de José Banús** (page 42)
4M	11. **Puerto de Marbella** (page 44
1M	12. **Marina de Bajadilla** (page 45)
	Punta Calaburras
7M	13. **Puerto Cabo Pino** (page 46)
9M	14. **Puerto de Fuengirola** (page 48)
4M	15. **Puerto de Punta Negra** (page 50)
12M	16. **Puerto de Benalmádena** (page 50)
9M	17. **Puerto de Málaga** (page 52)
4M	18. **Puerto de El Candado** (page 54)
	⌁ Fondeadero de Vélez-Málaga
14M	19. **Puerto Caleta de Vélez** (page 56)
	Punta de Torrox
	⌁ Fondadero de Nerja
	⌁ Cala de la Miel

Miles	Harbours, anchorages & headlands
17M	⌁ Cala de los Cañuelos
	⌁ Ensenada de la Herradura
20.	**Marina del Este** (page 60)
	Punta de la Concepción
	⌁ Ensenada de los Berengueles
	⌁ Punta San Cristóbal and Almuñecar
	⌁ Fondeadero de Almuñecar
	⌁ Ensenada de Belilla
10M	⌁ Ensenada de Robaina
	⌁ Surgidero de Salobreña
21.	**Puerto de Motril** (page 62)
	⌁ Anchorage east of Cabo Sacratif
	Cabo Sacratif
	⌁ Cala Honda
	⌁ Anchorages to Castell de Ferro
26M	⌁ Fondeadero de Castell de Ferro
	⌁ Anchorages in La Rábita
	Punta Negra
22.	**Puerto de Adra** (page 66)
	⌁ Balerma
	⌁ Punta de los Baños
	Punta de los Baños
12M	⌁ Ensenada de las Entinas
23.	**Puerto de Almerimar** (page 69)
14M	24. **Puerto de Roquetas del Mar** (page 71)
4M	25. **Puerto de Aguadulce** (page 72)
4M	26. **Puerto de Almería** (page 74)
60M	⌁ Cabo de Gata anchorages
	Punta del Río
	Cabo de Gata
	27. **Isla de Alborán** (page 77)

PORTS

6. Puerto de La Atunara

36°10´.7N 05°19´.9W

Lights
0008 **Dique de Abrigo head** Fl.G.8s11m5M Green tower
0008.5 **Contadique head** Fl.R.6s8m3M Red tower

Some five miles north of Point Europa there has recently been built the small fishing port of La Atunara, a Mediterranean outlet for La Línea. It is solely for the use of commercial fishermen but it could be a possible refuge in storm conditions.

Apart from a fuelling point (for fishing trawlers only) there are no other facilities at the port apart from the normal café. It is a long way from any shops and the port is only included here to inform passing craft of a possible refuge.

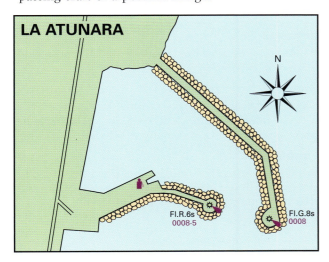

LA ATUNARA

Fl.R.6s 0008·5
Fl.G.8s 0008

⚓ **PUNTA CARBONERA**
36°16´.9N 5°17´.9W

This insignificant point just south of Sotogrande is now lit with light 0012 Oc.4s39m14M from a 14m white tower.

⚓ **RÍO GUADIARO**
36°16´.9N 5°16´.6W

The bar has been impassable in 2006. In the river, holding and depths are variable but, should the situation on the bar change, there was an anchorage in 4m mud between it and the road bridge 300m inland.

Approach
The river has a house with a conical blue roof on its right (SW) bank and training wall of rocks on its opposite bank. There are three dinghy pontoons upriver of the wall. To NNE is the massive development of Puerto de Sotogrande.

Entrance
If there is a channel through the bar, it is usually close to the training wall. The river in spate may reach four to five knots in the entrance.

7. Puerto de Sotogrande

36°17´N 05°16´W

Charts
British Admiralty *3578, 773.* Imray *M11*
French *4717.* Spanish *453*

⊕12 36°17´N 05°16´.2W

Lights
0016 **Dique Levante S head** Fl(3)G.11s8m4M Masonry tower, green top 3m
0016.2 **Dique Levante N head** Q(3)10s8m4M E card (with ↕ topmark)
0016.8 **External espigón** Q.R.2m2M Red post 2m
0016.4 **Spur** Q.G.3m2M
0016.6 **Contradique head** Fl(4)R.14s4m2M Red post 2m

Port communications
VHF Ch 9. Port ☎ 956 79 00 00 *Fax* 956 79 01 09
Email puertosotogrande@telefonica.net
www.puertosotogrande.com

Major marina village
A marina complex close NNE of the Río Guadiaro. It has housing blocks with shops and restaurants around the north side of the harbour. The harbour is easy to approach and enter but in SE–S winds entrance could be difficult and despite additional breakwaters, a swell enters the yacht harbour.

Facilities are good; besides those listed below, there are sandy beaches either side of the harbour, golf, riding, polo, tennis, squash etc.

Yachts ashore may be lived in by special arrangement with the marina manager and winter lay-up prices may be negotiated.

Sotogrande is undergoing a huge development to make use of the lagoon to the west of the present marina. There are now 250 new berths over and above the 550 of the original marina with many more to come in the future.

Approach
From the south Having rounded Europa point follow the coast at 500m in a general NNE direction. Torre Nueva and Torre de Punta Carbonera may be identified. The mass of buildings at Puerto de Sotogrande can be seen from afar.

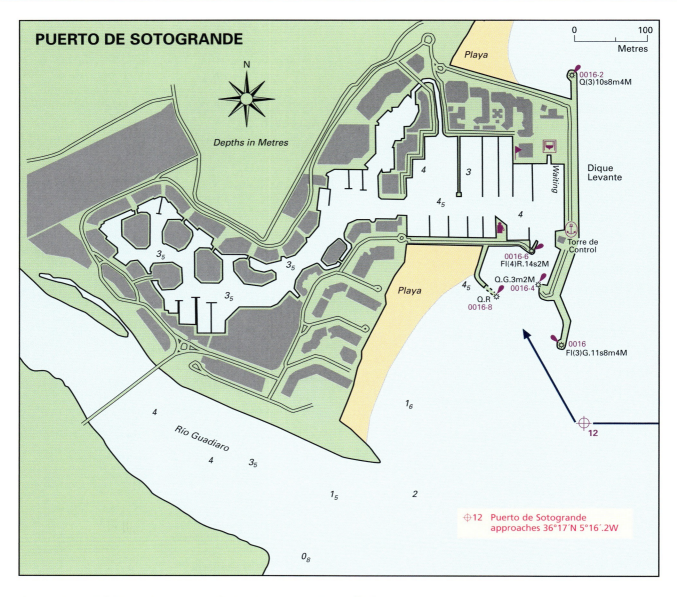

PUERTO DE SOTOGRANDE

N

Depths in Metres

Playa

0   100
Metres

0016·2
Q(3)10s8m4M

Dique
Levante

Waiting

4   3

4₅

4

Torre de
Control

0016·6
Fl(4)R.14s2M

Q.G.3m2M
0016·4

Playa   4₅

Q.R
0016·8

3₅   3₅

3₅

3₅

0016
Fl(3)G.11s8m4M

4

1₆

Río Guadiaro

4   3₅

12

1₅   2

⊕12   Puerto de Sotogrande
approaches 36°17′N 5°16′.2W

0₈

From the NE Follow the coast at 500m in a general SSW direction. The harbour and breakwaters of José Banús, Estepona and La Duquesa may be seen but caution is needed as there are a number of rocky sand-retaining breakwaters which can be mistaken for harbours.

In the closer approach the anchorage of Cala Sardina with a *torre* on each side and the harbour breakwater and a large red hotel located N of the entrance will be identified. The *torre de control* is a handsome, square, castellated stone tower with cupola and flag-staff.

GPS approach

Steer for ⊕12 from an easterly quadrant and then steer for the end of the breakwater (approximately 0.12M).

Anchorage in the approach

Anchor in 3m sand 300m offshore to N or S of the harbour.

Entrance

Approach S head of the Dique de Abrigo and round it leaving at 15m.

Berths

Secure beneath the *torre de control* and ask there for a berth which will be on one of the yacht harbour pontoons. Two bow lines may be needed.

Formalities

If entering from abroad (e.g. Gibraltar) the office in the *torre* will arrange for customs clearance, should that be required.

Facilities

Maximum length overall: 50m.
Most repair facilities including sailmaker, GRP.
150-tonne travel-lift, large hardstanding, slipways.
Chandlery shop beside the harbour.
Water taps on pontoons and quays.
Shower baths, WCs and sauna at sanitary block.
220v AC and 380v AC on quays and pontoons.
Ice from fuel station.
Gasoleo A, petrol.
Club Marítimo with restaurant.

Launderette near the harbour.
Supermarket and some shops at the harbour, more at Sotogrande 1M away.

Communications

Bus service along the coast. ☎ Area code 956.
Taxi ☎ 61 60 78 or 907 59 26 09 (mobile).

⚓ CALA SARDINA

36°18´.5N 5°15´.3W

A pleasant anchorage 1.5M N of Sotogrande. Punta de la Chullera is a low sloping point with a conspicuous tower and a few houses in the trees. On the other side of the bay a square fort-like building, Casa Cuartel, is easily seen. Anchor in 3m sand and pebbles about 75m off. There is foul ground 100m off Punta de la Chullera which is sometimes called Punta Europa. The main coast road is behind the beach.

8. Puerto de la Duquesa

36°21´.3N 05°13´.7W

Charts

British Admiralty *3578, 773.* Imray *M11*
French *4717.* Spanish *453*

⊕13 36°21´.1N 05°13´.6W

Lights

0018 **Dique de Levante S head** Fl.G.7s8m5M White truncated tower green lantern and base 4m
0018.3 **Dique de Levante N head** Q(3)10s7m5M Yellow truncated tower black band 4m
0018.4 **Contradique head** Fl(2)R.7s6m3M White tower red top 4m
0018.41 **External espigón head** Fl.R.5s7m3M Metal strucure, red top 5m

Port communications

VHF Ch 9. Port ☎ 952 89 01 00 *Fax* 952 89 01 01
Email duquesa@marinasmediterraneo.com
www.marinasmediterraneo.com/duquesa.htm

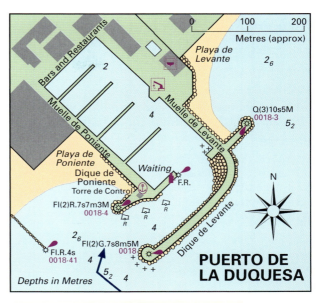

⊕13   Puerto de la Duquesa 36°21´.1N 5°13´.6W

Useful marina near Gibraltar

A marina surrounded by blocks of apartments and with good facilities. Approach and entrance are easy and good shelter is available inside. It is a useful first port of call after Gibraltar which is less than 20M away. Good beaches on either side of the harbour.

Approach

From the south Punta de la Chullera, with a tower, has rocks extending up to 100m offshore. Castillo de la Duquesa just SSW of the harbour is conspicuous.

From the north Punta de Salto de la Mora with its old watch tower can be seen. Foul ground extends 200m off this point. The new buildings around the harbour and its breakwater are visible during the closer approach.

Puerto de la Duquesa

GPS approach

Steer for ⊕13 from an easterly quadrant and then steer for the end of the breakwater (approximately 0.13M).

Anchorage

Good anchorage is available to the NE of the harbour, about 150m offshore in 5m sand.

Entrance

Approach the head of the Dique de Levante on a NW course, round it and enter on a NE course. Give the breakwaters a 25m berth; underwater obstructions are marked by small buoys.

Berths

Secure alongside fuelling berth on the port hand side of the entrance and ask at the *torre de control* or call on Ch 9.

Formalities

If entering Spain, the *capitán de puerto* and *aduana's* offices are in the *torre de control*.

Facilities

Maximum length overall: 20–25m.
Limited workshops on E side of harbour.
75-tonne crane on NE side of harbour.
Water taps on pontoons and quays.
Showers at *torre de control*.
220V AC on pontoons and quays.
Ice on fuel quay.
Gasoleo A and petrol.
Clubhouse with pool.
Local supermarket. Other shops in Manilva village 1½ M away and Las Sabinilla ½ M away.
Washing machine in *torre de control*.

Communications

Bus service. Airfield at Gibraltar. ☎ Area code 95.
Taxi ☎ 280 29 00.

Duquesa entrance and Capitania

9. Puerto de Estepona

36°24′.8N 5°09′.4W

Charts

British Admiralty *3578*. Imray *M11*
French *4717*. Spanish *453*

⊕15 36°24′.65N 05°09′.6W

Lights

Approach
0020 **Punta de la Doncella LtHo** Fl(1+2)15s32m18M Dark 8-sided tower, grey lantern, white house 21m
Harbour
0022 **Dique de Abrigo spike** Q(6)+LFl.15s9m5M Black tower, yellow top 6m
0022.2 **Dique de Abrigo head** 36°24′.8N 5°09′.4W Fl.G.5s9m5M Green pole 7m
0024 **Dique de Poniente** Fl(2)R.7s9m3M Truncated tower 4m
21010(S) **Buoy** 36°25′.2N 5°08′.4W Q(6)+LFl.15s6m2M ⚑ card S

Port communication

VHF Ch 9. Capitanía de Marina ☎ 95 280 18 00
Fax 95 280 24 97 *Email* estepona@eppa.es
Club Náutico de Estepona ☎/*Fax* 952 80 09 54
Email cnestepona@teleline.es
www.clubnauticoestepona.es

Harbour and tourist resort

A town of Roman origin developed from a fishing village into a close-packed tourist resort with restaurants, shops and a supermarket. There is an early morning fishmarket at the harbour. Local holidays are from 24 to 29 June.

Approach

The harbour is backed by four tower blocks of flats. The dark octagonal lighthouse 31m high capped by a grey lantern is to the NE of the harbour entrance. The outer breakwater (Dique de Abrigo) has been extended westwards leaving the old entrance tower in its original position.

GPS approach

Steer for ⊕15 from a SE quadrant and then make for the breakwater head (approximately 0.1M).

Anchorage in the approach

Anchor 200m to the NE of head Dique de Abrigo in 5.5m sand.

Entrance

Approach the head of Dique de Abrigo on a N course, round it at 20m and enter on a NE course.

In a SW gale the entrance could be dangerous. The breakwaters have underwater projections. Dredgers may be in operation as this harbour's mouth frequently silts up. Most harbours along this coast have reported severe reduction in entrance depths in spring due to winter storms.

Berths

Secure to the Muelle de Espera, which is at the end of Pantalan 5, and ask at the *capitanía* which is in a blue building, like a towered wedding cake with white icing, on the north side of the harbour. The *pantalanes* have lockable gates at their shore ends.

Estepona from the south

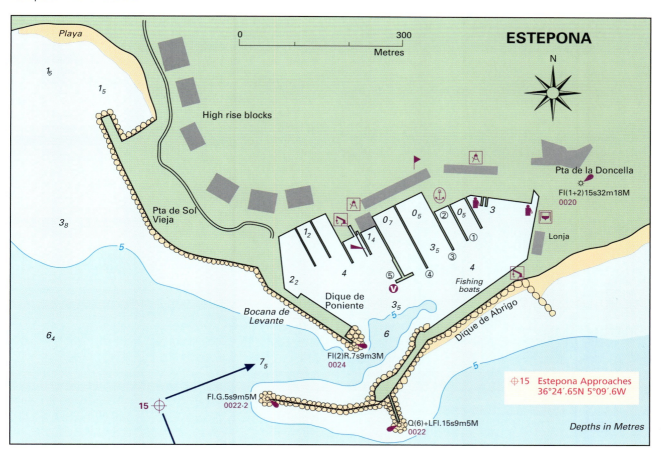

ESTEPONA

0   300
Metres

N

Playa

1₅

1₅

High rise blocks

Pta de la Doncella
Fl(1+2)15s32m18M
0020

Pta de Sol
Vieja

3₈

5

1₂

0₇   0₅

② 0₅   3

①

Lonja

3₅

③

2₂

4

④

4

⑤

Fishing
boats

Dique de
Poniente

Bocana de
Levante

3₅

5

6

6₄

7₅

Dique de Abrigo

Fl(2)R.7s9m3M
0024

5

⊕15   Estepona Approaches
36°24´.65N 5°09´.6W

15 ⊕

Fl.G.5s9m5M
0022·2

Q(6)+LFl.15s9m5M
0022

Depths in Metres

Harbour charges

Medium to high.

Facilities

Maximum length overall: 30m.

Repairs (most services) at a shipyard to NE of the harbour.

Sailmaker under the club nautico is Magnusson Sails (Antonio Rodriguez Carrasco) ☎ 952 79 12 41 (the only sailmaker on the west of Costa del Sol. Excellent work has been reported and English is spoken).

80-tonne travel-lift and 3.5-tonne mobile crane.

Yachts up to 25-tonnes may be hauled out on the slipway immediately SW of the *club náutico*.

Hardstandings.

Chandlery in harbour.

Life-raft servicing.

Water taps on quays and pontoons.

Butane: the Marina can arrange refills for 10lb Calor bottles.

220V AC on the Dique de Poniente and pontoons, 380V on berths 20–35m.

Ice from the fish auction building or waiting quay.

Gasoleo A and petrol.

Club Náutico de Estepona has showers, a restaurant and bar and is usually open to non-members.

Provisions from shops in the town about 1M away and from supermarket on N side of the harbour.

Laundry in port, launderettes in the town.

Communications

Bus services. ☎ Area code: 95 Taxi ☎ 280 29 00

⚓ FONDEADERO DE ESTEPONA

An anchorage to the NE of the harbour off the town of Estepona, 500m from the shore in 5m sand. To E of the harbour where five breakwaters were built is a submerged breakwater parallel to the coast and about 400m offshore marked by a S card buoy. The anchorage is somewhat protected by Punta de los Marmoles, a small cliffed headland with a tower surrounded by trees.

Note Further East, anchoring is forbidden between Torre del Padrón and Punta de Guadalmaza because of submarine cables.

Banús Capitania and light

10. Puerto de José Banús

36°29′N 04°57′.2W

Charts

British Admiralty *3578, 773*. Imray *M11* French *4717*. Spanish *454*

⊕16 36°28′.9N 05°57′.4W

Lights

0030 **Groyne Centre** Q(6)+LFl.15s10m5M Truncated masonry tower 6m

0031 **Dique de Benabolá elbow** Fl.R.3s7m4M Siren 60s Truncated masonry tower red lantern 4m

0032 **Dique de Levante W head** 36°29′.1N 04°57′.2W Fl.G.4s13m8M Truncated masonry tower 9m

0032.2 **E head** Q(6)+LFl.15s10m4M Tower, yellow top 6m

Port communications

VHF Ch 9. *Capitanía* ☎ 952 90 98 00 *Fax* 952 81 08 99 *Email* torrecontrol@puertobanus.com www.puertojosebanus.es Club de Mar de José Banús ☎ 952 81 77 50 *Fax* 952 81 68 62 *Email* infoclubdemar@purtobanus.com

Upmarket marina

An up-market marina handling large and very large yachts, motor and sail, and correspondingly pricey. The enclave also contains apartments, shops boutiques, restaurants, night clubs, casinos and so forth, patrolled by armed security guards and protected from the outside world by automated barriers allowing the passage of selected vehicles. However, it has good repair facilities.

There is a hotel beach and swimming pool to W of the harbour which is available to yachting visitors. Entrance tickets from third floor office of the tower. It is worth escaping to Ronda by taxi.

Approach

The lone rocky-peaked mountain Pico de la Concha in the Sierra Blanca, called Sierra de Marbella on British charts, can be seen from afar. Closer in, some yellow tower blocks 2M to W and the very large Hotel Nueva Andalucía, the bull ring close E and a white flag-poled terrace are conspicuous. The old stone tower with a number of windows at the entrance and the mass of buildings around the harbour are also conspicuous.

GPS approach

Steer to ⊕16 from southerly quadrant and steer for breakwater end (approximately 0.08M).

Anchorage in the approach

200m S of S head of Dique de Levante in 8m sand.

Entrance

Approach the S head of Dique de Levante on a N course, leave it 50m to starboard and enter on an E course.

In a SW gale, the entrance could be difficult except for powerful vessels as it involves turning sharply across the waves in a restricted area of disturbed water.

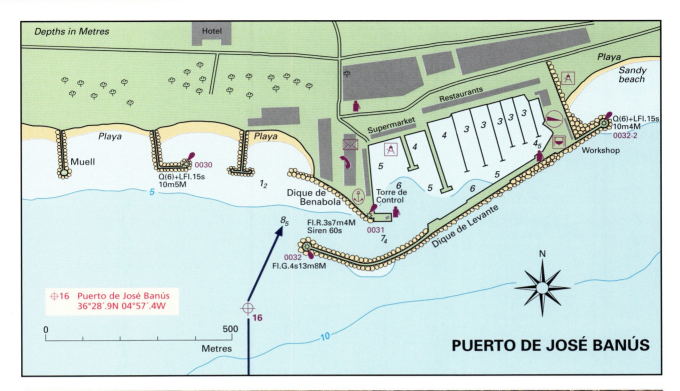

Puerto de José Banús

Berths

Secure alongside E side of Dique de Benabolá near the fuel station for the allocation of a berth from the control tower.

Harbour charges

High.

Facilities

Maximum length overall: 80m.

Two travel-lifts, 50 and 25 tonnes and a 5-tonne mobile crane.

Launching slipway at E of the harbour.

Most shipwright and electronic work possible.

Sailmaker on N side of harbour.

Two chandlers beside the harbour.

Water points on quays and pontoons.

Showers by the tower.

220V AC to berths and 380V AC to berths over 15m.

Petrol.

Ice from fuelling point or slipway.

Yacht Club: Club Náutico Internacional Nueva Andalucia.

Supermarket at the harbour but fresh food has to be obtained from Marbella, 15 minutes away by bus or taxi, or from San Pedro.

Laundry in port and launderette behind the house on Dique de Riberea.

Communications

Bus service. ☎ Area code 95. Taxi ☎ 278 38 39.

II.i COSTA DEL SOL

11. Puerto de Marbella

36°30′.3N 04°53′.4W

Charts

British Admiralty *3578, 773*. Imray *M11*
French *4717*. Spanish *454*

⊕17 36°30′·25N 04°53′·55W

Lights

Approach
0056 **Marbella LtHo** Fl(2)14·5s35m22M White round
   tower 29m
Marina
0056·2 **Dique de Levante** Fl(2)G.7s7m4M White tower,
   green top 4m
0056·6 **Dique de Poniente** Fl.R.4s6m2M Red tower 3m
Note There may be several fish farms off this harbour
   which normally have four buoys, Fl.Y.5s marking their
   extent

Port communications

Capatania VHF Ch 9 ☎ 952 77 55 24 *Fax* 952 90 01 74
Email puertodeportivo@marbella.es
www.marbella.es/puertodeportivo

Noisy tourist town

One of the original tourist towns on this coast, a
mass of high rise blocks. The approach and entrance
to the marina are easy but could be dangerous in
strong SW–W winds. Strong winds from that
quarter as well as from the east produce a serious
surge in the harbour which may become untenable.
If sitting out a blow, use your own gear and double
up on the lines.

During the early part of 2006 there was a build-
up of sand at the entrance which has reduced the
depth at the entrance by an unspecified amount.
Until this build-up has been removed all craft

entering and leaving the port have been advised to
exercise caution.

The harbour is noisy at night during the high
season and during the day the long sandy beaches on
either side of the harbour are often crowded.

The local holidays are 10–18 June, Ferias de San
Bernabé. 18–24 August, Semana del Sol. 18 October,
San Pedro de Alcantara.

Approach

The mass of skyscraper apartments and hotels along
the seafront and the high Sierra Blanca mountain
range behind make the whereabouts of the marina
easy to locate. The marina itself is immediately S of
Marbella light; in day time the lighthouse is difficult
to spot as it is the middle of a group of high-rise
buildings. Do not be confused by a number of rocky
jetties between the marina and the fishing harbour,
built as breakwaters to retain sand for bathing

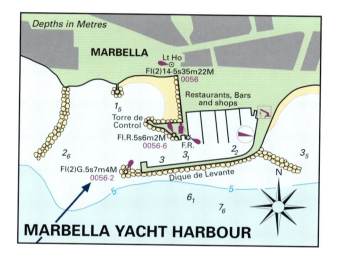

MARBELLA YACHT HARBOUR

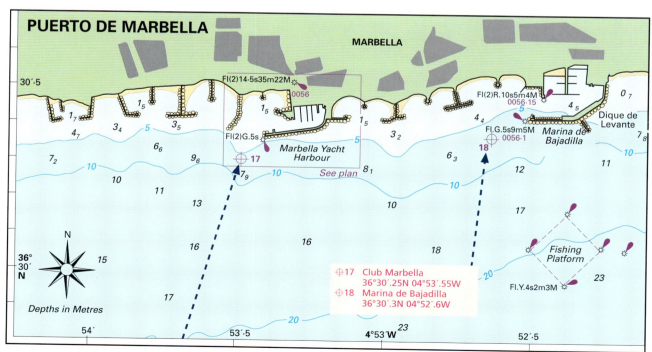

Marbella

beaches, and look out for a fishing platform at 36°30′.0N 04°52′.4W, about half a mile off the fishing harbour. The marina breakwater has been heightened to give extra protection within.

GPS approach

Steer to ⊕17 from southerly quadrant and steer for breakwater end (approximately 0.04M).

Anchorage in the approach

Anchor in 5m sand anywhere 200m to SW of the entrance to the yacht harbour.

Entrance

Give the jetty heads a good berth as they are not vertical at the foot. Line of small red can buoys on the north side of the entrance and a wreck on the south side, leave to port and starboard respectively.

Berths

Secure to the fuelling station on the port side of the entrance and ask at the *capitanía*, behind the fuel station.

Facilities

Maximum length overall: 15–20m.
A fork-lift type hoist on a tractor, rated at 16 tonnes.
A small slipway in NE corner of the harbour and a slipway on the W side of the harbour.
Small hardstanding.
Chandlery shop in the town.
Water from club marítimo and on pontoons and quays.
125V, 220V AC on quayside and pontoons and 380V on berths of 20m.
Gasoleo A and petrol.
Ice from factory 100m NE of the club marítimo.
Club Marítimo de Marbella is really a high quality hotel and restaurant with showers and other services in the basement.
There is a market about 1M to N of the club marítimo. Buy food from shops in back streets, they have better quality provisions and are cheaper.
Several launderettes in town.

Communications

Bus service along the coast. ☎ Area code 95.
Taxi ☎ 277 44 88.

12. Marina de Bajadilla

36°30′.4N 04°52′.5W

Lights

0056.1 **Dique de Levante head** 36°30′.4N 04°52′.5W
Fl.G.5s9m5M White tower, green top 4m
0056.15 **Dique de Poniente head** Fl(2)R.10s5m4M Grey tower, red top 3m

⊕18 36°30′.3N 4°52′.6W

Port Communications

VHF Ch 9. *Capitanía* ☎ 952 85 84 01 *Fax* 952 85 84 26
Email marbellad@eppa.es

Fishing harbour turned marina

This used to be the fishing harbour where yachts were definitely not welcome but recently it has been developed into a 260-berth marina with all the usual facilities. The entrance is quite straightforward but the harbour is subjected to swell from W and SW.

GPS approach

Steer to ⊕18 from southerly quadrant and steer for breakwater end (approximately 0.07M).

Approach

Marbella with its line of high-rise buildings can be seen from afar but the tall (35m) Marbella lighthouse is difficult to spot amongst them. Close the coast aiming at the east end of the high-rise buildings until the breakwater and/or the lighthouse can be identified. The marina is just over half a mile east of the lighthouse.

Berths

Moor to the fuel berth, at the end of the Dique de Poniente immediately to port on entering and obtain a berth at the *capitanía* which is at the very NE corner of the harbour.

Facilities

Maximum LOA 15m.
Crane, travel-lift, hardstanding etc.
Water and electricity on pontoons.
Showers etc at base of main pier.
Restaurant in marina.
Shops in town.

Marina de Bajadilla

13. Puerto Cabo Pino

36°29′N 04°44′.4W

Charts

British Admiralty *3578, 773*. Imray *M11*
French *4717*. Spanish *454*

⊕19 36°28′.8N 04°44′.5W

Lights

Note 3F.R vertical means port closed.
To the east
0058 **Punta de Calaburras** Fl.5s46m18M White tower,
house with red roof, 25m

Port communications

VHF Ch 9. Port manager ☎ 952 83 19 75
Fax 952 83 02 37.
Email marinacabopino@terra.es

Puerto Cabo Pino

Small private harbour

An attractive small private harbour with houses
built in the local style; it is one of the less oppressive
in terms of not being surrounded by high rise
buildings and boutiques. The approach and entrance
may be problematic – see below – but there is good
protection once inside. Facilities are good and there
are beaches on either side of the harbour.

As of June 2006 the Spanish and UK light lists
expunged all lights at this port except the Dique de
Levante head which is now three vertical fixed reds
(with three round shapes as a day mark) which
indicates the port is closed to all vessels. Dredging
was ongoing during the November 2007 visit but
there is no advice as to when this port may reopen.
This port should not be approached for the
foreseeable future.

Approach and entrance

Cabo Pino lies 8M to the E of Marbella and 4M to
WSW of Punta Calaburras lighthouse, both of which
are easily recognised. The high white apartment
blocks and harbour breakwater can be seen from
afar. The partly ruined square, Torre de Cala Honda,

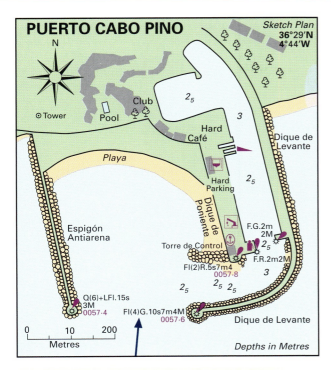

PUERTO CABO PINO

Sketch Plan 36°29'N 4°44'W

⊕19 Puerto Cabo Pino approaches 36°28'.8N 04°44'.5W

GPS approach

Steer to ⊕19 from southerly quadrant and steer for breakwater end (approximately 0.14M).

Anchorages

The sea floor near the harbour is mainly stony with poor holding, particularly on the E side, though some sandy patches may be found.

In the approach

Cala Moral 36°29'.8N 04°40'.7W 2M to ENE has a sandy bottom. Anchor between Torre Pesetas on Punta de la Torre Nueva and Torre de Cala Moral 200m from the shore in 3m sand.

Berths

Secure to the fuel berth which is just inside the harbour to port and near the F.R light and ask at the *torre de control* for berthing instructions.

Harbour charges

High.

Facilities

Maximum length overall: 16m (Four berths only).
Small yard which can pressure clean and apply anti foul.
8-tonne crane and 26-tonne travel-lift.
Slipway on W side of the harbour.
Engine mechanics.
Water points on all quays.
Showers at *torre de control*.
220V AC points on all quays. Some at 380V by the larger berths.
Gasoleo A and petrol.
Ice from the bars or from fuel quay.
Supermarket behind the harbour.
Launderettes near harbour.

Communications

Bus along the coast. ☎ Area code 95.
Taxi ☎ 277 44 88.

located just to W of the harbour will be seen closer in.

The approach and entrance silt and are dredged by the marina to a least depth of 1.5m though there is usually more water than that and yachts drawing 2m and more have entered without difficulty. Enter on the flood, sounding, and pass the Dique de Levante at about one third the distance between it and the Espigón Antiarena; sand builds up off the head of the Dique de Levante. Care is particularly necessary in strong SW–W winds or swell which may effectively reduce depths. If in doubt, call the marina and inquire about depths.

Cabo Pino tower

Punta de Calaburras

14. Puerto de Fuengirola

36°32′.5N 04°36′.9W

Charts

British Admiralty *3578, 773*. Imray *M11*
French *4717*. Spanish *455, 454*

⊕21 36°32′.6N 04 36°65′W

Lights

0059 **Dique de Abrigo** 36°32′.6N 04°36′.8W
  Fl(4)R.12s10m4M Red metal pyramidal tower 4m
0059.4 **Contradique** Fl(2)G.7s6m3M Green truncated
  pyramidal tower 4m
0058.5 **Espigón S head** 36°32′.8N 04°36′.7W Fl.G.5s5m5M
  Green tower 4m (on submerged groyne to the north
  of entrance)
To the west
0058 **Punta de Calaburras** 36°30′.5N 04°38′.3W
  Fl.5s46m18M White tower, house with red roof, 25m

Port communications

VHF Ch 9. Port ☎ 952 46 80 00 *Fax* 952 46 99 89
Email fuengirola@terra.es

Harbour with good shelter and facilities

Planned as a harbour in two parts, only the western
side has been built. It has good shelter and facilities.
All necessary provisions may be bought from large
modern tourist town nearby. Usually the approach
and entrance are easy but could be difficult with
strong NE–E winds and/or swell. In these conditions
parts of the harbour are uncomfortable.

The town is very busy and noisy in the season.
There are good beaches each side of the port but
they are crowded in summer. Local holidays: three
days in August and 7–10 October for their Patron
Saint.

Approach

From the SW The low headland of Punta Calaburras
with its conspicuous lighthouse and a mast 6.2M to
N, is about 2M SW of Fuengirola. An old castle on
a small hill lies halfway between this point and the
harbour. The town of Fuengirola with its high-rise
hotels and apartments is easily seen.

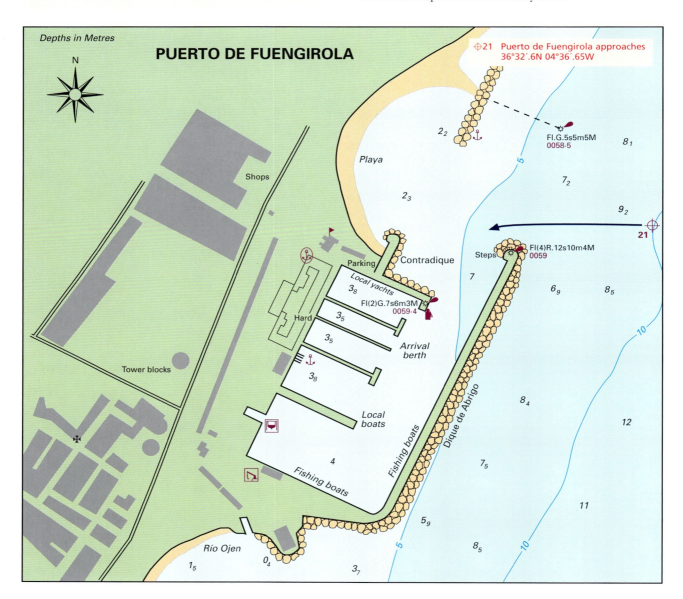

Fuengirola. Note submerged breakwater running SE from groynes to NE

From the NE The massive high-rise tourist development around Torremolinos continues with minor interruptions along the coast as far as Fuengirola after which it peters out.

The four minarets of the marina, although they do not compete in altitude with the buildings in the background, are conspicuous and catch the sun. As of 2007 there were only three minaret roofs visible as the SW one had lost its cover and only a framework remains.

GPS approach

Steer to ⊕21 from easterly quadrant and steer for breakwater end (approximately 0.13M).

Anchorage in the approach

Anchor 200m to N of the head of the breakwater in 3m sand. An alternative deeper anchorage lies 500m to SE of the harbour in 15m sand.

Entrance

Approach the head of the Dique de Abrigo on a NW course and round it. A shallow area has developed on the starboard side of the entrance; keep in mid-channel.

Berths

Pick up a mooring line and go bows- or stern-to one of the new concrete pontoons and check with the office near SW corner of the port.

Facilities

Maximum length overall: 20m.
Repairs – limited; there is a small yard to the SW of the harbour.
35-tonne travel-lift and 6-tonne crane.
Chandlery.
Water taps on quay and pontoons.

220V AC on pontoons and quays.
Gasoleo A and petrol.
Ice at the SW end of the harbour.
Club náutico – inquire about using its facilities.
Shop in the town for provisions.
A market near the centre of town and an open market on Tuesdays.
Launderettes in the town.

Communications

Rail and bus service. Airport at Málaga. ☎ Area code 95. Taxi ☎ 247 10 00.

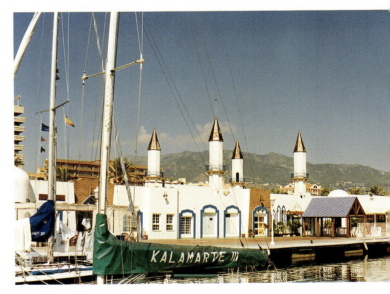

The minarets at Fuengirola

15. Puerto de Punta Negra

36°34′.7N 04°32′.43W
For charts, lights etc. see Fuengirola page 36.

Small private harbour

This very small private harbour for small yachts and runabouts is part of the casino complex.

Approach

The harbour lies 4M to NE of Fuengirola and ½M to SW of Puerto Principe at Torremolinos. The casino building is conspicuous.

Anchorage in the approach

Anchor 200m to S of the entrance in 7m sand.

Entrance

Approach the casino building heading NNW and identify the entrance in the centre of the harbour breakwater. Go in to either basin. Depths believed to be 2m or less.

16. Puerto de Benalmádena

36°35′.7N 04°30′.7W

Charts

British Admiralty *773*. Imray *M11*
French *4717*. Spanish *455, 455A*

⊕22   36°35′.5N 04°30′.5W

Lights

0060·3 **Laja de Bermeja** Q(3)10s7m5M ⬥ E card post 4m
0060.4 **Dique Sur SW head** Fl.G.5s9m10M White tower, with green band 5m
0060.5 **Dique Sur NE corner** Q(3)10s9m4M ⬥ Truncated conical masonry tower 5m
0060.7 **Dique Sur inner head** Fl(3)G.10s4m4M White tower, green band 2m
0060.6 **Dique del Oeste head** Fl.R.5s4m4M Truncated conical masonry, red band 2m

Port communications

VHF Ch 9. *Capitanía* ☎ 952 57 70 22 *Fax* 952 44 13 44
Email info@ puertobenalmadena.org
www.puertobenalmadena.org
Club Nautico Maritimo ☎ 952 44 42 34 *Fax* 952 57 64 61
Email info@cnmbenalmadena.com
www.cnmbenalmadena.com

Huge yacht harbour

This is a huge artificial yacht harbour enclosing 150,000 square metres of water located at the SW end of Torremolinos. The area near the harbour is a mass of soulless high-rise buildings and as it is very difficult to find a berth in Málaga, Benalmádena is a good alternative. Good beaches on each side of the harbour.

Approach

The approach requires care to avoid the shoal, Laja de Bermeja (see below) which breaks in heavy weather. The entrance is easy and good protection is offered once inside though there is some swell in outer harbour with W gale.

From the west The prominent walls of Benalmádena can be seen when passing the large casino building and small harbour of Punta Negra. Keep over ½M off the coast to pass south of the Laja de Bermeja and make for a position where the S end of the harbour is due W.

From the east Passage is forbidden through the area of an oil terminal located 1M to S of Puerto de Málaga. This area is about ½M square and lies ¾M off the coast. From Puerto de Málaga keep ½M off coast and pass inside prohibited area. Pay attention to an exposed wreck in the area. The mass of high rise blocks of flats at Torremolinos ends shortly before Benalmádena. Keep well to the east of Laja de Bermeja.

GPS approach

Steer to ⊕22 from easterly quadrant and steer for breakwater end, leaving the Laja de Bermeja post well to port (approximately 0.3M).

Anchorage in the approach

Anchor 200m to the NE of the E end of the Dique Sur in 5m sand.

Entrance

The Laja de Bermeja (2.5m), lying some 250m S of Dique Sur head light, is the easterly outlier of a large rock strewn and shallow area to the west of the actual rock. The E cardinal post marks this large shallow area (although to the west of the actual Laja de Bermeja!)

From a position ½M out and where the S end of the harbour is due W, approach on this course leaving the Laja de Bermeja post well to port. Follow the Dique Sur to its head then round it, keeping at least 30m clear and enter on an east-northeasterly course. In late 2007 there was a small red buoy moored some 40m north of the Dique Sur end. Vessels seemed to pass this buoy on either side but the larger yachts appeared to leave it to port on leaving and to starboard on entering.

Berths

Go to the fuelling point and ask at the control tower for a berth. (There may be significant swell on outer wall).

Facilities

Maximum length overall: 30m.
Most yacht maintenance services including sailmaker.
Slipway in the E corner of the harbour.
50-tonne travel-hoist and 5-tonne crane.
Chandleries inside and outside the port.
Water taps on all quays.

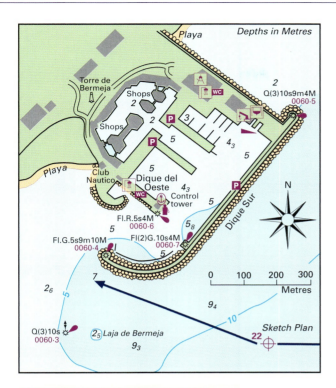

⊕22　Puerto de Benalmádena approaches
36°35′.5N 04°30′.5W

Benalmádena

Showers.

220V AC and 380V AC on berths between 18–30m.

Gasoleo A and petrol pumps by the control tower.

Ice on fuel quay.

Supermarket in port.

Shops and supermarkets in Benalmádena Costa and Torremolinos, 1M away. Good shops and market (Friday) at Arroya del Miel 1½M inland.

Laundry collected within the port and launderettes in the town.

Diving school.

Communications

Bus and rail services to most parts of Spain, bus stop on main road near the marina. Airport at Málaga.

☎ Area code 95. Taxi ☎ 244 15 45.

Benalmádena Club Nautico Maritimo

II.i COSTA DEL SOL

17. Puerto de Málaga

36°43´N 04°25´W

Tides

Time differencesr based on Gibraltar

HW	LW	MHWS	MHWN	MLWS	MLWN	*Mean level*
+0005	−0005	−0.3	−0.1	0.0	+0.1	0.45

⊕23 36°41´.7N 04°25´.0W

Currents

Offshore these are normally E-going but a counter-current sometimes runs off the entrance. The tidal streams up to 0.5 knots run NE and SW in the entrance.

Charts

British Admiralty *1850, 1851*. Imray *M11*
French *4717, 7294*. Spanish *455, 455A, 4551*

Lights

Approach
0062 **Málaga LtHo**
Fl(3+1)20s38m25M 243°-vis-047° White truncated conical tower on white two-storey building 33m

Harbour
0064 **Dique del Este head** Fl(2)G.7s13m3M 000°-vis-200° Conical masonry tower 7m
0064.5 **New Dique de Levante N head** Q(3)10s12m3M Black tower, yellow band 2m
0065 **New Dique de Levante S head** Fl.G.5s7m5M Green tower 4m
0065.3 **Submerged breakwater head** Q(6)+LFl.15s3M ⍚ cardinal post 4m

0065·5 **Contradique SW corner** Q(6)+LFl.15s3M ⍚ card. post 4m
0065.7 **Contradique E head** Fl.R.5s5M Red pyramid 5m.
0066 **Dique del Oeste head** Fl(2)R.7s13m4M 374°-vis-231° Conical masonry tower 7m
0067 **Puerto Pesquero Espigón Sur** Q.R.4m2M Conical stone tower 3m
0067.5 **Puerto Pesquero Espigón Norte** Q.G.5m2M Conical stone tower 3m
0068 **Dique Transversal del Este head** SE corner Fl(2)G.7s6m2M Conical masonry tower 5m
0070 **Muelle Transversal del Oeste head** Fl(2+1)R.12s7m2M Tower with red top 4m
0070.2 **Muelle de Romero Robledo** Fl(4)R.11s7m2M Tower with red top 4m
0069 **Small craft basin. Dique Norte** Fl(3)R.9s6m2M Red metal column
0069.2 **Small craft basin. Dique Sur head** Fl(3)G.8s6m2M Green metal column
0069.4 **Muelle Canovas del Castillo head** Fl(2+1)G.12s6m2M Tower with green top 4m

Port communications

Port VHF Ch 9, 11, 12, 13, 14, 16
☎ 952 22 85 28
Real Club Mediterraneo VHF Ch 9
☎ 952 22 62 03 *Fax* 952 21 63 11
Email cbotes@realclubmediterraneo.com
www.realclubmediterraneo.com

Storm signals

Storm signals may be displayed at the signal station.

Puerto de Málaga

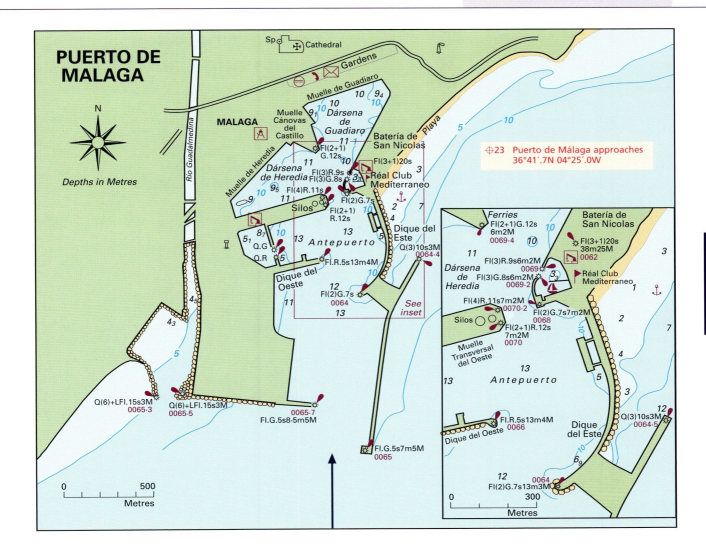

Major working port

This is a port to be avoided unless prior arrangements have been made for a berth especially now with the extensive works going on in the harbour. A new Dique de Levante and a new *contradique* have been constructed and much work is still going on in the harbour. It is the major commercial and fishing port of the Costa del Sol without special provision for yachts and there is very limited room at the Real Club Mediterráneo de Málaga which is an exclusive club. Yachts are turned away from Málaga by the harbour authorities and sent to Benalmádena and it has been reported that even in difficult conditions this applies as there is now, effectively, no room for pleasure craft in Málaga.

During a November 2007 visit it was noticed that there were a number of large yachts (>25m) moored in the NE corner of the Darsena de Guardiaro. It was understood that this area was under the direct control of the port authorities.

Local holidays 27 August for 10 days. Fair, 1–9 August.

Approach by day

From the west The line of high-rise apartments and hotels at Torremolinos and Puerto de Benalmádena are conspicuous, as are the round storage tanks and the power station with two very tall chimneys 1.5M to SW of the port. Keep within ½M of the shore or more than 1½M off-shore to avoid the Passage Prohibited Area. Pay attention to the exposed wreck in the area.

From the east A grey cement factory about four miles to E of the port is identifiable and the wide flat valley between high ranges of mountains where the port and city are located can be seen from afar. Avoid the prohibited area.

GPS approach

Steer to ⊕23 from a south easterly quadrant and steer for breakwater end (approximately 0.2M).

Prohibited area

There are a number of mooring buoys and yellow lit buoys 1½M S of the port, opposite the oil terminal, about 1M offshore and surrounding an oil pipeline terminal. Passage is forbidden through these buoys. Pass inside within ½M of the shore or more than 1½M offshore.

Anchorage in the approach

Anchor to E of port with lighthouse about 300m to NW in 6m sand.

Entrance

Enter on a NE course between breakwater heads. Then on a N course between the inner two quays, the port hand quay being very low.

Berths

The Real Club Mediterráneo de Málaga is on the E side of Darséna de Heredia.

Try the E side of the quay that separates the Puerto Pesquero from the Ante Puerto or stern to quay with anchor from the bow in SW corner of Dársena de Heredia either side of the large floating dock; use an anchor trip line and before heaving it up, make sure the deck wash is working. Larger yachts are sometimes allowed alongside the N side of the Dique Transversal del Oeste while on other occasions yachts have been directed to the NE corner of the Dársena del Guadiaro where the quay wall is high.

Harbour charges

Very high.

Formalities

Check with the harbour authorities on VHF Ch 9.

Facilities

Geared towards large commercial vessels. There are points for electricity and water (contact Obras de Puerto, office at the main gate), cranes (no travel hoist), a slipway, ice etc. all something of a hassle to organise.

Chandleries, shops, supermarkets in town but the harbour is enclosed and only the main gate (which has to be negotiated) is open at night.

Spanish chart agency at the Comandancia de Marina near the lighthouse.

Communications

Málaga airport is halfway between Málaga and Benalmádena and has year-round international services. Ship ferry service to Tanger, Barcelona, Canary Islands, Genoa and Marseille. Rail and bus services. Railway. ☎ Area code 95.

British Consulate Málaga
Edificio Eurocom, Calle Mauricio Moro Pareto, 2-2°, 29006 Málaga ☎ 95 235 23 00 *Fax* 95 235 92 11.

RC Málaga

The coast between Málaga and Candado

There are several bathing beaches along this stretch of the coast which are protected by breakwaters. From the sea they may appear to be harbours. They are not.

18. Puerto de El Candado

36°42´.8N 04°20´.8W

Charts

British Admiralty *773*. Imray *M11*
French *4717, 7294, 6569*. Spanish *455*
⊕25 36°42´.8N 04°20´.9W

Lights

0071 **Dique de Levante head** 2F.R(vert)7m4M

Port communications

Club náutico VHF Ch 9 ☎ 952 290 547 *Fax* 952 295 804
Email info@clubelcandado.com www.clubelcandado.com

Small shallow harbour

A very small harbour some 3½M to E of Málaga. Only suitable for yachts and vessels drawing 2m or less – and there is not much room for manoeuvre. The narrow entrance tends to silt up and is occasionally dredged to 4m. It is open to W. It would be uncomfortable to remain there in strong SW–W winds and difficult to enter or leave in those conditions. As of January 2002 it is understood that this port is to be used in daylight hours only and there is also a draught restriction of 2m on entering craft.

There was a build-up of sand in March 2006 at the entrance and following a number of attempts to clear the entrance it was decided to shut the port and the lights were withdrawn in mid 2006 and replaced with two fixed vertical lights showing the port was closed.

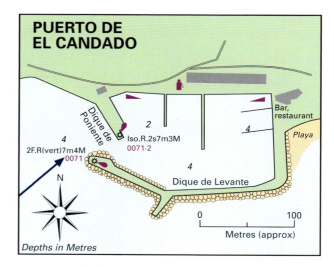

⊕25 Puerto de El Candado approaches 36°42´.8N 04°20´.9W

Puerto de El Candado

The club appears to be thriving, however, and there are port and starboard buoys laid to lead the locals into the harbour (all berths are privately owned and full). The depth in the entrance was stated to be 1.5m with a lot of hand-waving so it is probably less than that! This is another marina to bypass.

Approach

There is a large, grey cement factory just to the E of the harbour.

GPS approach

Steer to ⊕25 from a southerly quadrant and steer for breakwater end (approximately 0.08M).

Anchorage in the approach

Anchor 200m to SW of entrance in 10m sand.

Entrance

Approach a point 200m to NW of the entrance of the harbour, sounding continuously. Leave three small red buoys to port and four small green buoys to starboard. Leave the head of the Dique de Levante 10m to starboard.

Berths

Berth stern-to the quay or pontoon with anchor or mooring buoy from the bow.

Harbour charges

Low.

Facilities

Maximum length overall: 10m.
A hard in the corner of the harbour.
Water and Electricity (220V AC) on the pontoons and
 quays.
Chandlery to N of harbour.
Club náutico with bar, showers.

Communications

Bus service. ☎ Area code 95.

⚓ FONDEADERO DE VÉLEZ-MÁLAGA
36°44′.2N 4°05′.5W

An open anchorage off the town of Torre del Mar. Anchor in 6m sand 100m offshore, E of the lighthouse (0072 Fl(1+2)10s30m13M white tower 28m) or further NE. Everyday supplies from the town which has a *club náutico*. The new Puerto Caleta de Vélez lies 1½M to NE.

II.i COSTA DEL SOL

ENSENADA DE VELEZ-MALAGA

19. Puerto Caleta de Vélez

36°44′.8N 04°04′W

Charts

British Admiralty *773*. Imray *M11*
French *6569*. Spanish *455*

⊕26 36°44′.7N 04°04′.4W

Lights

To the west
0072 **Torre del Mar (Torre de Vélez)** Fl(1+2)10s30m13M
   White round tower 28m
Harbour
0073.2 **Dique de Abrigo head** Fl.G.5s9m5M White
   truncated conical tower, green top 4m
0073.6 **Contradique** Fl(2)R.7s4m3M White post, red band
   2m
0073.7 **Espigón head** Fl.R.4s8m3M Red tower 4m
To the east
0074 **Punta de Torrox** Fl(4)15s29m20M White tower and
   building 23m

Port communications

VHF Ch 10. *Capitania* ☎ 952 51 13 90 *Fax* 952 55 05 26
Email caleta@eppa.es www.eppa.es

Quiet fishing harbour

A quiet, in terms of it not being full of tourists, fishing harbour at the head of the Ensenada de Vélez Málaga. It is one of eleven yacht harbours run by the *Junta de Andalucía*. It is easy to approach and enter though care is necessary with heavy onshore wind and/or swell. Facilities for yachts are limited but it is a useful place to spend a day or two on passage between Málaga and Motril. Sand and pebble beaches either side of the harbour.

Approach

From the west The sandy coast from Málaga eastward is relatively featureless, lined with small housing estates. Punta de Vélez Málaga, which is the delta of a river, is not prominent. Only after rounding it, will Torre del Mar light become plain among the houses and flats of the town. A factory chimney to its NE is conspicuous.

From the east Punta de Torrox is on a low, flat sandy delta which itself is not prominent. The lighthouse is conspicuous. The large block of flats at La Mezquitilla, 1M to the E of the harbour, and the road bridge over the Río del Algarrobo will also be seen. In the closer approach the harbour walls are conspicuous.

GPS approach

Steer to ⊕26 from a southerly quadrant and steer for breakwater end (approximately 0.1M).

Anchorage in the approach

Anchor 200m offshore in 5m sand either side of the harbour.

Entrance

Approach the W end of the breakwater on a northerly course and round the head of the Dique de Levante, giving it a berth of at least 40m. This is to avoid a small espigón running N from the head of the dique. Also keep a look out for fishing craft leaving at speed as they can be obscured by the high dique.

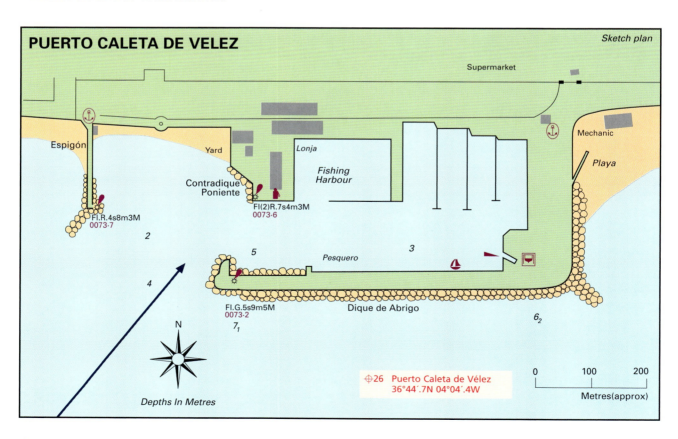

Puerto Caleta de Vélez

Caleta digue, espigón and nets

Berths

Secure stern to the quay or pontoon at the E end of the harbour. There are mooring buoys but they are private.

Harbour charges

Medium.

Facilities

Maximum length overall: 20m.
45-tonnes hoist. The whole E side of the harbour is hard.
Electricity and water on the quay.
Gasoleo A, petrol 0900–1230, 1600–2000hrs.
Supermarket 100m from the port, more in Torre del Mar and a hypermarket about 3km from the port towards Torre del Mar.

Communications

Bus service along the coast. ☎ Area code 95.

II.ii Pta del Torrox to Cabo de Gata and Isla del Alboran

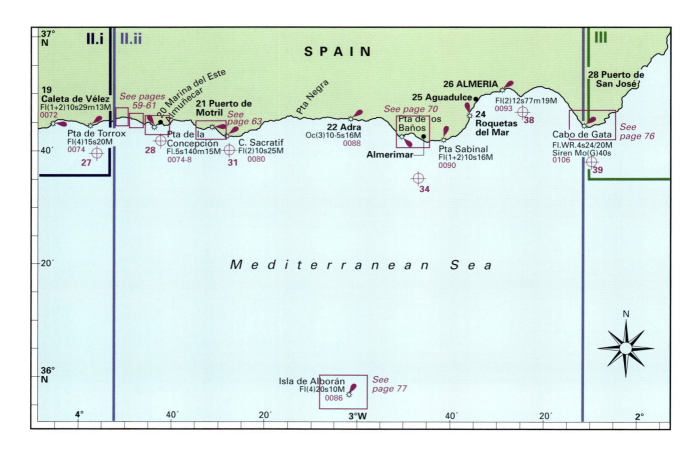

PORTS

20. Marina del Este Puerto de la Mona
21. Puerto de Motril
22. Puerto de Adra
23. Puerto de Almerimar
24. Puerto de Roquetas de Mar
25. Puerto de Aguadulce
26. Puerto de Almería
27. Isla de Alborán

COASTAL WAYPOINT LIST

The waypoints listed form a series with which one is able to steer from off Gibraltar to Cabo de Gata. It is essential to keep a lookout at all times while making a coastal passage in this area.

⊕27	Pta del Torrox	36°42′N	03°57′.4W
⊕28	Pta de la Concepción	36°42′.5N	03°44′W
⊕31	Cabo Sacratif	36°41′N	03°28′W
⊕34	SSE of Pta de las Entinas	36°37′.5N	02°46′W
⊕38	S of Pta del Río	36°46′.5N	02°25′.5W
⊕39	Cabo de Gata	36°41′N	02°10′W

Punta del Torrox

Anchorages between Pta del Torrox and Motril

⚓ FONDEADERO DE NERJA
35°45′N 3°51′.8W

A pleasant anchorage just E of Nerja where everyday supplies are available. Anchor 100m from the Playa de Barranja in 5m, sand, or 400m off in 18m, stones.

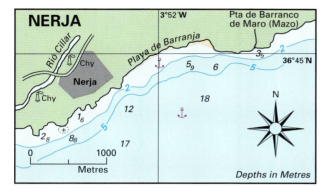

⚓ CALA DE LA MIEL
36°45′.1N 3°49′.5W

An interesting and attractive open anchorage with a stony beach and a track to the main road on the cliffs behind. Anchor in 5m sand and pebbles. Conspicuous ruined tower on cliff to W of bay with three small disused houses. There is a freshwater spring.

⚓ CALA DE LOS CAÑUELOS
36°44′.6N 3°47′.5W

Anchor in 5m sand and pebble off the centre of the shingle beach which has isolated rocks at either end of the beach. The track leads to the main road.

⚓ ENSENADA DE LA HERRADURA
36°44′N 3°44′.8W

A bay a mile wide between Puntas Cerro Gordo and de la Mona. Anchor in 5m sand 100m from the beach or 200m out in 11m mud. Additonal shelter at either end but beware rocks. Everyday supplies from the town.

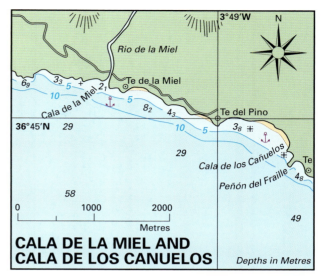

Above Cañuelos   *Below* Herradura

Ensenada de la Herradura west and, opposite, east

II.ii COSTA DEL SOL

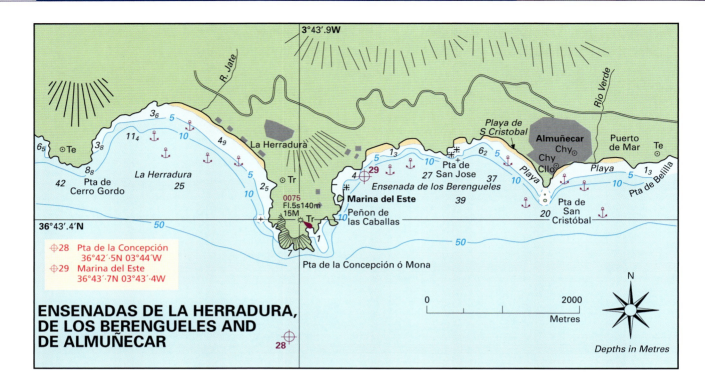

ENSENADAS DE LA HERRADURA, DE LOS BERENGUELES AND DE ALMUÑECAR

⊕28 Pta de la Concepción
       36°42′·5N 03°44′·W
⊕29 Marina del Este
       36°43′·7N 03°43′·4W

Pta de la Concepción ó Mona

0   2000
      Metres

Depths in Metres

20. Marina del Este Puerto de la Mona

36°43′.7N 03°43′.5W

Charts

British Admiralty *773*. Imray *M11*
French *4717, 6569*. Spanish *456*

⊕29 36°43′.7N 03°43′.4W

Lights

To the south
0074.8 **Punta de la Mona** Fl.5s140m15M Masonry tower 14m
Harbour
0075 **Dique de Abrigo** Fl.R.5s13m4M Red tower 5m
0075.2 **Contradique** Fl(2)G.6s5m3M Green tower 3m
To the east
0080 **Cabo Sacratif** Fl(2)10s98m25M White tower and building 17m

Port communications

Capitania VHF Ch 9. ☎ 958 640 801 *Fax* 958 827 240
Email marinaeste@marinasmediterraneo.es
www.marinasmediterraneo.es

Small harbour in beautiful area

A small artificial yacht harbour which is part of a huge housing development in a beautiful area. The approach and entrance are easy and good protection is provided especially from the W. Some swell is experienced with NE–E winds and is sometimes unpleasant due to deflected waves. Basic facilities are provided. This harbour together with the Puerto Caleta de Vélez (Torre del Mar) form useful stopping places between Málaga and Motril, but prices are high. A small beach near the harbour, pool at yacht club.

The prehistoric caves at Nerja, the old villages in the hills and the famous city of Granada can all be visited. The mountains of Sierra Nevada lying inland are very beautiful.

Approach

From the west Nerja and the Punta de Cerro Gordo are easily recognised. The high prominent Punta de Mona (Concepción) is unmistakable; the harbour lies round the corner.

From the east After passing the delta of Río Guadalfeo the coast becomes hilly. Almuñecar with an old fort above it is conspicuous at the beginning of the Ensenada de los Berengueles. The harbour lies on the W side of this Ensenada, about half-way along the ridge leading to Punta de la Mona.

GPS approach

Steer to ⊕29 from a easterly quadrant and steer for breakwater end (approximately 0.06M).

Anchorage in the approach

Anchor 100m off the beach in 5m sand in the NW corner of the Ensenada de Berengueles.

Entrance

Approach the W side of the Ensenada de los Berengueles keeping 400m from the coast, due to off-lying rocks, until the N end of the harbour bears W then approach and round the head of the breakwater leaving it 25m to port and enter on a S course.

Berths

Secure to fuel berth on the starboard side on entering and ask at control tower.

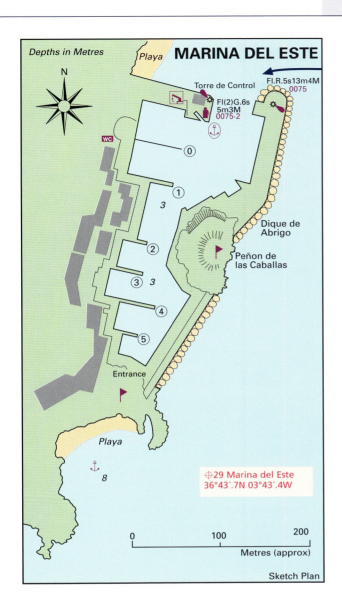

Depths in Metres

Playa

MARINA DEL ESTE

N

Torre de Control

Fl.R.5s13m4M
0075

Fl(2)G.6s
5m3M
0075·2

WC

0

1

3

2

3 3

Dique de Abrigo

Peñon de las Caballas

3

4

5

Entrance

Playa

8

⊕29 Marina del Este
36°43´.7N 03°43´.4W

0   100   200

Metres (approx)

Sketch Plan

Harbour charges

Low in low season (1 November to 1 March). Medium in summer.

Facilities

Maximum length overall: 30m.
30-tonnes travel-lift and a 3.3-tonne crane.
A large hard for laid-up yachts.
Limited repair facilities. The marine engineer and chandler can find specialists.
Water points on the quays and pontoons.
Showers at yacht club.
220V AC points on the quays and pontoons, 380V on large berths.
Gasoleo A and petrol.
Ice near the fuel quay.
Small supermarket and laundry in the marina. Other shops in Herradura 2M over the hill.

Communications

Bus service on the main road 1M away – a long, steep climb. ☎ Area code 958. Taxi ☎ 63 00 17.

⚓ ENSENADA DE LOS BERENGUELES

36°43´.9N 3°43´W
(See plan on page 60)

Another large anchorage on the E side of Punta de la Mona in attractive surroundings. There are several places where anchorage is possible – 100m off the Playa de San Cristóbal that lies to the W of Almuñecar in 5m sand or off the two beaches in the NW corner of the bay. All normal facilities from the town of Almuñecar and some repairs possible. Almuñecar fort is conspicuous.

⚓ PUNTA DE SAN CRISTÓBAL AND FONDEADERO DE ALMUÑECAR

36°43´N 3°42´.2W
(See plan on page 60)

Anchor 200m off the beach in 5m sand or 400m out in 20m stones. Punta de San Cristóbal gives protection from the west. Almuñecar has a conspicuous fort. Everyday supplies in the town.

II.ii COSTA DEL SOL

Marina del Este

Almuñecar

⚓ ENSENADA DE BELILLA
36°43′.7N 3°41′.1W
(See plan on page 60)

An anchorage 150m off the Playa de Belilla in 5m clay and sand, or further out in 30m stones. Modern holiday development along the coast where everyday supplies may be found.

⚓ ENSENADA DE ROBAINA
36°44′.5N 03°39′.4W

A pleasant small anchorage 50m off a small pair of sand and pebble beaches in 5m sand. A conspicuous small fort is located on Punta de Jesus o del Tesorillo and a large block of flats behind the W beach.

⚓ SURGIDERO DE SALOBREÑA
36°44′.1N 03°35′.7W

Peñón and Surgidero de Salobreña: anchor either side of the conspicuous peñon, 100m off the coast in 5m, sand and pebbles, or 400m out in 25m, mud. The Moorish castle above the town of Salobreña is easily seen.

Salobreña

21. Puerto de Motril
36°43′.4N 3°30′.7W

Charts
British Admiralty *773, 774*. Imray *M11*
French *4717, 6569*. Spanish *4571, 457*

⊕30 36°42′.7N 03°30′.7W

Lights
To the west
0074.8 **Punta de la Mona** Fl.5s140m15M Masonry tower 14m
Harbour
0077 **Dique de Poniente head** Fl(2)R.6s11m10M Red truncated conical tower 5m
0077.5 **Dique del Este** Fl(2)G.7s9m5M Metal post 4m
0079 **Nuevo Dique de Levante elbow** Fl(3)G.12s6m5M Green truncated conical tower 4m
0079.2 **Nuevo Dique de Levante head** Fl.G.5s6m2M Green truncated conical tower 5m
0078 **Dique de Levante head** Fl(2+1)G.12s6m5M Green tower, red band 5m
0078.4 **Espigón head** Fl.R.5s6m2M Red truncated conical tower 5m
To the east
0080 **Cabo Sacratif** Fl(2)10s98m25M White tower and building 17m

Port communications
VHF Port Ch 12 (Tugs), 13. Marina Ch 9. ☎ 958 60 00 37
Fax 958 60 12 47 *Email* info@nauticomotril.com
www.realclubnauticomotril.com

Primarily a commercial harbour
A small fishing harbour that has developed into a commercial harbour which has recently been doubled in size. It has an easy approach and entrance but rather poor facilities for yachtsmen. The harbour is uncomfortable in strong easterly winds but some shelter can now be found behind the huge new *contradique*. The little village near the harbour can provide basic needs but there are many

Puerto de Motril from SE

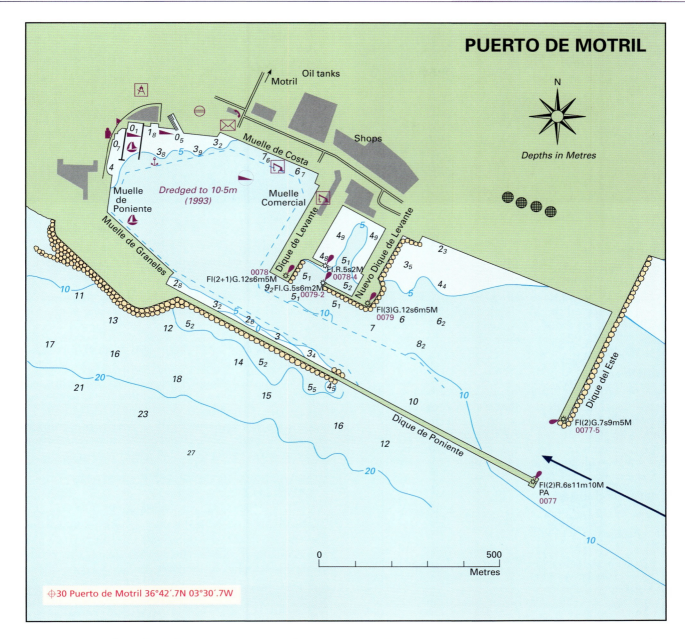

PUERTO DE MOTRIL

N

Depths in Metres

Oil tanks

Motril

Shops

Muelle de Costa

Muelle de Poniente

Dredged to 10·5m (1993)

Muelle Comercial

Muelle de Graneles

Dique de Levante

Nuevo Dique de Levante

Dique del Este

Dique de Poniente

Fl(2+1)G.12s6m5M 0078

Fl.R.5s2M 0078·4

Fl.G.5s6m2M 0079·2

Fl(3)G.12s6m5M 0079

Fl(2)G.7s9m5M 0077·5

Fl(2)R.6s11m10M PA 0077

0   500

Metres

⊕30 Puerto de Motril 36°42´.7N 03°30´.7W

more shops in Motril itself, two miles away. Local holidays occur on 15 August and 15 October.

Inside the new Dique del Este a large area has been reclaimed from the harbour in front of the oil tanks but there is still space to anchor behind the groyne SW of the oil tanks.

Approach

From the west The flat open plain of the delta of the Río Guadalfeo and the cranes, buildings and tall silos just to the W of Cabo Sacratif show the location of this harbour. Several large blocks of flats line the coast just to the W of this harbour. The town of Motril 2M inland shows in the closer approach.

From the east Cabo Sacratif, a distinctive headland with an isolated conspicuous lighthouse at its summit can easily be recognised from afar. There are two white radar domes on the mountain Sierra do Pelaos 4M to NE of this cape.

The *contradique* had four large columns and a crane at its end in the September 2004 visit but they were all been removed in late 2006. Further work has gone on infilling the east corner of the harbour in front of the oil tanks which has removed the chance of anchoring east of the Nuevo Dique de Levante.

GPS approach

Steer to ⊕30 from a southerly quadrant and steer for breakwater end (approximately 0.27M).

Entrance

Approach the new head of the Dique de Poniente on a N course. Round it and enter between the heads, and steer parallel to the *dique* up the harbour on a WNW course.

II.ii COSTA DEL SOL

Puerto de Motril Club Náutico from S

Calahonda

Berths

If there is space, go stern-to on the pontoons at the *club náutico* in the NW corner of the harbour. Otherwise go stern-to either side but clear of the diesel pumps on the Muelle de Poniente on the west side of the harbour. In strong SE or E winds, lie alongside the Muelle Comercial with permission of the *capitanía*.

Anchorage

Along with most of the commercial harbours on this coast anchoring in the port is frowned on, if not expressly forbidden. As mentioned above the new infilling east of the new Dique de Abrigo has radically reduced the space available for anchoring and it is probable that anchoring is now prohibited in the port.

Harbour charges

Low. Yachts at anchor may escape charges.

Facilities

Maximum length overall (*club náutico*): 20m.
Slipways at the yard in the NW corner of the main harbour and in the Puerto Pesquero can handle up to 100 tonnes.
Cranes up to 2.5 tonnes.
Engine and mechanical workshops outside the harbour.
A small chandlery shop in the village.
Water from points on quays and pontoons. For water hose, contact a harbour official if using water from quays.
220v AC points on quays and pontoons.
Gasoleo A on west side of harbour.
Ice from the ice factory in the village or from restaurant.
Club Náutico de Motril has bars, lounge, terrace and restaurants, also showers and a pool. Visiting yachtsmen are welcomed.
Supermarket just outside harbour area. Market and many more shops in Motril.

Communications

Frequent bus service to Motril. Buses to Granada and back (a long day's outing). ☎ Area code 958.
Taxi ☎ 60 18 54.

⚓ ANCHORAGE E OF CABO SACRATIF
36°41′.5N 03°28′W

An open coastal anchorage tucked under the E end of the rocky cliffed Cabo Sacratif. Anchor 100m offshore in 5m sand and pebbles. The main road runs a little way inland.

⚓ CALAHONDA
36°42′.1N 03°24′.7W

There are now yellow swimmers buoys all along the beach and the available area for anchoring is in 20+ metres of water. The village, which has a church tower like a lighthouse, has everyday supplies.

⚓ ANCHORAGES BETWEEN CALAHONDA AND CASTELL DE FERRO

This 3M stretch of high, rocky cliffed coast is broken into several deep bays. It is possible for experienced navigators to anchor at the heads of these bays in good conditions providing the water is clear enough to see the odd isolated rock. The coast road runs along the top of the cliff.

⚓ FONDEADERO DE CASTELL DE FERRO
36°43′.1N 03°21′.6W

Anchor in the corner of the bay near Punta del Melonar (at the left of the photograph), 100m from the shingle beach, 5m sand and mud or further out in 10m, mud. Good protection from the west. Everyday supplies in the village.

Fondeadero de Castell de Ferro

⚓ ANCHORAGES IN LA RÁBITA
36°44′.7N 03°10′.5W

A useful coastal anchorage at the W end of a gravel beach. Anchor 100m offshore in 5m sand and stones. The small village is readily recognised by the small blocks of flats 'hung' on a cliff face behind the village with a tower nearby. There is a small fort to the E of the tower. Everyday supplies from the village. Another possible anchorage is small bay to E of Punta Negra.

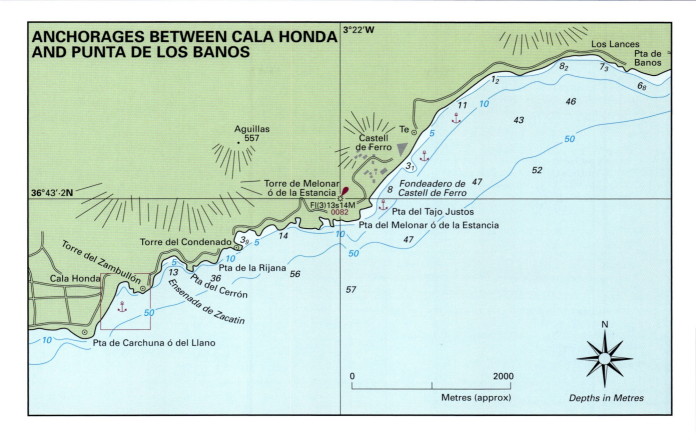

ANCHORAGES BETWEEN CALA HONDA AND PUNTA DE LOS BANOS

3°22'W

Los Lances
Pta de Banos
Aguillas
· 557

Te
Castell de Ferro

Torre de Melonar ó de la Estancia
36°43'·2N
Fl(3)13s14M
0082

Fondeadero de Castell de Ferro
Pta del Tajo Justos
Pta del Melonar ó de la Estancia

Torre del Condenado
Torre del Zambullón
Cala Honda
Pta de la Rijana
Pta del Cerrón
Ensenada de Zacatin
Pta de Carchuna ó del Llano

N

0   2000

Metres (approx)

Depths in Metres

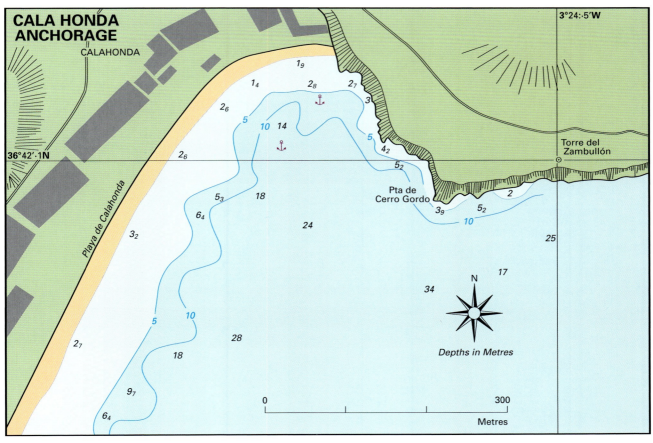

CALA HONDA ANCHORAGE

CALAHONDA

3°24:·5'W

36°42'·1N

Torre del Zambullón

Playa de Calahonda

Pta de Cerro Gordo

N

Depths in Metres

0   300

Metres

II.ii COSTA DEL SOL

22. Puerto de Adra

36°44′.7N 03°01′.2W

Charts

British Admiralty *773, 774.* Imray *M11*
French *4717, 6569.* Spanish *457, 458*

⊕32 36°44′.25N 03°01′W

Lights

To the west
0082 **Castell de Ferro** Fl(3)13s237m14M White tower 12m
0088 **Adra lighthouse** 36°44′.9N 03°01′.8W
   Oc(3)10.5s49m16M White tower, red bands 26m
Harbour
0088.4 **Dique de Poniente head N end** 36°44′.6N
   03°01′.1W Fl(2)R.6s8m5M Red masonry tower 6m
0088.6 **Inner breakwater head** Fl(3)R.10s5m2M Red post
   3m
0089 **Dique de Levante head** Fl(2)G.10s8m3M Green
   masonry tower 5m
0089.2 **Inner breakwater head** Fl(3)G.9s5m2M Green post
   3m
To the east
0089.5 **Punta de los Baños** Fl(4)11s22m11M Rectangular
   white tower 21m
0090 **Punta Sabinal** Fl(1+2)10s34m16M Tower above
   white houses 32m

Port communications

Capitanía VHF Ch 9. ☎ 950 40 10 53 *Fax* 950 56 05 93
Email adra@eppa.es
Club náutico ☎ 950 40 14 17 *Fax* 950 40 07 12
Email rcna@larural.es www.eppa.es

A working harbour

A rather desolate commercial and fishing harbour, established by the Phoenicians, who called it Abdera, and in use ever since. It has accommodation for small motor boats but is less suitable for keeled yachts. The approach and entrance is easy in normal conditions but in strong winds, especially those from the E, the entrance can be dangerous and the harbour very uncomfortable. The harbour is also disturbed by the constant movement of fishing boats. Work was started in late 2007 infilling to the NW of the inner breakwater which will make the harbour even more uncomfortable for visitors during the work. Facilities for yachtsmen are poor but there are sandy beaches on either side of the harbour. The town is small and without much tourist development. Local holidays September 6 to 10 in honour of Our Lady of the Sea and St Nicholas of Tolentino.

Approach

From either direction the harbour can be identified by the lighthouse and by the very large and tall Torre de Perdigones which has windows. The upper half is brown brick and the lower painted white. A smaller similar tower is located further inland. There is a deep grey sandy beach along the SW side of Dique de Poniente which makes identification somewhat difficult from seaward as it merges into the shore

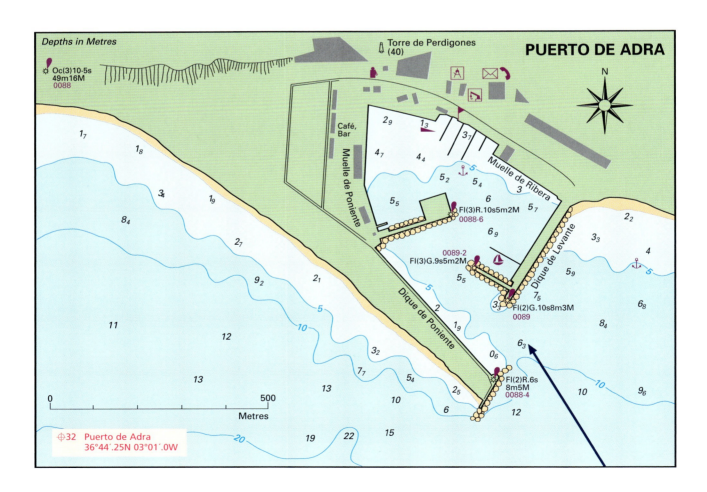

Puerto de Adra from SE – infilling work started (November 2007) at the end of the interior jetty

line. However there is a sand elevator and other machinery and blocks of flats. A conspicuous factory with a pair of grey chimneys stands some 2M to W of the harbour.

GPS approach

Steer to ⊕32 from a southerly quadrant and steer for breakwater end (approximately 0.28M).

Anchorage in the approach

Anchor 200m to E of Dique de Levante in 5m sand and pebbles. Alternative anchorage in deep water S of the harbour.

Entrance

The head of the Dique de Poniente is T-shaped and the NE spur extends about 30m in that direction from the light. Give it a good berth and pass between the two inner moles. The depths in the entrance and harbour frequently change and are sometimes dredged; depths are approximate.

Berths

Alongside or stern-to the off-shore end of the Dique de Levante. The *club náutico* is crowded with small boats. It has four visitors berths but check to see if you will fit.

Harbour charges

High.

Anchorage

Anchor in 3m mud near centre of harbour using an anchor with a trip line. Anchor light and shape are necessary.

Facilities

Maximum length overall: 20m for berthing.
Shipyards geared towards fishing boats.
150-tonnes travel hoist and hardstanding in fishing harbour.
5-tonnes crane.
Several slipways which will take the largest yachts.
Chandlers shop in town.
Water from points on quay or from *club náutico*.
125V and 220V AC supply point near water point.
Ice factory on NE side of the harbour.
Club náutico with a bar and restaurant.
Supermarket and shops in the village.

Communications

Bus service along the coast. ☎ Area code 950.

Balerma

⚓ BALERMA
36°43′.6N 02°53′.7W

An open coastal anchorage some 100m off the beach in 5m sand and pebbles, opposite the low Torre de Balerma which has a few buildings around and a factory to NE. A somewhat unattractive flat coast with plastic-covered greenhouses stretching for miles.

⚓ PUNTA DE LOS BAÑOS
36°41′.6N 02°51′.2W

An extraordinary and rather exposed anchorage between the double spurs of a point. Anchor about 50m from the coast in 3m sand and stones. The very conspicuous Castillo de Guardias Viejas stands on a small hill just within the double point and Punta de Los Baños light is on the eastern side. There are a few buildings and shacks in the area but the nearest small village is about 2M away.

⚓ ENSENADA DE LAS ENTINAS
36°41′.8N 02°49′.0W

Spanish chart 3550. A wide bay where anchorage is possible anywhere along the coast in three to 5m and 50 to 100m offshore. The shore is flat and the whole area covered with plastic greenhouses. The Castillo de Guardias Viejas on Punta de los Baños and the high-rise flats and buildings around the Puerto de Almerimar near Punta Entinas are both very conspicuous. Supplies from the Puerto de Almerimar.

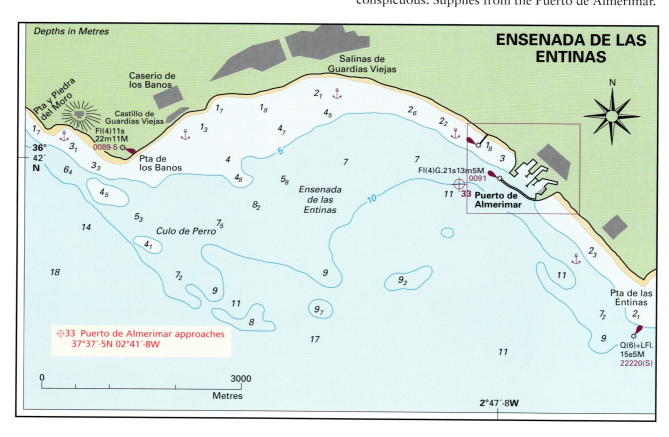

23. Puerto de Almerimar

36°41′.7N 02°47′.6W

Charts
British Admiralty *774*. Imray *M11*
French *6569*. Spanish *45B*

⊕33 36°41′.65N 02°48′.1W

Lights
To the west
0089.5 **Punta de los Baños** Fl(4)11s22m11M Rectangular white tower 21m
Harbour
22187(S) **Red port hand buoy** Fl.R.7.5s2M
0091.6 **Espigón** Fl(4)R.11s3m3M Post on red turret 1m
0091 **Dique Sur head** Fl(4)G.21s13m5M Green tower 8m
0091.3 **Dique Sur Middle** LFl.G.9.5s2m2M Green turret 1m
0091.35 **Contradique head** Fl(2)R.9.5s2m2M Red tower 1m
0091.4 **Ldg Lts** *Front* Iso.10s3m2M White tower, winged top 2m
0091.41 *Rear* Oc.10s4m2M White tower, winged top 3m
To the east
22220(S) **Bajo Punta de las Entinas** Q(6)+LFl.15s5M ⸸ card buoy
0090 **Punta Sabinal** Fl(1+2)10s34m16M Tower on white buildings 32m
Buoys There may be five or six small yellow buoys marking the starboard and port hand of the entrance channel as the leading lines are sometimes difficult to make out.

Port communications
VHF Ch 9. Port Control ☎ 950 60 77 55, 950 49 73 50
Fax 950 49 73 53
Email infomarina@almerimarpuerto.com
www.almerimarpuerto.com

Welcoming good yacht harbour
This artificial yacht harbour is very pleasant. Much of the hinterland is a sheet of plastic under which a major proportion of north Europe's winter vegetables are grown. The marina is built to an ambitious plan and not only provides good facilities for yachts but also for crews. Approach and entrance are easy except in strong SW winds which sometimes send a swell into the harbour. Very secure with good shelter from easterly gales. Rates, which are on the low side, can be examined on the internet website.

Winter liveboard community.

Almería and the Alcazaba are worth a visit. There are beaches on either side of the harbour. Fishing, wind surfing, diving, golf, tennis and horse-riding are possible.

Approach
From the west The coast from Adra is low and flat, Puerto de Adra and the Castillo de Guardias Viejas which is on a small hill near Punta de los Baños are easily recognised while the high blocks of flats to the E of Puerto Almerimar can be seen from afar.

From the east The conspicuous lighthouse on the low flat Punta del Sabinal will be seen and also the blocks of flats mentioned above.

GPS approach
Steer to ⊕33 from a southwesterly quadrant and steer for breakwater end (approximately 0.17M).

Puerto de Almerimar

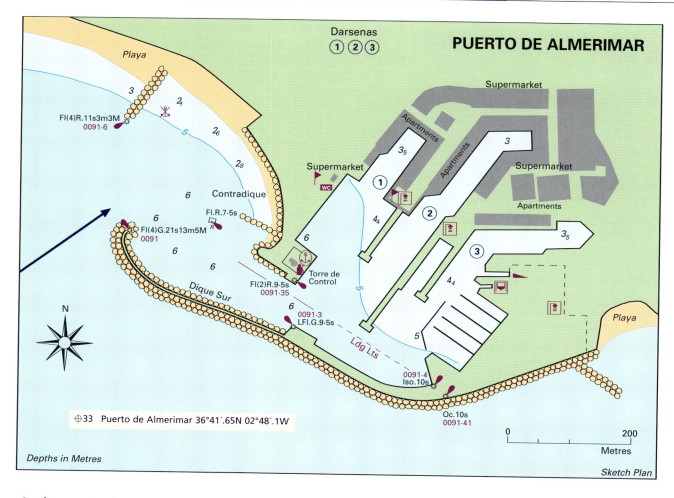

PUERTO DE ALMERIMAR

Darsenas
① ② ③

Playa

Fl(4)R.11s3m3M
0091·6

Contradique

Fl.R.7·5s

Fl(4)G.21s13m5M
0091

Dique Sur

Fl(2)R.9·5s
0091·35

Torre de Control

0091·3
LFl.G.9·5s

Ldg Lts

Supermarket

Apartments

Apartments

Apartments

Supermarket

Supermarket

Apartments

Playa

0091·4
Iso.10s

Oc.10s
0091·41

N

⊕33 Puerto de Almerimar 36°41'.65N 02°48'.1W

Depths in Metres

0   200
Metres

Sketch Plan

Anchorage in the approach

It is possible to anchor either side of the harbour about 100m to 150m from the coast in 5m sand.

Entrance

The harbour entrance silts but is frequently dredged to 6m. In spite of frequent dredging it has been reported that there is a shallow patch running out along the breakwater. Exercise care and watch the echo-sounder on entry, giving the hooked end of the breakwater a reasonable berth (50m or so). Leave the red buoy to port and enter between two lines of small yellow buoys or pick up the leading lines at night.

Berths

Secure to fuel berth and ask at the control tower.

Note The four pontoons shown at the east of the harbour are for small craft only.

Harbour charges

Medium.

Facilities

Maximum length overall: 60m.
Most repair and maintenance facilities.
Volvo dealer and servicing.
110 and 60-tonne travel-lift.
5-tonne crane.
Slipways on the E side of the harbour.
Large hardstanding.
Two chandlers in the port plus other useful shops.
Water points on all quays and pontoons – potable but taste before filling tanks.
Showers in the service block and in the port.
220V AC points on all quays and pontoons. 380V AC on the larger berths.
Gasoleo A and petrol.
Ice available from control tower and bars.
Club náutico.
A small supermarket at the west end of the harbour and a well-stocked one near the boatyard.
Launderettes.
An active Live-Aboard Club has a small club room near the boatyard.
A hypermarket is on the bus route to the town of El Ejido. Restrictions 2004. Yachtsmen may not work on their boats.

Communications

Regular bus service to El Ejido whence further buses.
Airport at Almería, year round services to Barcelona, Madrid and Melilla, summer charter flights from other European countries. ☎ Area code 950.
Taxi ☎ 57 06 11, 48 00 63.

24. Puerto de Roquetas de Mar

36°45′.4N 02°36′.3W

Charts

British Admiralty *774*. Imray *M11*
French *4718, 6569*. Spanish *459*

⊕35 36°45′.5N 02°36′.15W

Lights

To the west
0090 **Punta Sabinal** Fl(1+2)10s34m16M Tower on white
buildings 32m
Harbour
0092 **Dique Sur head** Fl(3)R.9s10m5M Round concrete
tower 4m
0092.4 **Dique Norte head** Fl(3)G.9s5m3M Round tower on
square base 3m
0092·5 **Interior Quay** Fl(4)G.10s6m2M Green post 5m
To the east
0106 **Cabo de Gata** Fl.WR.4s55m24/20M 356°-W-316°-R-
356° Siren Mo(G)40s White tower, grey lantern 19m

Port communications

Capitanía VHF Ch 9 ☎/*Fax* 950 32 08 90
Email roquetas@eppa.es
Club náutico ☎ 950 32 07 89 *Fax* 950 32 01 44
Email info@realclubnauticoroquetas.es
www.realclubnauticoroquetas.es

Primarily for fishing boats

A small harbour for sardine fishing boats and a few
yachts. Easy to approach and enter but would be
uncomfortable in heavy weather between SE and
NE. Attractive in a simple way but tourist
development is taking place around this area. There
are a few facilities, some basic shops near the
harbour and other, better, shops in the village about
two miles away.

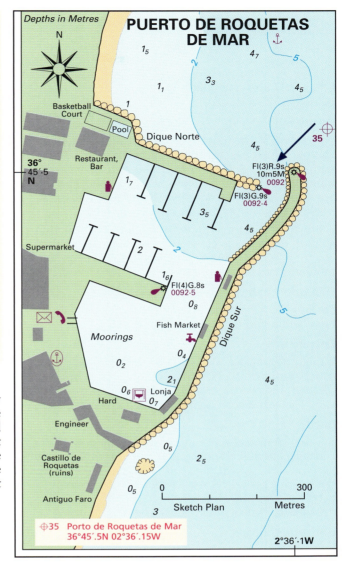

Roquetas de Mar from NE showing new promenade in the
inner basin but missing four pontoons running N from
inner jetty

II.ii COSTA DEL SOL

The fuel point on the Dique Sur is for fishing vessels only. The yachts' fuel point is on the NW corner quay but it is very shallow there and fuel can only really be obtained with jerrycans.

Fine beaches each side of the harbour. Local holidays 7 and 8 October in honour of the Virgen del Rosario.

Approach

From the SW The low flat-topped headland of Punta Sabinal which has an isolated lighthouse and tower with radomes. A large tourist complex of high-rise buildings is located between this headland and the port. The old disused yellow lighthouse and small castle just S of the harbour are recognisable.

From the NE From Almería the cliffs reach within 4M of Roquetas which is at the edge of a plain covered with plastic greenhouses. There are buildings and blocks of flats behind the harbour.

GPS approach

Steer to ⊕35 from an easterly quadrant and steer for breakwater end (approximately 0.05M).

Entrance

Straight-forward between *dique* heads which have small stone towers. Give Dique Sur head a reasonable berth in case sand has built up off the end. The entrance is dredged and depths vary.

Berths

Bow or stern to pontoons on the north side of the entrance but make up wherever possible in the outer harbour and ask at the *club náutico*. Due to the shallow harbour, keel yachts should only attempt to berth at the easternmost pontoon. The harbour becomes crowded when the fishing fleet returns.

Harbour charges

Low.

Facilities

Maximum length overall: 15m.
50-tonnes travel hoist and 8-tonnes crane.
220V and 380V AC points on quays.
Water on the quays.
Club náutico with restaurant and bar.
Several small shops and a supermarket in the village. A market and some other shops 2M away.

Communications

Bus service to Almería. ☎ Area code 950.

25. Puerto de Aguadulce

36°48′.9N 02°33′.7W

Charts

British Admiralty *774*. Imray *M11*
French *4718*. Spanish *459*

⊕36 36°48′.7N 02°33′.8W

Lights

To the west
0090 **Punta Sabinal** Fl(1+2)10s34m16M Tower on white buildings 32m
Harbour
0092.6 **Dique head** Fl(2)G.6s5m5M Green pyramid 4m
0092.8 **Contradique head** Fl(2)R.7s6m3M Red concrete tower 4m
To the east
0093 **San Telmo LtHo** Fl(2)12s77m19M White square tower oblong black stripes 7m
0106 **Cabo de Gata** Fl.WR.4s55m24/20M 356°-W-316°-R-356° Siren Mo(G)40s White tower, grey lantern 19m

Port communications

Capitanía/club náutico VHF Ch 9 ☎ 950 34 31 15
Fax 950 34 31 64
Email contacto@puertodeportivoaguadulce.es
www.puertodeportivoaguadulce.es

Popular harbour

Aguadulce provides a useful alternative to Puerto de Almería. It harbour is easy to enter and provides good shelter except in strong ESE winds when some swell enters making it uncomfortable. Facilities are good. The Alcazaba at Almería should be visited. Long sandy beaches to SW. Popular for winter liveaboards.

Local holidays: The ten days before the last Sunday in August and the first two weeks in January.

Approach

From the SW Round the low headland of Punta del Sabinal with its conspicuous white, round lighthouse tower. Follow the low featureless coast dotted with various housing estates in a NE direction until Puerto de Roquetas del Mar which has a disused lighthouse, a small square fort and a breakwater, has been passed. Puerto de Aguadulce is located just beyond the point where a range of rocky hills reaches down to the coast. The rocky breakwaters, *torre de control* and low blocks of flats will be seen in the close approach.

From the east Round the unmistakable Cabo de Gata and cross the Golfo de Almería on a WNW course. The mass of buildings of Almería surmounted by the Alcazaba castle and fronted by the harbour breakwater are all conspicuous. The S cardinal light buoy, Q(6)+LFl, off Punta del Río may also be seen. This harbour is located near where the rocky range of coastal hills drops back and the low flat coast commences.

GPS approach

Steer to ⊕36 from a southeasterly quadrant and steer for breakwater end (approximately 0.09M).

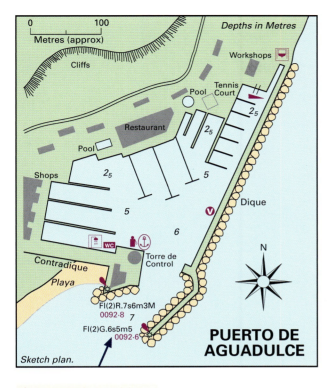

PUERTO DE AGUADULCE

Sketch plan.

⊕36 Puerto de Aguadulce
36°48′.7N 02°33′.8W

Entrance

Approach the head of the *dique* on a course between SW and N, round it and then the head of the *contradique* to port.

Berths

Secure to the quay by the *torre de control* and report to the office for allocation of a berth.

Facilities

Maximum length overall: 25m.

Workshops at N end of harbour for mechanical, electrical and hull repairs; maintenance, painting etc. Work on own boat permitted.

50-tonnes travel-lift.

Slipway at N end of the harbour.

Hardstanding at N end of the harbour; additional space for 100 yachts under cover.

Sailmaking.

Water taps on quays and pontoons.

Showers.

220V AC on quays and pontoons.

Gasoleo A and petrol.

Ice at fuel quay.

Club náutico with good facilities.

Many shops and a large market at Almería about 5M away.

Swimming pool beside the harbour.

Communications

Bus to Almería on road behind the harbour. Airport (11 miles) and rail (five miles) at Almería. ☎ Area code 950. Taxi ☎ 34 05 46.

Puerto de Aguadulce

II.ii COSTA DEL SOL

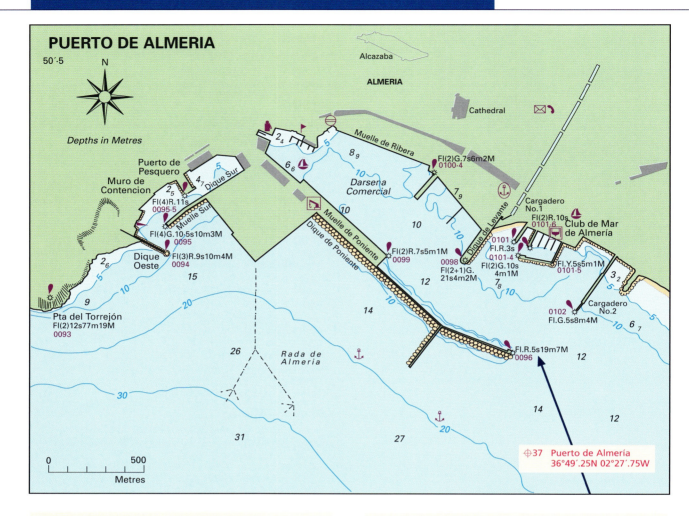

PUERTO DE ALMERIA

50´·5

N

Depths in Metres

ALMERIA

Alcazaba

Cathedral

Puerto de Pesquero

Muro de Contencion

Dique Sur

Muelle de Ribera

Fl(2)G.7s6m2M
0100·4

Darsena Comercial

Fl(4)R.11s
0095·5

Muelle Sur

Fl(4)G.10·5s10m3M
0095

Dique Oeste

Fl(3)R.9s10m4M
0094

Muelle de Poniente

Dique de Poniente

Fl(2)R.7s5m1M
0099

Fl(2+1)G.
21s4m2M

Fl(2)G.10s
4m1M

Dique de Levante

Cargadero No.1

Fl(2)R.10s
0101·6

Club de Mar de Almería

0101

Fl.R.3s
0101·4

Fl.Y.5s5m1M
0101·5

Cargadero No.2

0102
Fl.G.5s8m4M

Fl.R.5s19m7M
0096

Pta del Torrejón
Fl(2)12s77m19M
0093

Rada de Almería

⊕37 Puerto de Almería
36°49´.25N 02°27´.75W

0   500

Metres

---

26. Puerto de Almería

36°49´.8N 02°27´.9W

Tides

Time differences
based on HW Gibraltar   Height difference   Mean

HW	LW	MHWS	MHWN	MLWS	MLWN	*level*
+0010	−0010	0.5	0.4	0.3	+0.3	0.40

Current

There is a constant E-going current across the mouth of the bay.

Charts

British Admiralty *1515, 774*. Imray *M11*
French *7504, 4718*. Spanish *4591, 459*

⊕37 36°49 25N 02°27 75W

Lights

To the west
0093 **San Telmo LtHo** Fl(2)12s77m19M White square tower oblong black stripes 7m
Puerto Pesquero
0094 **Dique del Oeste head** Fl(3)R.9s10m4M Red tower 5m
0095 **Dique Sur head** Fl(4)G.10·5s10m3M Green tower 5m
0095·5 **Interior mole head** Fl(4)R.11s5m1M Red tower 3m
Main harbour
0096 **Dique de Poniente head** Fl.R.5s19m7M White 8-sided tower, red top and base 12m
0102 **Cargadero No. 2 head** Fl.G.5s8m4M Green metal structure 3m
0101 **Cargadero No. 1 head** Fl.R.3s7m1M

0101.5 **Corner** Fl.Y.5s5m1M Yellow concrete tower
0101.4 **Club de Mar del Almería Dique de Abrigo** Fl(2)G.10s4m1M Green inclined concrete tower 3m
0101.6 **Club de Mar del Almería Contradique** Fl(2)R.10s4m1M Red inclined concrete tower
0099 **Muelle de Poniente o Comercial E corner** Fl(2)R.7s5m1M Red concrete structure 3m
0098 **Dique de Levante head** Fl(2+1)G.14·5s4m2M Green structure, red band 10m
0103 **Power station wharf head** Q(9)15s11m5M ⚡ on yellow metal framework tower, black band 9m F.R on building 360m E
To the east
0106 **Cabo de Gata** Fl.WR.4s55m24/20M 356°-W-316°-R-356° Siren Mo(G)40s White tower, grey lantern 19m
Buoys
Black and yellow S card lightbuoy Q(6)+LFl ⚡ topmark off Punta del Río de Almería

Port communications

Port VHF Ch 12, 14 and 16. Club de mar VHF Ch 9
☎ 950 23 07 80 *Fax* 950 62 11 47
Email cma@clubdemaralmeria.es
www.clubdemaralmeria.es

Useful commercial harbour

A commercial and fishing port with an old and interesting town and castle nearby. Approach and entrance can be made in almost any conditions and good shelter obtained but winds from the E cause an uncomfortable swell inside the harbour. The town,

Almería

which is the capital of the province of the same name has good shops and markets. Yachts use the Club de Mar del Almería, outside the Dique de Levante; they are not welcome in the main harbour.

Note that the fishing port has its own separate harbour to the west of the main harbour. In 2004 there was construction work beginning outside the root of the Dique de Poniente. This work is still continuing and a large area is being reclaimed from the sea. At present it looks more like the basis of a container terminal than a yacht marina. However there is further construction of a series of jetties going on outside and towards the end of the Dique de Poniente which may be the start of a yacht harbour but only time will tell.

The Moorish Alcazaba (castle) is most impressive and attractive and should be visited. There are four interesting churches, many old buildings and an archaeological museum. Miles of beaches to the E of the harbour.

Local holidays: the ten days before the last Sunday in August and the first two weeks in January.

Approach

From the SW Almería lies at the head of a wide bay at the foot of the mountains. The low flat headland of Punta del Sabinal with its isolated lighthouse is recognisable 10M to SW. The Alcazaba (castle) on a hill near the town is conspicuous at a distance but is dwarfed by tower blocks of flats to E. The town buildings and the long Dique de Poniente are seen in the closer approach.

From the east After Cabo de Gata, a rugged high promontory, the coast is low and flat. The town and harbour are visible from afar; there is a very tall port authority building on the end of the Dique de Levante which is prominent.

GPS approach

Steer to ⊕37 from a southerly quadrant and steer for breakwater end (approximately 0.35M).

Anchorage in the approach

Anchor to SW of Dique de Poniente.

Entrance

Straight-forward but keep a lookout for commercial and fishing vessels leaving, sometimes at speed. Inside the harbour there are a number of unlit mooring buoys.

Berths

Visiting yachts are now sent four miles west to Puerto de Aguadulce. The Club de Mar moorings are reserved for members yachts although accasionally, and with a great deal of persuasion space can be found for a visitor.

Anchorage

Anchor in 6m sand and mud 150m S of club de mar, clear of moorings. Show anchor light and shape.

Harbour charges

High.

Facilities

Maximum length overall: 15m in the *club de mar*.
Shipyards geared to fishing boats beside the slipway and also at the W end of Puerto Pesquero.
Slipways in both the main of the harbour and the Puerto Pesquero.
Cranes 4–12 tonnes in the harbour and a 4-tonne crane at the *club de mar*.
Several engineering workshops in town and one on the quay on Muelle Sur.
Chandlers and Engineers in the NW corner of the main harbour.
Water and 220V AC on all berths at *club de mar*.
Gasoleo A and petrol at *club de mar*.
Ice from ice factory between Puerto Pesquero and Dársena Comercial.
The Club de Mar del Almería is a tennis and yachting club with a bar, restaurant, showers and terrace. Visitors should first contact the secretary for permission to use the facilities.
A number of small shops and a small market near the port. Many large and varied shops and a large market about 1M away in the town.
Several launderettes in the town.

Communications

Airport with summer charter flights from Europe and year-round services to Madrid or Barcelona. Railway. Occasional service by boat to Marseille, Algeria, Canary Isles and South America. ☎ Area code 950.
Taxis ☎ 25 11 11.

Club de Mar del Almería

⚓ CABO DE GATA ANCHORAGES

Anchor off the village of San Miguel de Cabo de Gata and its conspicuous tower in 5m of sand some 200m off the coast. One can also anchor 100m off Playa de los Corrales further to the SE in sand, well sheltered from N and E. There is a sheltered anchorage 150m NW of Cabo de Gata light in 5m sand and stone, or about 400m offshore in 10m. There is a small settlement and conspicuous church by the saltworks on the road to San Miguel de Gata. Tunny nets are sometimes laid in this area.

Cabo de Gata from the east

Cabo de Gata from the west

NOTES ON ROUNDING CABO DE GATA

1. Stay close inshore or 1.0M offshore to avoid Laja de Cabo de Gata shoal (3m) which breaks in heavy weather
2. Winds tend to increase around this cape
3. Current is normally east-going and can be very strong.

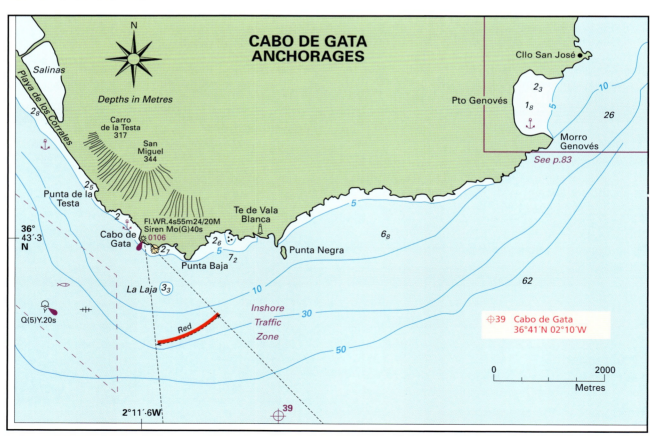

27. Isla de Alborán

35°56′.3N 03°02′.1W

Current

A permanent current of up to three knots runs past the island on an E and SE-going direction.

Charts

British Admiralty *774*. Imray *M11*
French *5864, 6569*. Spanish *4351, 435*

Lights

0086 **Alborán lighthouse** Fl(4)20s40m10M Grey conical
tower and house 20m
0087 **Puerto refugio E wharf head** Fl.R.3s4m3M Red
square column 3m
0087.1 **Dique de Abrigo head** Fl.G.2s4m3M Green square
column 3m

Isolated island S of Puerto de Adra

This small island lies some 49M to S of Puerto de Adra and about 30M from the African coast. It is a bare, low, reddish-cliffed island 700m long and 300m wide with two small landing jetties and several anchorages. The sole inhabitants are the staff for the lighthouse and a military detachment.

Facilities are non-existent and, officially, in order to visit, permission must be obtained from the Naval Commander in Almería. If you arrive without permission you may or may not be allowed to stay for a short visit depending on the officer on duty.

Approach

The island can be approached from any direction but as it is low, it will not be seen until within 10M. There are a number of sunken rocks extending in places to 200m from the coast.

Entrance

Approach the E jetty on a W course with the jetty in line with the lighthouse. Approach the W jetty on an ESE approach. In both cases keep a sharp lookout for submerged rocks during the last 200m of the approach.

Anchorages

There are several anchorages to suit the prevalent wind direction in about 6m sand and stone.

Formalities

Call on the military commander.

Facilities

In an emergency, water and food might be obtained from the garrison.

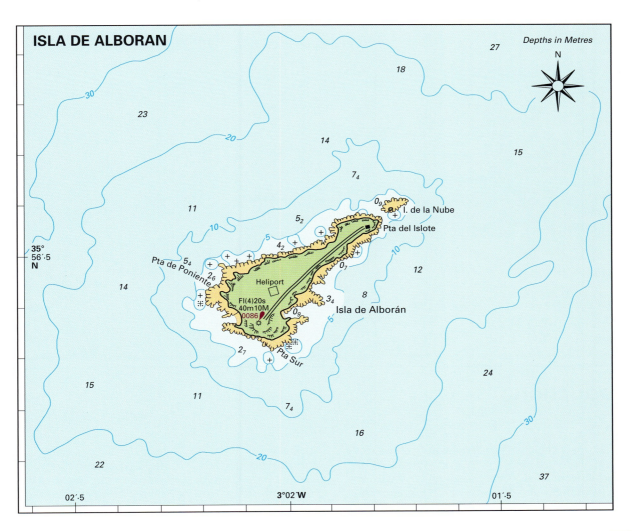

ISLA DE ALBORAN

II.ii COSTA DEL SOL

III. COSTA BLANCA

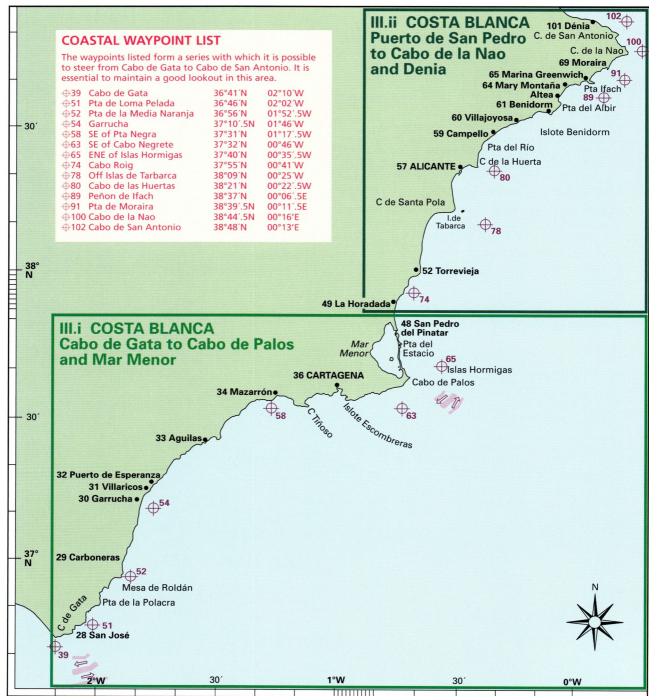

III.ii COSTA BLANCA Puerto de San Pedro to Cabo de la Nao and Denia

101 Dénia
C. de San Antonio
102
100
C. de la Nao
69 Moraira
65 Marina Greenwich
64 Mary Montaña
91
Altea
Pta Ifach
61 Benidorm
89
Pta del Albir
60 Villajoyosa
Islote Benidorm
59 Campello
Pta del Río
C de la Huerta
57 ALICANTE
80
C de Santa Pola
I.de
Tabarca
78
52 Torrevieja
49 La Horadada
74

COASTAL WAYPOINT LIST

The waypoints listed form a series with which it is possible to steer from Cabo de Gata to Cabo de San Antonio. It is essential to maintain a good lookout in this area.

39	Cabo de Gata	36°41′N	02°10′W
51	Pta de Loma Pelada	36°46′N	02°02′W
52	Pta de la Media Naranja	36°56′N	01°52′.5W
54	Garrucha	37°10′.5N	01°46′W
58	SE of Pta Negra	37°31′N	01°17′.5W
63	SE of Cabo Negrete	37°32′N	00°46′W
65	ENE of Islas Hormigas	37°40′N	00°35′.5W
74	Cabo Roig	37°55′N	00°41′W
78	Off Islas de Tarbarca	38°09′N	00°25′W
80	Cabo de las Huertas	38°21′N	00°22′.5W
89	Peñon de Ifach	38°37′N	00°06′.5E
91	Pta de Moraira	38°39′.5N	00°11′.5E
100	Cabo de la Nao	38°44′.5N	00°16′E
102	Cabo de San Antonio	38°48′N	00°13′E

30′

38°N

30′

III.i COSTA BLANCA Cabo de Gata to Cabo de Palos and Mar Menor

48 San Pedro del Pinatar
Mar Menor
Pta del Estacio
36 CARTAGENA
65
Islas Hormigas
Cabo de Palos
34 Mazarrón
58
C. Tiñoso
Islote Escombreras
63
33 Aguilas
32 Puerto de Esperanza
31 Villaricos
30 Garrucha
54

30′

37°N

29 Carboneras
52
Mesa de Roldán
Pta de la Polacra
C de Gata
51
28 San José
39

N

2°W   30′   1°W   30′   0°W

Introduction

CURRENTS

Along this coast the current is reasonably consistent and is not discussed under each port. Off Cabo de Gata the current is normally E-going and can be strong. It changes its direction to NE-going and becomes weaker along the coast, although it is stronger off Cabo de Palos. In the summer and autumn months this NE and ENE-going current is felt as far as Cabo de San Antonio but in the other months it is usually SW-going between Cabo de Palos and Cabo de San Antonio.

TIDES

Maximum spring range is less than 1m and its effects are small.

GALES – HARBOURS OF REFUGE

In the event of onshore gales and heavy seas, Cartagena, Torrevieja and Alicante are the safest to enter. Shelter may sometimes be found where a small harbour is located behind a promontory which protects the entrance from the wind and swell.

GENERAL DESCRIPTION

This 195M stretch of coast between Cabo de Gata to just beyond Cabo de San Antonio is called Costa Blanca (the White Coast). Much of the coastal rock is a light grey which appears white in the bright sunlight. There has been much development in the past two decades. Communications and services have been much improved, many harbours have been built and old harbours adapted for yachts but the discovery of the Costa Blanca by the developers has resulted in many of the once deserted *calas* becoming surrounded by holiday homes and, in some cases, high-rise buildings for package tourists.

However, some sections remain comparatively deserted and with isolated anchorages. By no means all anchorages are noted here and the cruising yacht should be able to find unlisted spots where there is peace and quiet.

The section begins with the impressive promontory of Cabo de Gata which has several white patches of rock on its E side. The high coastal cliffs are broken by many valleys and small coves with good anchorages. The major promontories are high with steep cliffs; Punta de la Media Naranja (half an orange!), Cabo Cope and Cabo Tiñoso are examples.

Beyond Cartagena, which is one of the few natural harbours, lies the long, low sand bar that separates the Mar Menor from the sea, now looking more like a high-rise breakwater. From here to Alicante and beyond, the coast is made up of low rolling hills coming down to broken cliffs with long sandy beaches. Inland ranges of higher hills can be seen and these mountainous features reach the sea in places such as Cabo de La Huerta, Sierra Helada, Cabo de la Nao and Cabo de San Antonio.

Outlying dangers are the small islands; Isla de los Terreros near Aguilas, Isla Grosa and some smaller islets off the Mar Menor, Isla de Tabarca off Cabo de Santa Pola, Islote de Benidorm off Benidorm and the Isla de Portichol. In general, deep water can be carried quite close to the coast with the exception of some areas bordering the Mar Menor.

VISITS INLAND

Apart from places mentioned in the text, there are many interesting places to visit and things to see further inland which may be reached by taxi, bus or, in some cases, by rail. The narrow gauge FEVE runs from the north station of Alicante to Dénia and puts on the 'Lemon Express' for tourists during summer – an expedition which includes a bottle of 'champagne'. Suggestions for other expeditions can be obtained from the various information offices but the following are worth considering: Lorca, a very picturesque old town; Murcia, the capital city of the province of the same name, which has interesting churches, museums and art galleries; Orihuela, with an old church and valuable paintings; Jijona, where the nougat-like sweet turrón is made and with a ruined Moorish castle; and Alcoy, an old Visigoth town with many ancient remains.

Pilotage and navigation

TUNNY NETS

In spring, summer and autumn tunny nets may be laid at the places listed below (see the Introduction, page 5).
- Off San José
- Near Punta del Esparto
- Off Punta de la Polacra
- In Cala de San Pedro
- 2M to SW of Punta de la Media Naranja
- 1½M to N of Villaricos
- 3M to SW of Isla de los Terreros
- ½M to N of Isla de los Terreros
- 2M and 1M to SW and 1M to E of Aguilas
- In Cala Bardina
- S of Cabo Cope
- 1M to NE of Punta de Calnegre
- 5, 3 and 1M to W of Punta Negra
- Off Punta de la Azohía
- Centre and E end of Ensenada de Mazarrón
- N of Cabo Tiñoso
- Off Puerto de Portmán
- Off Cap de Palos
- N of Cabo de las Huertas
- In the Ensenada de Benidorm
- W of the Peñón de Ifach
- Ensenada de Moraira

FISH HAVENS

There are extensive fish havens along this coast.

RESTRICTED AREAS

In Cartagena there are areas reserved for the Spanish navy which may not be entered by yachts. Submarines exercise in areas from Cabo de Gata to Cabo San Sebastian and there is a firing area S of Cartagena. Anchoring is prohibited in an area to the S of Puerto de Jávea where there are underwater cables.

MAGNETIC VARIATION

Costa Blanca (Cartagena) 01°25′W (2008) decreasing 7′ annually.

PLANNING GUIDE AND DISTANCE TABLES

See page 80.

Planning guide and distances

⚓ Anchorage

Miles	Harbours & Anchorages	Headlands
21M	⚓ Puerto Genovés	Cabo de Gata
	⚓ Ensenada de San José/Cala Higuera	
	28. Puerto de San José page 84	
	⚓ Ensenada de los Escullos	
	⚓ Ensenada de Rodalquilar	
18M	⚓ Las Negras	
		Punta de la Polacra
	⚓ Cala de San Pedro	
	⚓ Ensenada de Agua Amarga	
	29. Puerto de Carboneras page 87	
	⚓ 2 commercial harbours – emergency only and Puerto Pescaro	
14M	⚓ Marina de las Torres	
	⚓ Punta de la Media Naranja	
	30. Puerto de Garrucha page 89	
5M	⚓ Palomares y Villaricos	Río de Aguas
	31. Puerto de Villaricos page 91	Río Almanzora
0.3M	**32. Puerto de Esperanza** page 91	
	⚓ Anchorages 2M to N of Río Almanzora	
14M	⚓ Ensenada de Terreros	
	⚓ Punta Parda	
	33. Puertos de Aguilas y del Hornillo page 94	
		Punta Parda
19M	⚓ Cala Bardina	
	⚓ Ensenada de la Fuente	
	34. Club Regatas, Mazarrón page 97	
3M		Punta Negra
	35. Puerto Deportivo de Mazarrón page 99	
	⚓ Ensenada de Mazarrón	
	⚓ Cala Cerrada	
15M	⚓ Rincón de la Salitrona	
	⚓ El Portús	Cabo Tinoso
	36. Puerto de Cartagena page 102	
8M	⚓ Cala del Gorguel	
	37. Puerto de Portmán page 105	
9M		Cabo del Agua
	38 Puerto de Cabo de Palos page 107	
	⚓ Cabo de Palos	
	⚓ Playa de Palos	
8M	⚓ Isla Grosa	
	39. Puerto de Tomás Maestre page 110	
	40. Puerto de Dos Mares page 114	
	41. Puerto de la Manga page 114	
	42. Puerto de Mar de Cristal page 115	
	43. Puerto de las Islas Menores page 116	
	44. Puerto de los Nietos page 116	
5M	**45. Puerto de los Urrutias** page 117	
	46. Puerto de los Alcázares page 118	
	⚓ Puerto Santiago de Ribera	
	47. Puerto de Lo Pagan page 119	
	⚓ Ensenada del Esparto	

Miles	Harbours & Anchorages	Headlands
3M	**48. Puerto de San Pedro del Pinatar** page 121	
3M	**49. Puerto de la Horadada** page 122	
2M	**50. Puerto de Campoamor** page 124	
5M	**51. Puerto de Cabo Roig** page 125	
9M	**52. Puerto de Torrevieja** page 126	
	53. Marina de la Dunas (Puerto de Guardamar)	
6M	page 128	Cabo Cervera
	⚓ Bahía de Santa Pola	
	54. Puerto de Santa Pola page 130	
2M	**55. Puerto de Espato** page 132	
4M	**56. Puerto de Isla de Tabarca** page 132	
11M	**57. Puerto de Alicante** page 134	
3M	⚓ Ensenada de la Albufereta	
	58 Puerto de San Juan page 138	
7M	⚓ Playa de la Huerta	
	59. Puerto de Campello page 139	
9M		Cabo de las Huertas
	60. Puerto de Villajoyosa (Alcoco) page 140	
6M	**61. Puerto de Benidorm** page 142	
	⚓ Ensenada de Benidorm	
	⚓ Cabezo del Tosal	
7M	⚓ Anchorage E of Punta de Canfali	
	⚓ Anchorage W of Punta de la Cueva del Barbero	Punta de la Esalata
	⚓ Anchorages NW of Punta del Albir	
		Punta del Albir
2M	**62. Puerto de Altea** page 144	
1M	**63. Puerto de la Olla de Altea** page 146	
1M	**64. Puerto de Mary Montaña** page 147	
2M	**65. Marina Greenwich (Mascarat)** page 148	
	⚓ Punta Mascarat	
2M	**66. Puerto Blanco** page 150	Cabo Toix
	⚓ Ensenada de Calpe	
	67. Puerto de Calpe page 152	
3M	⚓ Cala la Fosa	Punta Ifach
	68. Puerto de las Basetas page 154	
	⚓ Cala Canaret	
3M	⚓ Cala Blanco	
	⚓ Cabo Blanco	
	⚓ Cala del Dragon	Cabo Blanco
	69. Puerto de Moraira page 156	
	⚓ El Rinconet	
	⚓ Anchorages between Cabo Moraira and Jávea	
	⚓ La Grandadilla	
11M	⚓ Isla del Descubridor	
	⚓ Punta Negra	
	⚓ Isla del Portichol	Cabo de la Nao
	⚓ Cabo de San Martin	
	⚓ Cala Calce	
	⚓ Cala de la Fontana	
	100. Puerto de Jávea page 160	
5M	**101. Puerto de Dénia** page 162 Cabo de San Antonio	

III.i Cabo de Gata to Cabo de Palos and Mar Menor

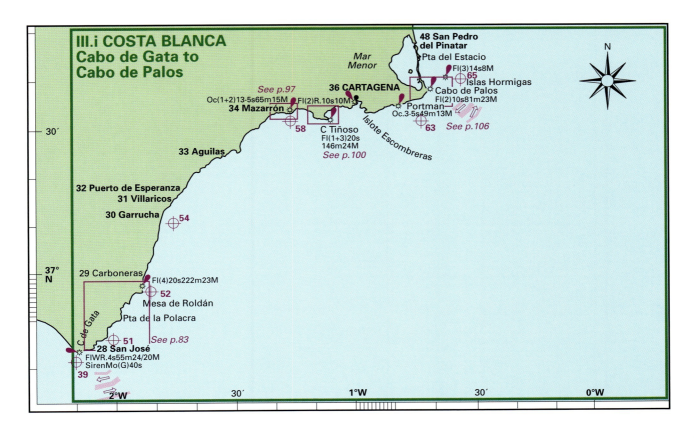

III.i COSTA BLANCA
Cabo de Gata to
Cabo de Palos

Mar
Menor

48 San Pedro
del Pinatar
Pta del Estacio
Fl(3)14s8M

65
Islas Hormigas
Cabo de Palos
Fl(2)10s81m23M

See p.97
Oc(1+2)13·5s65m15M
34 Mazarrón
36 CARTAGENA
Fl(2)R.10s10M

Portman
Oc.3·5s49m13M

63   *See p.106*

58

C Tiñoso
Fl(1+3)20s
146m24M
See p.100

Islote Escombreras

33 Aguilas

32 Puerto de Esperanza
31 Villaricos

30 Garrucha   **54**

37°
N

29 Carboneras
Fl(4)20s222m23M
52
Mesa de Roldán
Pta de la Polacra

C. de Gata

51   *See p.83*
28 San José
FlWR.4s55m24/20M
SirenMo(G)40s
39

30´   2°W   30´   1°W   30´   0°W

N

PORTS

28. **Puerto de San José**
29. **Puertos de Carboneras**
30. **Puerto de Garrucha**
31. **Puerto de Villaricos**
32. **Puerto de Esperanza**
33. **Puertos de Aguilas y del Hornillo**
34. **Puerto Deportivo de Mazarrón**
35. **Puerto de Mazarrón**
36. **Puerto de Cartagena**
37. **Puerto de Portmán**
38. **Puerto de Cabo de Palos (Cala Avellán)**

THE PORTS OF MAR MENOR

39. **Puerto de Tomás Maestre**
40. **Puerto de Dos Mares**
41. **Puerto de la Manga**
42. **Puerto de Mar de Cristal**
43. **Puerto de los Islas Menores**
44. **Puerto de Los Nietos**
45. **Puerto de los Urrutias**
46. **Puerto de los Alcázares**
47. **Puerto de Lo Pagan**

COASTAL WAYPOINT LIST

The waypoints listed form a series with which it is possible to steer from Cabo de Gata to off Cabo de Palos. It is essential to maintain a good lookout in this area.

⊕39	Cabo de Gata	36°41′N	02°10′W
⊕51	Pta de Loma Pelada	36°46′N	02°02′W
⊕52	Pta de la Media Naranja	36°56′N	01°52′.5W
⊕54	Garrucha	37°10′.5N	01°46′W
⊕58	SE of Pta Negra	37°31′N	01°17′.5W
⊕63	SE of Cabo Negrete	37°32′N	00°46′W
⊕65	ENE of Islas Hormigas	37°40′N	00°35′.5W

III.i COSTA BLANCA

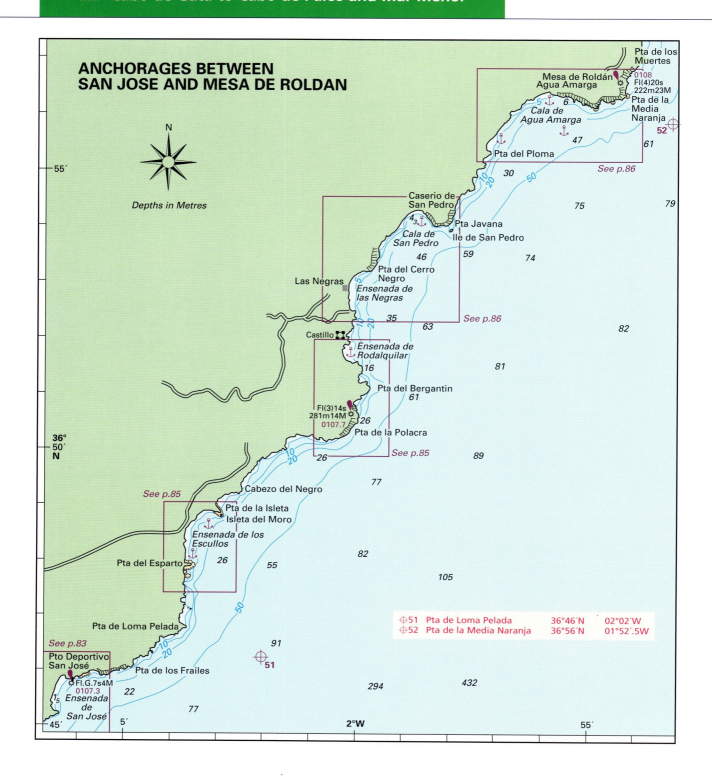

**ANCHORAGES BETWEEN
SAN JOSE AND MESA DE ROLDAN**

N

Depths in Metres

55′

See p.86

Pta de los
Muertes

0108
Fl(4)20s
222m23M
Pta de la
Media
Naranja

52

Mesa de Roldán
Agua Amarga

5   6

*Cala de
Agua Amarga*

47

Pta del Ploma

10
20   30   50   61

Caserio de
San Pedro

75   79

4 3   Pta Javana
*Cala de
San Pedro*   Ile de San Pedro

46   59   74

Pta del Cerro
Negro

Las Negras

*Ensenada de
las Negras*

5
10
20   35   63   See p.86   82

Castillo

*Ensenada de
Rodalquilar*

16   81

Pta del Bergantin

61

Fl(3)14s
281m14M
0107.7   26

Pta de la Polacra

89

36°
50′
N

10
20   26   See p.85

77

See p.85   Cabezo del Negro

Pta de la Isleta
Isleta del Moro

*Ensenada de los
Escullos*

82

Pta del Esparto   26   55   82   105

Pta de Loma Pelada

50

See p.83

Pto Deportivo
San José   Pta de los Frailes

Fl.G.7s4M   10
0107.3   22   20

1 5   *Ensenada
de
San José*

45′   5′   77

91

51

294   432

2°W   55′

| ⊕51 | Pta de Loma Pelada | 36°46′N | 02°02′W |
| ⊕52 | Pta de la Media Naranja | 36°56′N | 01°52′.5W |

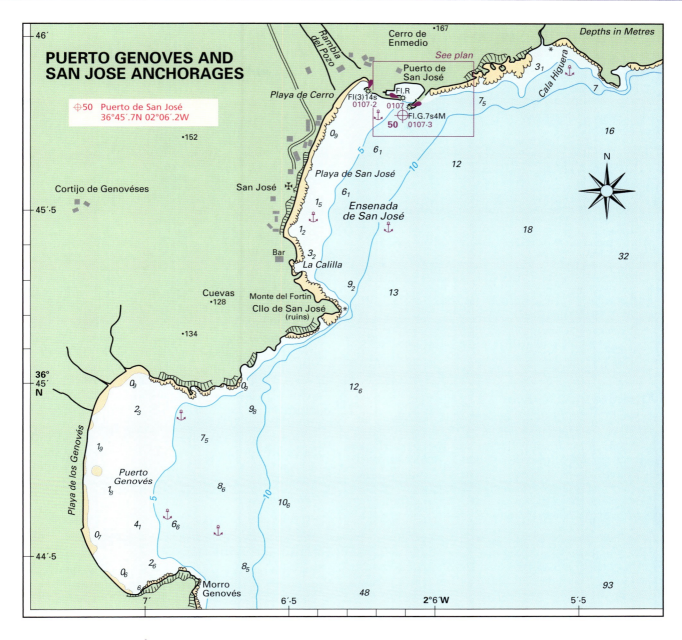

PUERTO GENOVES AND
SAN JOSE ANCHORAGES

⊕50 Puerto de San José
36°45'.7N 02°06'.2W

Cerro de
Enmedio

•167

Depths in Metres

See plan

Puerto de
San José

Cala Higuera

Playa de Cerro

Fl(3)14s
0107·2

Fl.R

0107

Fl.G.7s4M
0107·3

50

Cortijo de Genovéses

•152

Playa de San José

San José

Ensenada
de San José

Bar

La Calilla

Cuevas
•128

Monte del Fortin
Cllo de San José
(ruins)

•134

Playa de los Genovés

Puerto
Genovés

Morro
Genovés

N

16

32

18

13

12₆

Puerto Genovés. The word 'Puerto' covers both an enclosed harbour and a bay with some shelter

⚓ PUERTO GENOVÉS
36°44'.6N 2°07'W

A bay with a gently sloping sandy bottom. Open between NE and SE with good protection from other winds especially close inshore at N and S sides of bay. Anchor to suit wind in 5m, sand and mud.

Note that there are rocks to the SE of Morro Genovese so do not pass too close to the cliffs on entering bay from the south.

⚓ ENSENADA DE SAN JOSÉ/CALA HIGUERA
36°45'.6N 2°06'.3W

Similar open bay to Puerto Genovés but with sandy and rocky beach with developments. A small village now exists with a road to Almería. Protection from N–NE winds at NE end of bay under cliffs.

In strong S to SW winds the swell curls round the headland into this ensenada and Porto Genovés is quieter and should be used in these conditions.

28. Puerto de San José

36°46′N 02°06′W

Charts

British Admiralty *774*. Imray *M11*
French *4718*. Spanish *461*

⊕50 30°45′.7N 02°06′.2W

Lights

To the southwest
0106 **Cabo de Gata** Fl.WR.4s55m24/20M 356°-W-316°-R-356° Siren Mo(G)40s White tower, grey lantern 19m
Harbour
0107.3 **Dique Este head** Fl.G.7s8m4M Green ▲ on truncated tower 3m
0107 **Dique Sur E head** Fl.R.6s7m3M Red ■ on truncated tower 3m
0107.2 **Dique Sur W head** Fl(3)14s4m2M White masonry tower 1m
To the northeast
0108 **Mesa de Roldán** Fl(4)20s222m23M White octagonal tower 18m
0107.7 **Punta de la Polacra** 36°50′·6N 02°00′·1W Fl(3)14s281m14M Tower 14m

Port communications

Capitanía VHF Ch 9. ☎ 950 38 00 41 *Fax* 950 38 02 09
Email correo@clubnauticodesanjose.com
www.clubnauticodesanjose.com

Attractive small harbour

A small yacht harbour in attractive surroundings which is a useful break in the 50M stretch of coast between Almería and Garrucha. The harbour is subject to swell from E–SE but is otherwise well protected. A small village nearby can supply basic requirements. There are walks in empty country, fine views from the hills, caves near top of Monte del Fortin and excellent sandy beaches.

Approach

From the south Round the prominent Cabo de Gata (344m), either close inshore or 1M offshore to avoid the Laja de Cabo de Gata shoal (3.3m) which breaks in heavy weather. It lies 1300m SSE of Cabo de Gata light and in its red sector. 1M to E of the lighthouse there are some conspicuous white rock patches on the dark cliff face which, seen from afar, resemble sails. Keep ½M offshore rounding onto a NE course after the Morro Genovés which is conically shaped and lies at the S side of Puerto Genovés, a deep bay with a sandy beach. The Monte del Fortin, which has a ruined fort, separates Puerto Genovés from

San José

Ensenada de San José. This bay is lined with houses and the harbour lies in the N corner under a small white rock patch.

From the north The Mesa de Roldán is a high plateau (221m). The lighthouse is on Punta de la Media Naranja and can be seen from afar. Agua Amarga is just to the west of Media Naranja. These features can easily be identified. To the SW Punta Javana has a small island, Isla de San Pedro, off its point. Punta de la Polacra (263m) with a tower on its summit and Punta de Loma Pelada which has the high Cerro de los Frailes (489–444m) inland should be recognised. San José lies SW of this high ground. Keep over ¼M offshore.

GPS approach

Steer to ⊕50 from a southeasterly quadrant and steer for breakwater end.

Anchorage in the approach

The whole of the Ensenada de San José is suitable for anchorage – 200m to SW of the harbour entrance in 5m sand is recommended. If wind is strong from N an alternative is in a small bay off Playa de Cala Higuera, just under ½M E of the harbour.

Entrance

Approach the harbour heading N and give the head of Dique Sur 10m clearance.

Berths

Secure to starboard-hand quay or fuel berth to port and ask at the *capitanía* for a berth.

Charges

High.

Facilities

Maximum length overall: 14m.
Slipway.
8-tonne crane.
A few taps on pontoons but water may be salty.
220V AC.
Gasoleo A and petrol.
Shops in village.

Communications

Bus service to Almería. ☎ Area code 950.

⚓ ENSENADA DE LOS ESCULLOS
36°48′.2N 02°03′.2W

An open bay anchorage with sloping sandy bottom, some sandy beaches. Coast road, some development. The ruined castle, *guardia civil* barracks and a point with a white, skull-shaped rock, lie near the centre of the bay. The bay is wide open to E but some protection from NE in N corner of the bay is possible under Punta de la Isleta.

⚓ ENSENADA DE RODALQUILAR
36°51′.6N 02°00′W

The holding is reportedly poor in places. Open between NE and SE.

Punta de la Isleta

Los Escullos

Rodalquilar

III.i COSTA BLANCA

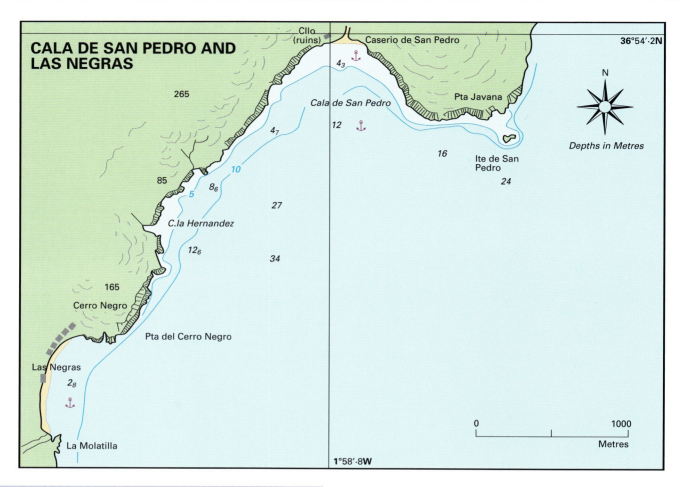

CALA DE SAN PEDRO AND LAS NEGRAS

San Pedro

⚓ **LAS NEGRAS** 36°52′.6N 01°59′.9W

Anchor in 3m sand and weed off the village. Open between NE and SE. The beach is sand and rock. The village has some shops.

⚓ **CALA DE SAN PEDRO** 36°53′.9N 01°58′.7W

An imposing anchorage where fluky and strong gusts may be expected. Anchor to suit draught in sand and weed.

⚓ **ENSENADA DE AGUA AMARGA (BITTER WATER BAY)** 36°56′.0N 01°56′.0W

Anchor outside the small boat moorings in six to eight metres of water. Excellent shelter from the NE winds but open between E and S. Alternative anchorages lie off the hamlet of El Ploma 2M to SW or off a small cove 1M to SW of Agua Amarga. Use these with care.

ENSENADA DE AGUA AMARGA

29. Puertos de Carboneras

36°59′.3N 01°53′.8W

Charts

British Admiralty *1515, 774.* Imray *M12*
French *4718.* Spanish *4621, 462*

⊕53 36°59′.2N 01°53′.5W

Lights

South Harbour (Puerto de Hornos Ibéricos SA)
0109 **Dique Este head** Fl(2)G.10s12m5M Green round
   tower 3m
0109.2 **Dique Este elbow** Q(3)10s12m3M ♦ card BYB
   tower 3m
0109.3 **Dique Oeste head** Fl(2)R.10s7m3M Red round
   tower 3m
**Middle harbour (PUCARSA – Puerto de Generar
Electricidad)**
0109.4 **Dique de Abrigo** 36°58′.5N 01°53′.6W
   Fl.G.10s14m5M Green metal post 4m
0109.5 **Dique auxiliar N head** Fl(2)R.9s10m1M Red metal
   framework tower 3m
North harbour (Puerto Pescaro de Carboneras)
0109.6 **Dique Este** Fl(3)G.12s10m5M Green hexagonal
   tower 4m
0109.7 **Contradique** Fl(3)R.12s8m3M Red hexagonal
   tower 6m

Port communications

Puerto de Hornos Ibéricos VHF Ch 9, 12.
Puerto Departivo (northern harbour) ☎/Fax 950 13 07 39

Commercial and fishing harbours

Three harbours, two commercial, large and forbidding, the Puerto de Hornos Ibéricos SA and the Puerto Generar del Electricidad and the third a working fishing harbour. However the first two offer good refuge from winds from all directions except SE though they should only be used in an emergency. Local facilities are about zero but provisions can be found in Carboneras village. The immediate area is dominated by the huge cement plant and electric generating station but the hinterland is wild and attractive. The fishing harbour is busy and has no special facilities for yachts. In poor weather it is likely to be crowded and a yacht would have to take its chance alongside a fishing boat.

Approach

From the south After Cabo de Gata the coast is broken by headlands enclosing sandy bays. Puerto Genovés is a wide sandy bay and the Ensenada de San José, which has a small harbour and village, can be identified. Further N, El Fraile (489m) is conspicuous as are the Isleta del Moro and Punta de la Polacra (263m) which has a tower. Cala de San Pedro which has a few houses and Agua Amarga may also be seen. The white lighthouse of Mesa de Roldán (221m) can be seen from afar. Once the points of Le Media Naranja and Los Muertos have been rounded the large breakwaters and the industrial buildings belching smoke will be seen.

From the north From Puerto de Garrucha, backed by the town of the same name, the coast is flat, sandy and unbroken, with high ranges of hills inland and some low cliffs. The town of Mojacar may be

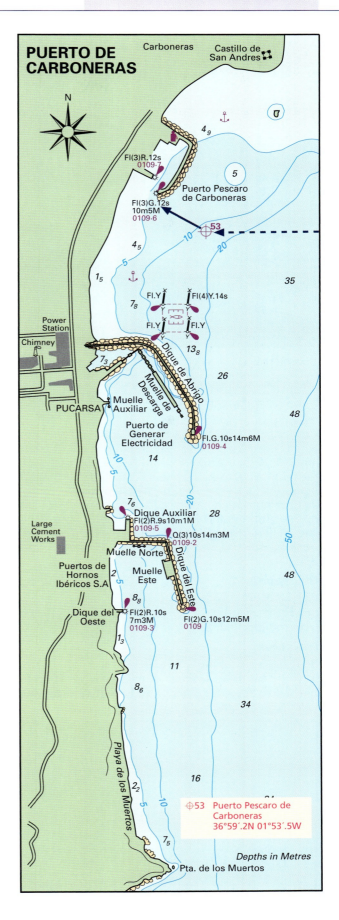

III.i COSTA BLANCA

The two commercial harbours at Carboneras with Puerto Pescaro at top right

seen on its hill ¼M then the buildings stop and the mountains begin, which last until shortly before Carboneras. The village of Carboneras stands behind a rather inconspicuous point with El Islote and Isla de San Andreas (14m) extending 600m off the point. Foul ground stretches nearly ½M from this point in a SE direction, otherwise the coast is free of dangers and can be followed at 400m. Once the Isla de San Andreas has been passed, the harbour walls and buildings may be seen. A 3.5m deep passage, running NE–SW, 150m wide, exists between this island and El Islote.

GPS approach

For the Puerto Pescaro steer to ⊕53 from an easterly quadrant and steer for breakwater end (approximately 0.3M).

Entrances

Both big harbours may be entered on a NW course leaving the head of either Dique Este 50m to starboard. Pay attention to and keep out of the way of any commercial vessel manoeuvring. The entrance to the Puerto Pescaro is straightforward but shoals and may be alive with traffic.

Berths

A temporary berth may be available in the S harbour alongside the quay if not in use. It has been rumoured that the fishing harbour is to be extended and become a fishing and yacht harbour. However during a visit in September 2004 only one small pontoon for local small craft was seen in the NE corner and no plans for further pontoons were forthcoming.

Anchorages

A temporary anchorage may be available in 5m sand and stone on the E side of the south and middle harbours, close inshore and clear of commercial works.

Outside, there are two possibilities: between Puerto de Carboneras and Puerto Pescaro and between Puerto Pescaro and El Islote. Both are open to the SE but the latter has better shelter from the NE. Sand, stone and weed.

Formalities

In the commercial harbours, contact the shore by radio for permission to stay. In the fishing harbour, inquire ashore.

⚓ MARINA DE LAS TORRES
37°09′.7N 01°49′W

An open coastal anchorage off the mouth of Río de Aguas in 5m sand, stone and weed. Exposed between NE and SE. The towns of Mojacar and Garrucha lie 2M and 1M away. There is a small landing jetty nearby. A road runs behind the beach and there is a conspicuous old factory chimney.

Puerto Pescaro de Carboneras

30. Puerto de Garrucha

37°11′N 01°49′.1W

Charts

British Admiralty *1515, 77*. Imray *M12*
French *4718*. Spanish *462*

⊕55 37°10′.5N 01°48′.8W

Lights

0110 **Garrucha LtHo** Oc(4)13s19m13M White tower house 10m Reserve light 8M
0110.5 **Espigón head** Q(3)10s4m3M ✦ card BYB 3m
0111·5 **Dique (unattached)** Q(3)10s4m3M ✦ card BYB 3m
0111 **Dique de Levante head** head Fl(3)G.9s13m5M Green tower 11m
0112 **Dique de Poniente head** Fl(3)R.9s6m3M Red tower 3m

Port communications

Capitania ☎ 950 46 02 36 *Fax* 950 13 26 36
Email garrucha@eppa.es
VHF Ch 9. Club Maritimo ☎ 950 46 00 48
Fax 950 13 24 10 *Email* pdgarrucha@distrito.com
www.eppa.es

Busy fishing harbour

A small fishing harbour, which is usually crowded, with a commercial quay. The harbour is easy to approach and enter but is open towards the SE. The little village has simple facilities, shops and a market where everyday requirements can be obtained. The harbour is clean and there is a slipway and small shipyard. The W side of the harbour has been converted into a promenade. A short walk to the disused factory by the prominent chimney gives a good idea of the coast and surrounding area. The hill top town of Mojacar is worth a visit by bus or taxi. Good sandy beaches on each side of the harbour.

Approach

From the south The Sierra Cabrera, whose foothills are easily identified, lead to Garrucha; one of these hills is covered with tourist housing development. An isolated obelisk-like chimney on a small hill behind the town is conspicuous. The lighthouse shows at close range.

From the north The low plain and dry river mouths SSW of Sierra Almagrera lead to Garrucha which has an isolated chimney and cranes on the Dique de Levante.

GPS approach

Steer to ⊕*55* from an easterly quadrant and steer for breakwater end (approximately 2.5M).

Anchorage in the approach

Anchor 200m S of elbow of Dique de Poniente in 5m sand.

Entrance

Straightforward but commercial vessels have right of way.

Berths

There is a small marina in the NW corner of the harbour. Secure near the fuel point at head of the 'T'-shaped pontoon near the centre of the harbour projecting from the NW side. Alternatively, berth alongside the broad commercial quay in NE corner of the harbour on the inside of the Dique de Levante. In the SW corner a possible berth is stern-to between fishing craft on N facing side of Dique de Poniente near the landward end; anchor with trip-line from the bow. Confirm berthing arrangements with the office near slipway.

Garrucha

III.i COSTA BLANCA

Anchoring in the N end of the harbour is very reluctantly accepted but not with any imminent big ship movements. In strong southerlies a big surge enters the harbour.

Facilities

Maximum length overall: 12m

Simple wood hull repairs by yard on slipway or in workshop in terrace to W of port.

12-tonne crane on Dique de Levante.

Slipways.

Water on quays.

Showers in the office block (key from harbourmaster).

125V and 220V AC supply point on Dique de Poniente and on pontoons.

Gasoleo A and petrol.

Ice from factory on front near *capitán de puerto*'s office.

Club Cultural y Marítimo de Garrucha.

A number of shops and a small market in the village SW of the harbour.

Litter bins around the harbour.

Communications

Bus service to Vera. ☎ Area code 950.

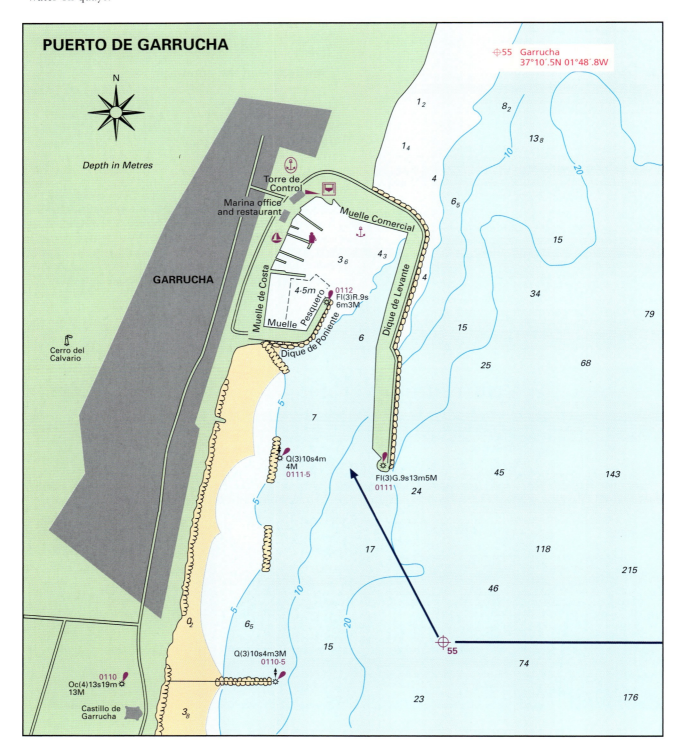

31. Puerto de Villaricos

37°14′.8N 01°46′W

Charts

British Admiralty *774*. Imray *M12*
French *4718*. Spanish *46A, 462*

Lights

0112.5 **Villaricos. Balsa breakwater head** 37°14′.8N
01°46′.1W Fl(4)G.12s8m5M Green truncated tower 3m
0112.51 **Outer breakwater head** Fl(4)R.15s4m3M Red
truncated tower 3m

No room for visitors

A pleasant but very small artificial harbour built for the town's pleasure craft (at last sighting there were only small motor boats). There is little or no room for visitors, no harbour facilities. Max length 5.6m.

⚓ PALOMARES Y VILLARICOS

Open anchorages either side of the mouth of the Río Almanzora. Note the shoals of the delta.

The village of Villaricos is right of centre in the photograph below.

32. Puerto de Esperanza

37°15′N 01°46′W

Charts

British Admiralty *774*. Imray *M12*
French *4718*
Spanish *46A, 462*

Lights

0113 **Dique de Abrigo head** Q(2)G.6s8m5M Green tower
3m
0113·1 **Contradique (centre)** Fl(2)R.10s3m3M Red post 1m
0113·2 **Espigón** Fl(3)G.10s3m3M Green square column 2m
0113·4 **Contradique head** Fl(3)R.10s4m3M Red tower 3m

Port communications

Capitania ☎/*Fax* 950 46 71 37

Tiny fishing harbour

Villaricos' tiny fishing harbour is only suitable for small (<8m) craft for a short stay. It is an attractive setting but even one visiting craft may be too many. Depths are reported to be 2m in the approach and port but caution and careful sounding is advised during any approach.

Approach

From the south The coast north of Garrucha is flat and sandy with few features and can be followed at about 200m offshore except off the delta of the River Almanzora when 400m should be maintained. The village of Palomares may be seen south of the river mouth with the village of Villaricos north of the river.

From the north From the easily identified Ensenada de Terreros with its off-lying island (24m) and small village, the coast is cliffed with small sand and stone beaches in breaks of the cliffs. Inland the hills rise to 350m. The coast is steep-to, two off-lying shallows (6m) – Piedra del Celor and Losa del Payo – break in heavy seas.

Entrance

Approach the head of the Dique de Abrigo on a W to NW course, round it at 10m and pass fairly close to the quay extension with its small green tower.

Facilities

Slipway in SW corner
Shops in village 200m to SW.

⚓ ANCHORAGES 2M TO N OF RÍO ALMANZORA

At least 10 small anchorages in *calas*, some with piers and quays – use with care.

Delta of Río Almanzora

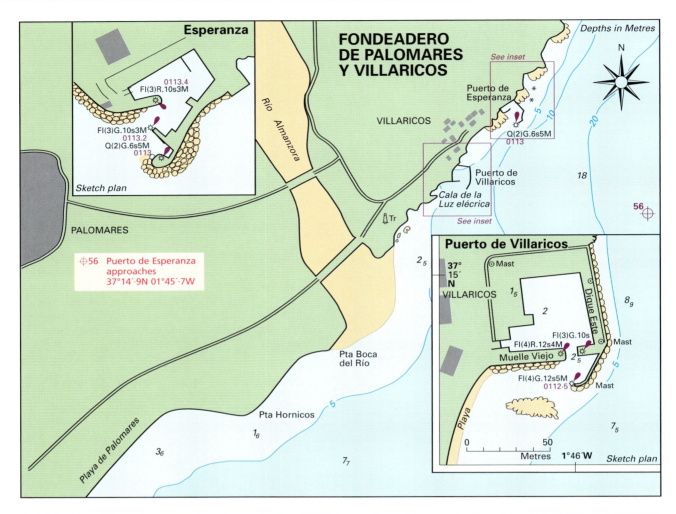

Esperanza

FONDEADERO DE PALOMARES Y VILLARICOS

Depths in Metres

See inset

Puerto de Esperanza

VILLARICOS

0113.4
Fl(3)R.10s3M

Q(2)G.6s5M
0113

Fl(3)G.10s3M
0113.2
Q(2)G.6s5M
0113

Sketch plan

PALOMARES

Puerto de Villaricos

Cala de la Luz elécrica

See inset

⊕56 Puerto de Esperanza approaches
37°14´·9N 01°45´·7W

Río Almanzora

Tr

Pta Boca del Río

Pta Hornicos

Playa de Palomares

Puerto de Villaricos

37° 15´ N

VILLARICOS

Mast

Dique Este

Fl(3)G.10s

Mast

Fl(4)R.12s4M

Muelle Viejo

Fl(4)G.12s5M
0112·5

Mast

Playa

0   50
Metres   1°46´W   Sketch plan

Puerto de Villaricos with Esperanza at the right of the photo

Anchorages to the SW of Aguilas

⚓ ENSENADA DE TERREROS
37°21′N 01°39′.7W

A well-protected anchorage but open to SE and subject to swell from E. The 600m passage between the Punta el Cañon and Isla de los Terreros (34m) is 6m deep. Anchor off San Juan de los Terreros in N part of bay. A few shops and the main road.

Looking N into Cala Cerrada with Punta Parda at right foreground; Cama de los Novios is just showing behind the point

⚓ PUNTA PARDA
37°22′.5N 01°37′.5W

At the N end of Ensenada de los Tarais, which is open between E and S, there are two anchorages on the west side of Punta Parda, off Cala Reona and Cala Cerrada, and one on the east, Cama de los Novios (beware of the small island in the entrance to this bay). Anchor according to draught, sand and weed. Whether the name, Cama de los Novios, the bed of the newly-married, reflects turbulent or peaceful nights is anyone's guess.

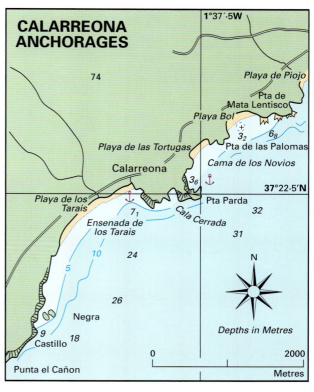

III.i COSTA BLANCA

33. Puertos de Aguilas y del Hornillo

37°24´.4N 01°34´.4W

Currents

Currents inside these two bays tend to set in the direction of recent winds.

Charts

British Admiralty *1515, 774.* Imray *M12*
French *6341, 4718.* Spanish *463*

⊕57 37°24´N 01°34´.2W

Lights

Approach
0114 **Punta Negra** Fl(2)5s30m13M Black and white bands 23m
0117.5 **Islote de la Aguilica** Fl.G.3s19m3M Square white building
Commercial Harbour
0116 **Mole** head Fl(2)R.6s9m3M Red post 5m
0116·1 **Contradique head** Fl(3)G.9s5m2M Grey Post 3m
Yacht Harbour (Darsena Deportiva)
0116.2 **Dique Sur head** Fl(2)G.5s6m2M White truncated tower, green top 5m
0116·4 **Dique Oeste** Oc.R.5s5m2M White truncated tower, red top 4m

Port communications

Port VHF Ch 9 ☎/Fax 968 41 02 28
Club Náutico de Aguilas VHF Ch 9 ☎/Fax 968 41 19 51
Marina *mobile* 670445725 *Email* admon@cnaguilas.com
www.cnaguilas.com

Useful anchorage harbour

Two bays, separated by a headland with a tourist development. The western bay, Aguilas, has a small fishing port on its west shore and a small crowded yacht harbour on its north shore. To the east, the other side of the headland, is El Hornillo, an old anchorage with a project for a marina close to the north east. Both bays are open to the ESE and uncomfortable in a wind from this direction but have attractive surroundings.

Aguilas was an important Roman port which fell into disuse after repeated invasions by the Berbers. In 1765 the village and harbour were rebuilt and the castle restored by Count Aranda, a minister of Charles III. A climb to the castle of San Juan (18th century) on Montaña de Aguilas above the harbour is worthwhile for the view. Good beaches on either side of the harbour.

Note that there are two headlands with lights named Punta Negra in this area: Punta Negra de Aguilas, normally listed under Punta Negra and Punta Negra de Mazarrón, normally listed under Mazarrón.

Approach

From the SW Follow the coast, passing the conspicuous Isla de los Terreros. In the distance four high, steep-sided headlands will be seen (Mt de Aguilas, Mt de la Aguilica, Isla el Fraile and Mt Cope). Aguilas lies behind the first headland, which

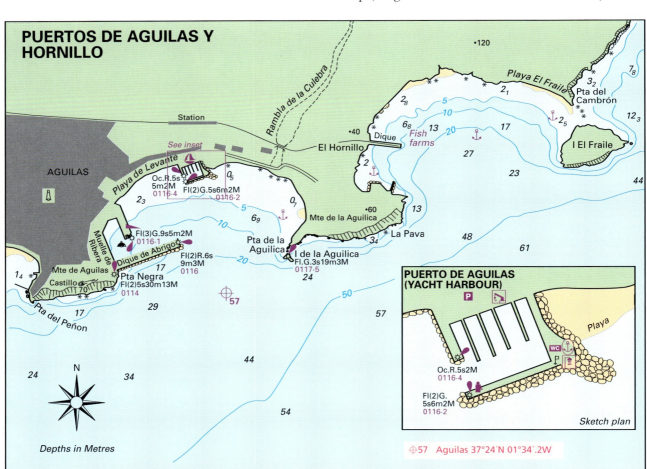

The fishing harbour at Puerto Aguilas and the yacht haven at upper right

has a small castle on its summit. A tall lone chimney stands in the bay to the W of the first headland.

From the NE Having rounded the large promontory of Mt Cope, a group of tree high, steep-sided rocky headlands will be seen, the first actually on an island. The harbour lies between the second and third headland.

GPS approach

Steer to ⊕57 from a southeasterly quadrant and steer for breakwater end (approximately 0.2M).

Entrance

In Aguilas, give the head of mole a 50m berth; a buoyed channel leads to the yacht harbour. Fishing nets are sometimes laid near the entrance to both bays. In heavy weather the entrance to both harbours might be dangerous.

Berths

In Aguilas yacht harbour secure to any vacant berth or as directed by harbour staff. In the fishing harbour a possibility is to go alongside at the root of the mole, clear of commercial craft; alternatively secure stern-to a fishing quay with a bow anchor using an anchor trip-line. Before arriving, check that there is room with the harbourmaster by radio.

Anchorages

It is possible to anchor almost anywhere in the bay clear of the quays. Suggested anchorages are shown on the plan.

Facilities

Aguilas Fishing Harbour
50-tonne travel-lift and hardstanding.
12-tonne crane.
Slipway at the SW corner.
Engine repair mechanics in the town.
Small repairs to woodwork and hulls can be carried out at workshop by slipway.
Chandlers shop near the fish quay, another near the yacht harbour.
Water on the commercial mole. Supply also available at lonja de pescadores.
Ice from a factory to W of the town or at the harbourmaster's office.
Darsena Deportiva
Maximum length overall: 12m.
Water and electricity on the quays.
Gasoleo A and petrol.
Club Náutico de Aguilas at yacht harbour.
A good selection of shops in the town and a small market.

Communications

Bus and rail services. ☎ Area code 968.

III.i COSTA BLANCA

Anchorages between Aguilas and Mazarron

⚓ CALA BARDINA
37°25′.6N 01°30′.5W

The first 50m offshore is cordoned off for swimmers and small boats. A channel for these boats is marked with a red and a green buoy – watch out for a submerged rock some 20m south of the green buoy! There is still plenty of room to anchor in six to eight metres outside the buoys. Well protected from the N and E by Mt Cope (244m) but open between SE and SW and with swell from E winds.

⚓ ENSENADA DE LA FUENTE
37°26′.1N 01°28′.7W

An anchorage open to NE but well protected by Mt Cope from other directions. Anchor in SW corner of the bay in 3m sand.

⚓ OTHER ANCHORAGES BETWEEN MONTAÑA COPE AND PUERTO DE MAZARRÓN

A large number of small coastal anchorages exist on this stretch of coast, see plan. Use with care. Most are off small, sandy beaches and any obstructions can be seen in the clear water. Some anchorages have a stony bottom but most are sand or shingle.

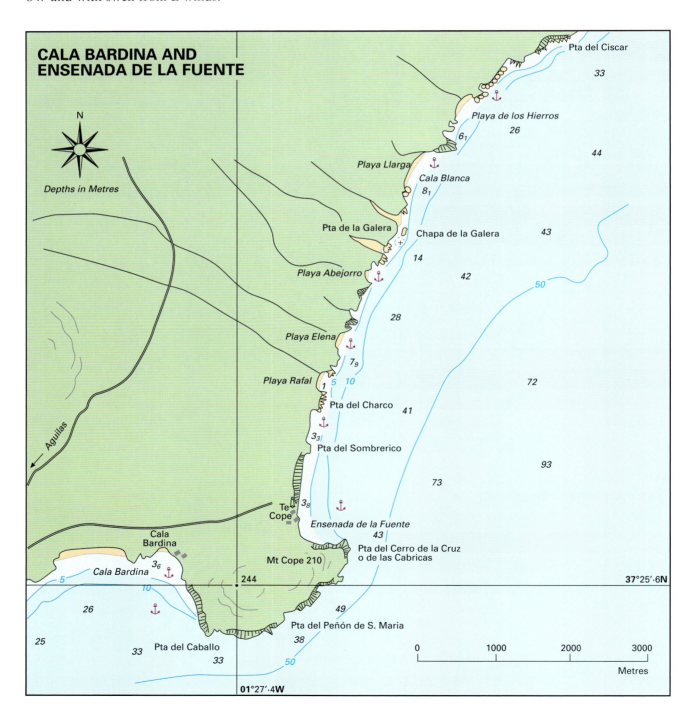

CALA BARDINA AND ENSENADA DE LA FUENTE

34. Club de Regatas, Mazarrón

37°33´.4N 01°16´.3W

Charts

British Admiralty *774*. Imray *M12*
French *6341, 4718*. Spanish *4632, 463*

⊕59 37°33´.3N 01°16´.3W

Lights

0122 **Yacht club jetty head** Fl(4)R.10s10m3M Red metal
tower, white band 4m
To the east
0120 **Mazarrón LtHo** Oc(1+2)13·5s65m15M White tower
11m

Port communications

VHF Ch 9. Yacht club ☎ 968 59 40 11 *Fax* 968 59 52 53
Email info@crmazarron.com
www.crmazarron.com

Pleasant harbour good shelter

Situated round the corner and about a mile west of
the old fishing harbour of Mazarrón. It offers very
good shelter from all directions. There are beaches
beside the harbour.

Note that there are two headlands with lights
named Punta Negra in this area: Punta Negra de
Mazarrón, normally listed under Mazarrón, and
Punta Negra de Aguilas, normally listed under Punta
Negra.

Approach

Tunny nets are sometimes laid off this section of
coast and there are presently fish farms 1M SE of Pta
del Calnegre and 1M S of Isla de Adentro.
Submarines exercise in the south of this area.

From the SW The Sierra de las Moreras, with two
peaks (458 and 429m), and the Isla de Adentro
(56m) are recognisable. Punta Negra de Mazarrón
with its lighthouse and large statue of Jesus is
unmistakable. The harbour lies to W of Isla de
Adentro.

From the NE The 4M-wide Ensenada de Mazarrón
is easy to identify as is Punta Negra, described
above, which has the appearance of an island from
this direction. When Punta Negra has been closed
Isla de Adentro will be seen; the harbour lies to W of
this island.

GPS approach

Steer to ⊕59 from a southerly quadrant and steer
for breakwater end (approximately 0.15M), leaving
the Isla de Adentro well to starboard.

Anchorage in the approach

Depths to the NE of the harbour are shallow and the
bottom is rocky so anchoring is not recommended
but there is a very attractive sandy cove just west of
the harbour with 3m in its centre.

Entrance

From the SW Approach Isla de Adentro on a NE
course and, when 200m from it, turn onto a N
course towards the harbour breakwater. Leave it
10m to port. Beware the rocky islet, Los Esculles,
lying just to the north of the line between the north
side of Isla de Adentro and the marina entrance.

From the NE Having identified the statue and Isla de
Adentro round the Isla leaving it 200m to starboard
(do not attempt to pass to the north of the Isla as the
water is shallow with rocky outcrops) and proceed on
a NNW course to close the breakwater end. Note the
warning about Los Esculles in previous paragraph.

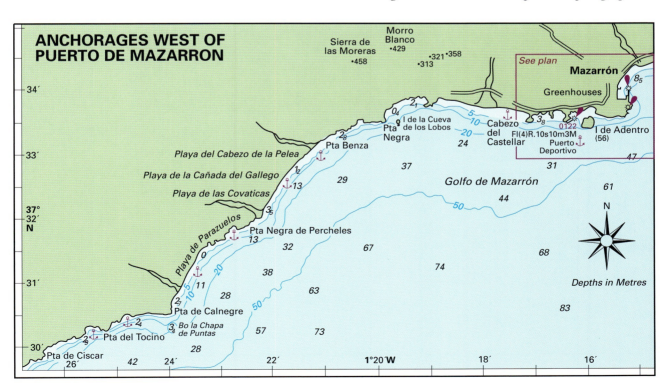

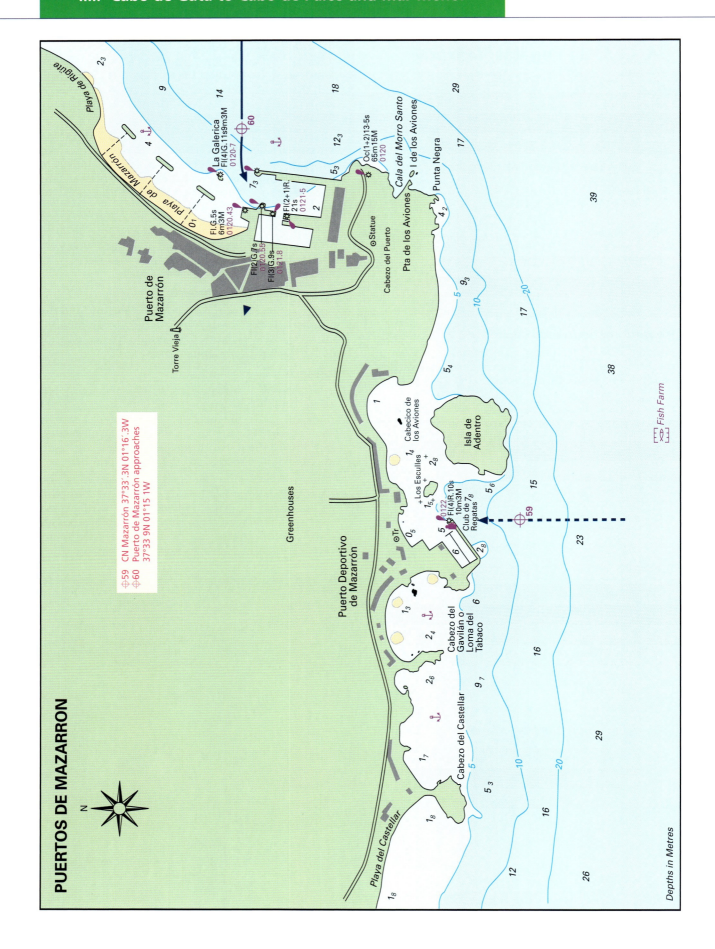

PUERTOS DE MAZARRON

N

⊕59 CN Mazarrón 37°33′·3N 01°16′·3W
⊕60 Puerto de Mazarrón approaches
      37°33′·9N 01°15′·1W

Puerto de Mazarrón

Playa de Ríguite

Playa de Mazarrón

La Galerica
Fl(4)G.11s9m3M
0120·7

Fl.G.5s
6m3M
0120·43

Fl(2+1)R.
21s
0121·5

Fl(2)G.7s
0120·55
Fl(3)G.9s
0121·8

Torre Vieja

Statue

Cabezo del Puerto

Pta de los Aviones

Cala del Morro Santo

Oc(1+2)13·5s
65m15M
0120

I de los Aviones

Punta Negra

Greenhouses

Puerto Deportivo
de Mazarrón

Tr

Cabecico de
los Aviones

Los Esculles

Isla de
Adentro

Fl(4)R.10s
10m3M
Club de
Regatas
0122

Fish Farm

Cabezo del
Gavilán o
Loma del
Tabaco

Cabezo del Castellar

Playa del Castellar

Depths in Metres

Club de Regatas, Mazarrón from the SW

Berths

Secure to quay on port-hand side of entrance near fuel pumps and ask at the Club de Regatas office for a berth. Visitors berths are limited to three at the end of the 'T' pontoon. Visitors may be put elsewhere if there is room.

Facilities

Maximum length overall: 25m (four yachts only; more at lesser length).
Marine Engineer (Volvo agency).
Slipway at N side of harbour and for dinghies at E side.
8-tonne crane.
Hardstandings.
Water taps on pontoons and quays.
220V AC points on pontoons and quays.
Gasoleo A and petrol.
Ice at entrance.
Club de Regatas de Mazarrón has a bar, restaurant, showers etc.
Provisions from village of Mazarrón.

Communications

☎ Area code 968. Taxi ☎ 59 51 22.

Mazarrón Capitania

35. Puerto Deportivo de Mazarrón

37°33´.9N 01°15´.W

Charts

British Admiralty *774*. Imray *M12*
French *6341, 4718*. Spanish *4632, 463*

⊕60 37°33´.9N 01°15´.1W

Lights

0120.5 **Dique de Abrigo head** Fl(4)R.11s7m5M Red post 3m
0120.6 **Dique de Abrigo corner** Q(3)10s7m3M E cardinal BYB 3m
0120.43 **Contradique N head** Fl.G.5s6m3M Green post 3m
0120.55 **Contradique Elbow** Fl(2)G.7s5m1M Green post 3m
0121.8 **Darsena N entrance** Fl(3)G.9s4m1M Green post 3m
0121·5 **Darsena S entrance** Fl(2+1)R.21s4m2M Red post, green band 3m

Port communications

Marina office VHF Ch 9. ☎ 609 36 02 60/ 968 15 40 65
Fax 968 15 57 53
Email boltursa@yahoo.es

Fishing, commercial and completely new marina complex

This fishing and commercial harbour at the W end of the Ensenada de Mazarrón is easy to enter and offers good protection from all directions except NE. Over the past five years there has been a vast injection of money and the rocky jetties of the nineties have been replaced with new quays and promenades with first class buildings and pontoons. It is still being developed but by the 2008 season it sould be a very nice place to visit with all facilities one expects from a top class marina. The town of Mazarrón, about 3M inland, has good shops and may be reached by taxi or bus. A climb to the lighthouse is worthwhile for the view. Good beaches in the bay.

Approach

Tunny nets are sometimes laid off this section of coast and there is a fish farm 1M south of Isla de Adentro. Submarines exercise in the south of the area.

From the SW The Sierra de las Moreras and a few islands close to the coast are recognisable. Punta Negra with its lighthouse and a large statue of Jesus is especially conspicuous.

From the NE Punta Negra resembles an island and, with its lighthouse and statue, is conspicuous across the wide Rada de Mazarrón.

GPS approach

Steer to ⊕60 from an easterly quadrant and steer for breakwater end (approximately 0.14M) leaving La Galerica well to starboard.

Entrance

Approach the head of the breakwater on a westerly course, keeping well clear of Isla de la Galerica and round the head at 25m.

III.i COSTA BLANCA

Puerto de Mazarrón

Berths

The new marina was predicted to be ready for visitors in 2008 so it is recommended to call ahead to ascertain whether the hoped for berths are available. With +300 berths there should be room for visitors but developers like to sell all the berths but it is hoped that the original plan for 10% of the berths being kept for visitors is maintained.

Anchorages

Anchor to E or N of the harbour entrance. Keep clear of La Galerica rock. In the E end of the bay anchor off village of La Subida (see plan below) and N of Punta de la Azohía outside small-craft moorings.

Miscellaneous

The beacons on Punta de la Azohía mark a measured distance of 1857.47m on the N side of the bay, near the centre, on an axis of 104°.

Facilities

Two hards ashore with large travel-lift on centre quay.
Water from fish quay.
Ice from a small factory.
Shops and a supermarket and market in the village. Many more in the town itself some 3M inland.

Communications

Bus to Mazarrón town. ☎ Area code 968.

⚓ ENSENADA DE MAZARRÓN
37°33′.4N 01°10′.6W

It is possible to anchor almost anywhere around this bay in 5M sand and weed. The recommended places are to the sides of the three *ramblas* (dry river beds) or just NE of Punta de la Azohía off the small hamlet of La Subida, both open to S. Watch out for fishing boat moorings. A pair of beacons are situated NE and SW of the hamlet. A small supermarket is located in a housing estate ½M along the road to

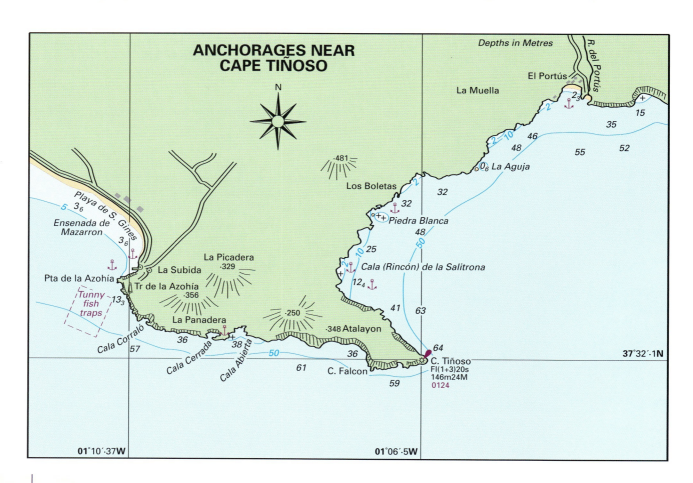

Punta de Azohía

Rincón de la Salitrona

Mazarrón. In the centre of the bay a small private harbour has been developed alongside and behind the Isla Plana.

There is a fish farm off Punta de la Azohía, but one can go between the farm and the point.

⚓ CALA CERRADA
37°32′.4N 01°09′.25W

Use with caution. Open to S. Anchor in the NE corner, in eight to 10 metres. The whole *cala* is very deep and is 8m even 20m from the beach.

⚓ RINCÓN DE LA SALITRONA
37°33′.2N 01°07′.5W

Anchor off the north beach, in 5m sand and weed, or the south beach which is more sheltered but deeper at eight to 10m. An alternative is off Los Boletas but pay attention to the rocks, Piedra Blanca.

⚓ EL PORTÚS
37°34′.8N 01°04′.4W

Anchor off the sandy beach. Open between SE and SW. Small shops.

Cala Cerrada

El Portús

III.i COSTA BLANCA

36. Puerto de Cartagena

37°35′.98N 00°59′.1W

Charts

British Admiralty *774, 1700, 1189, 1194.* Imray *M12*
French *4718, 4719.* Spanish *4642, 464A, 464*

⊕61 37°33′.5N 01°00′W

⊕62 37°35′N 00°58′.9W

Lights

To the west

0124 **Cabo Tiñoso** Fl(1+3)20s146m24M White tower and
  building 10m. A magnetic anomaly 3M to S of Cabo
  Tiñoso has been reported.

Approaches

Plan below

Western Approach

0125 **Dique, Algameca Grande** Fl(4)R.12s10m7M White and
  yellow tower 5m

0125·3 **The Point, Algameca Grande** Fl(3)G.12s8m3M White
  and yellow tower 3m

Entrance

0128 **Dique de Navidad** Fl(2)R.10s15m10M White tower red
  top 11m

23430(S) **Bajo de Santa Ana** Fl(2)G.7s5M Green conical 5m

Eastern Approach

0127 **Bajo Las Losas** Q(6)+LFl.15s5m5M ⌄ card 5m

Escombreras

0126.2 **Dique Muelle Bastarreche head** Fl(2)G.7s10m5M
  White tower 7m

0126.1 **Dique de Abrigo head** Fl.G.3s10m10M Green and
  white tower 7m

0126 **Islote Escombreras** Fl.5s65m17M Tower with
  aluminium cupola on white building 8m

Harbour Plan page 91

0128 **Dique de Navidad** Fl(2)R.10s15m10M White tower red
  top 11m

0130 **Dique de la Curra** Fl(3)G.14s14m5M Cylindrical white
  tower green cupola 11m

0130.2 **Espalmador floating breakwater** Q.R.4M Red post 3m

0130.5 **Muelle del Carbón head** Fl(2+1)R.14.5s8m3M Red
  post, green band 5m

0131.2 **Marina outer breakwater** Q.G.5m1M Green tower 4m

0131.5 **Muelle de Sta Lucia** Fl(4)G.12s5m1M Green post 3m

0132 **Muelle Santiago head** Fl(4)R.11s5m1M Red post 3m

0132.4 **Dolphin** Fl(2+1)G.16s5m1M Green column, red band
  3m

Yacht basin

0131.3 **Darsena de Yates breakwater head** 37°35′.7N
  00°58′.8W Fl(3)R.9s3m1M Red support 1m

0131.35 **Outer harbour elbow SW** Fl(2+1)G.12s3m1M Green
  column, red band

0131 **Club de Regatas mole SW corner** Q.G.3s5m1M Green
  post 5m

Port communications

Port VHF Ch 11, 12, 14. Marina VHF Ch 9.
Puerto Deportivo VHF Ch 9 ☎ 968 50 15 09 *Fax* 968 50 69 05
Real Club de Regatas Cartagena ☎ 968 50 15 07
Fax 968 52 36 22 *Email* rcrct@rcrct.net
www.clubregatascartagena.es
Yacht Port Cartagena ☎ 968 12 12 13 *Fax* 968 12 12 32
Mobile 636 877 374 *Email* marina@yachtportcartagena.com
www.yachtportcartagena.com

Storm signals

Flown from the signal station in Castillo de Galeras.

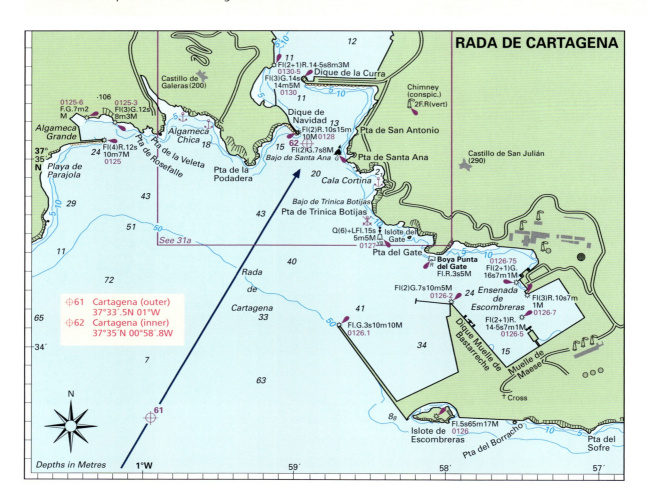

Major harbour with good facilities

A large naval, commercial and fishing port of great antiquity which is easy to approach and enter under almost any conditions. It is an attractive city with good shops. The yacht club is pleasant but is for members – an introduction is needed. Visiting yachts go to the marina. The harbour and quays are sometimes oily and with a SE wind, smoke and fumes from the refinery at Escombrera can be unpleasant.

As of 2004 the yacht club has been moved to a very modern building on the cruise liner landing in the centre of the Muelle de Alfonso XII. New piers have been constructed for berths for large (+25 metres) pleasure craft to the east of the old marina. During the visit in November 2007 the Real Club de Regatas Clubhouse is obviously well used by its members and the Puerto Deportivo to the west is still in operation from a small cabin at the gate of the puerto. The large new marina for super yachts to the east of the Clubhouse has clearly run into problems as it has hardly progressed in the last three years. The Real Club de Regatas have nothing to do with it now and it is being run by the Yacht Port Cartagena consortium. They have less ambitious plans and are pile-driving to make a marina for 12 to 25m yachts. A new jetty has been built on which they are planning to erect a club house with all facilities for visiting yachts. They are presently (2007) operating out of a couple of portacabins but there are yachts moored and there should be more berths by 2008.

Developed by Hasdrubal about 243 BC it became the centre of Carthaginian influence in Europe, helped by slaves working the gold and silver mines of the region. Hasdrubal's brother, Hannibal, used it a base for his expedition across the Alps and it became the primary target of Scipio the elder ('Africanus' – *Cathargo delenda est*). The Romans duly destroyed Carthaginian influence. St James the Great is said to have landed here in AD 36 bringing Christianity to Spain from Palestine (a sea passage which according to legend took four days). It subsequently passed into the hands of the Barbarians and then Moors. Philip II fortified the surrounding hills in the 16th century, Drake stole its guns in 1585 and took them to Jamaica, Charles III established the arsenal and naval base in the 18th century and the Republicans held out for months against Madrid during the Civil War in 1936. But the chief remnants of its troubled history lie in the minds of its

New works at Esperanza – from SE

Cartagena from the S – four pontoons now exist in the new marina east of the Puerto Deportivo

inhabitants, not its artefacts. There is a good view of the harbour from the Castillo de la Concepción and the old churches are worth visiting. A 10-day local holiday starts the Sunday before Trinity Sunday.

Approach

From all directions the entrance to Rada de Cartagena is made obvious by the high steep reddish cliffs of Cabo Tiñoso to the W and Islote de Escombrera to the E. The large oil refinery near this island is visible from afar. A large chimney, with black top and white band is conspicuous between Castillo de San Juan and Punta de San Antonio. There is vast construction work going on to enlarge the port of Escombrera. The passage between the Islote and Punta del Borracho has been closed while an 800 metre breakwater now runs NW from the west point of the Islote.

From the west The course goes past Puerto de Algameca Grande, a naval port on the W side of the Rada de Cartagena which is prohibited to yachts. Large unlit mooring buoys are located opposite Algameca Grande and Chico. A firing range exists to the S of this port and submarines exercise in the area.

From the east From Cabo de Palos follow the land keeping a good watch out for fish farms, which proliferate in this area especially off Portman and Cala de Gorguel. Pass south of Cabo del Agua and Islote de Escombreras and steer parallel to the new breakwater until the entrance to Cartagena proper opens up. It is recommended to keep well clear of all the ongoing construction work Although the port may be still used in dire emergency one will normally be sent away to the marina.

GPS approach

Steer to ⊕61 from the southerly sector and make towards ⊕62. Leave Bajo de Sta. Anna to starboard and make for the end of the Dique de la Curra.

Anchorages

Anchoring is forbidden in the harbour or its immediate approaches. Anchoring is possible in Rincón de la Salitrona behind and to N of Cabo Tiñoso, El Portús 4M to W of the harbour, Algameca Chica and Cala Cortina (pay attention to rock on N side). Algameca Chica is smelly and may have fishing nets. Cala Cortina has a rocky bottom. Expect to be moved if you finish up in a defence or commercial area.

III.i COSTA BLANCA

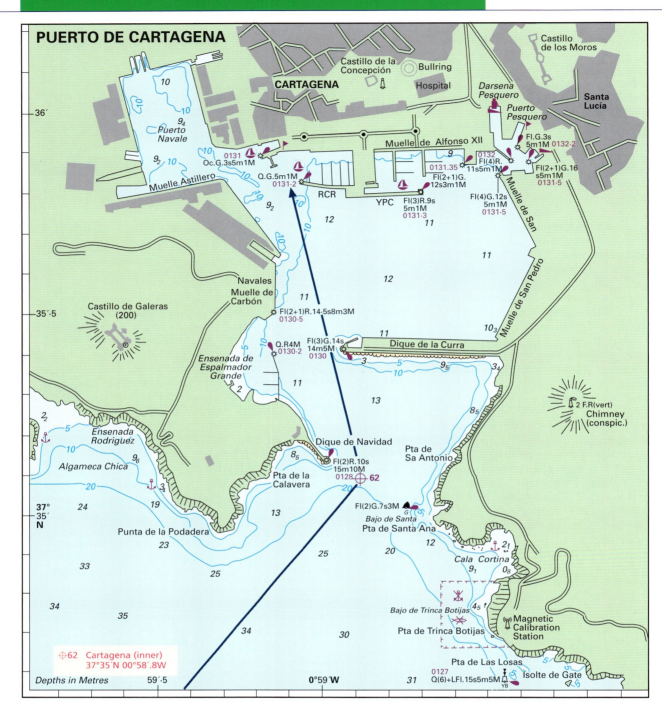

PUERTO DE CARTAGENA

⊕62 Cartagena (inner)
37°35′N 00°58′.8W

Depths in Metres

Entrance

Straightforward but check that there are no large vessels entering or leaving port.

Berths

There are two marinas to choose from and although the eastern one is the newer its facilities may not yet be fully developed. It is recommended to call ahead to see which one has a vacant berth.

Charges

Low.

Facilities

Maximum length overall: 25m.

All types of repairs, mostly by the naval workshops; contact the marina for advice.

Cranes up to 20 tonnes; contact *capitán de puerto*.

Marine radio shop next to the Scandinavian Consul's office in the Muralla del Mar.

Several chandlers, two near Dársena Pesquera.

Charts from Esqui Náuticas, Campos.

Water and 230/380V AC on marina pontoons.

Gasoleo A and petrol at the marina.

Hypermarket 'Continente' about a kilometre away – ask for directions or take a taxi. Many varied provision shops and two markets in the town, none near.

Launderette in Plaza de San Francisco.

Communications

Murcia airport 30 minutes by taxi, international flights.

Railway to Murcia from FEVE and Los Nietos from RENFE station and bus services. An occasional service by sea to the Canary Isles.

☎ Area code 968. Taxi rank at marina.

37. Puerto de Portmán

Lights

0134 **Punta de la Chapa** Oc.3.5s49m13M tower on white
building 8m
0134.5 **Breakwater head** Fl(2)R.6s6m2M Red post 4m
0134.3 **Bajo de la Bola** Q(6)+LFl.10s5M ⚑ card buoy 4m

Silted up port with fish farms

Called Portus Magnus by the Romans, Portmán has been completely silted up by effluent from the lead and zinc mines inland. The scars in the hillside and the new wind farm on the top of the hill inland make recognition of Portmán relatively easy. There is a huge fish farm to the west of the bay which leaves little space to anchor. The small dinghy harbour, on the east side, has a breakwater running out from the beach with a red column at its end. The harbour is totally sheltered but only has about 0.5m depth at

Puerto de Portmán

Cala de Gorguel

the entrance and is only for dinghies and RIBS. There is a *club náutico* on the west side of the beach but there are no facilities at all in the small village. Anchor between the two buoys in the bay in about 4m and land on the beach by dinghy – open between SE and SW.

⚓ CALA DEL GORGUEL
37°34′.4N 0°52′.5W

An unlit fish farm virtually blocks the entrance to this *cala*, approach with care from the east. The *cala* is full of floating gear and boats for the farm. Anchor (if there is room) in small rocky cove in 5m mud off the beach. There are off-lying rocks on W side of beach. Open between SE and S. There are also fish farms, mostly unlit, off-shore between La Manceba and Cabo Negrete.

III.i COSTA BLANCA

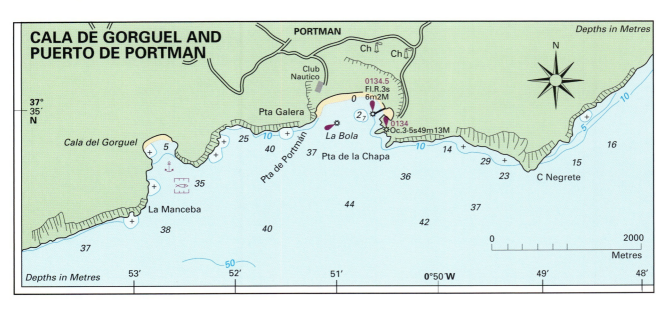

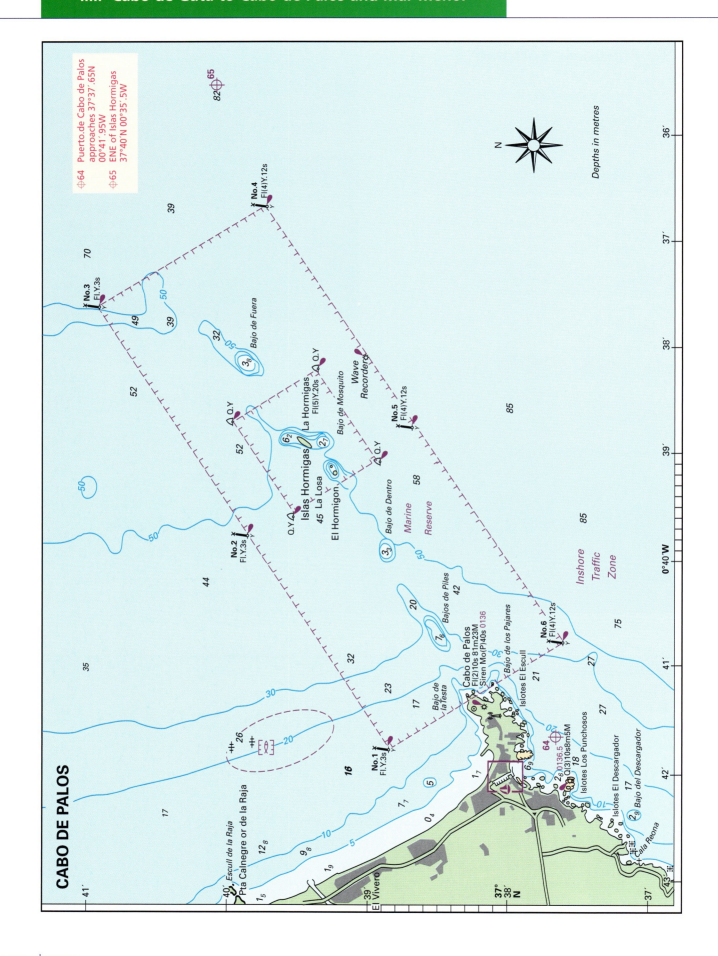

CABO DE PALOS

⊕64 Puerto.de Cabo de Palos
     approaches 37°37′.65N
     00°41′.95W
⊕65 ENE of Islas Hormigas
     37°40′N 00°35′.5W

Depths in metres

N

Inshore
Traffic
Zone

Marine
Reserve

Bajo de Fuera

La Hormigas
Fl(5)Y.20s

Islas Hormigas
45 La Losa
El Hormigon

Bajo de Mosquito

Wave
Recorder

Bajo de Dentro

Bajos de Piles

Cabo de Palos
Fl(2)10s 81m23M
Siren Mo(PI)40s 0136

Bajo de los Pajares

Islotes El Escull

Islotes Los Punchosos

Islotes El Descargador

Bajo del Descargador

Cala Reona

Bajo de
la Testa

El Vivero

Escull de la Raja
Pta Calnegre or de la Raja

No.1
Fl.Y.3s

No.2
Fl.Y.3s

No.3
Fl.Y.3s

No.4
Fl(4)Y.12s

No.5
Fl(4)Y.12s

No.6
Fl(4)Y.12s

Q.Y

Q.Y

Q.Y

Q.Y

Q.Y

64
Q(3)10s8m5M
0136.5

38. Puerto de Cabo de Palos (Cala Avellán)

37°37´.8N 00°42´.8W

Charts

British Admiralty *774, 1700.* Imray *M12*
French *4718, 4719.* Spanish *464, 471*

⊕64 37°37´.5N 00°41´.8W

Lights

0137 **Espigón de la Sal** Fl(2)G.10s6m5M Green post 3m
0137·3 **Beacon** Fl(2)R.12s5m3M White post (4m), on red
  concrete base 1m
0136.9 **Escollo Las Melvas** Q(6)+LFl.15s5m5M ⛛ card post
  YB 3m
To the northeast
0136 **Cabo de Palos** Fl(2)10s81m23M Siren Mo(P)40s Grey
  round tower 51m
To the southwest
0136.5 **Los Punchosos** Q(3)10s8m5M Grey pole 5m

Port communications

VHF Ch 9. ☎ 968 56 35 15

⊕ 64 37°37´.65N 00°41´.95W

Small yacht and fishing harbour

A small yacht and fishing harbour located at the western edge of a prodigious tourist development running along the edge of the Mar Menor. It and its surroundings are crowded. A pleasant short walk out to the lighthouse. Excellent sandy beaches to N.

The zig-zag entrance requires care and is not really suitable for yachts over 12m.

Approach

From the south From Cartagena to Cabo de Palos the coast has steep rocky cliffs with a few sandy bays lying between points. The hinterland is rugged and hilly. There are no dangers more than 200m off-shore and the coast is steep-to. Portmán may be recognised by the vast hillside of open-cast mining behind it with a wind farm with 8 turbines on top of the hill. The large lighthouse at Cabo de Palos (81m) is easily identified. The harbour lies ½M to the W of it. Pay attention to off-lying rocks in the approach to the harbour.

From the north Isla Grosa (95m) is unmistakable. The coast as far as the prominent Cabo de Palos, is low, flat, sandy and lined with high-rise buildings. No dangers lie more than 600m off-shore. Round Cabo de Palos at 200m paying attention to isolated rocks and islets in the western part of the bay inside this distance, in particular, the rock just under water southeast of Espigón de la Sal, which is now marked by a S cardinal beacon, Las Melvas.

GPS approach

Steer to ⊕64 from a southeasterly quadrant and steer for the end of Espigón de Sal (approximately 0.33M).

Anchorage in the approach

The bottom to the S of Cabo de Palos peninsula is rocky out to the 20m contour. It is better to anchor in 5m sand to the N of this peninsula.

Entrance

Approach the harbour keeping the church, which has an unusual open-work, tripod tower with a bell on a cross bar and a cross on top, approximately NNW (between 325° and 345°), keeping the awash rock, Las Melvas, with its S cardinal pole, well to starboard. Turn to starboard around the end of the Espigón de la Sal (with its green post) keeping close to the quay, leaving the white pole on the 2m diameter red beacon well to port. Then turn to port round the end of the Dique de Abrigo and go alongside the quay parallel to the *dique*.

Berths

Although there are pontoons inside the harbour these are for locals only and visitor berths are alongside the quay in the outer harbour.

Facilities

Maximum length overall: 10m.
A slipway at N end of the harbour and a small slipway in
  outer harbour to W of entrance to inner harbour.
Chandlery and diesel in the village.
Water taps and electricity on quays.
A few local shops.
See also the entry on facilities under Mar Menor, page 98.

Communications

Bus services to Cartagena, Murcia and La Manga where there is a large supermarket. ☎ Area code 968.

⚓ CABO DE PALOS

37°38´.1N 0°41´.55W

Anchorage in bay to NW of Cabo de Palos open to NE in 5m sand and stones. Shops in nearby Playa Honda and at La Barra. Note there is now a traffic separation scheme (TSS) some nine miles ESE of the lighthouse which should not seriously affect pleasure craft as they are closer to the point but one should be aware of its position.

III.i COSTA BLANCA

Puerto Cabo de Palos – note underwater rock in the lower right-hand corner (now marked by beacon) looking N to Mar Menor on left and Isla Grosa on right

MARINE RESERVE CABO DE PALOS

This low sandy point with its 51m-high grey lighthouse has a large marine reserve some 2M by 4M extending to the ENE. It is marked by six buoys, the three northern ones are Fl.Y.3s while the three southern ones are Fl(4)Y.12s. There is an inner reserve, around Islas Hormigas, marked with four buoys Q.Y some of which may be missing at times. There is also a yellow, spherical wave recorder buoy at 37°39′.3N 00°38′.2W with a light Q(5)Y.20s.

⚓ PLAYA DE PALOS
37°39′N 0°42′.7W

Coastal anchorage along a 6M stretch of sandy beach in 5m sand and weed. Wide open E and facing wall to wall high-rise buildings – access to the coast road is through private properties. A shallow patch, Banco El Tabal (1.7m), is near the centre of the beach.

⚓ ISLA GROSA
37°43′.5N 0°42′.6W

Anchorage in the W quarter of the island to suit draught in clay with weed. The island, 95m high, offers some protection from sea and wind. There are houses on the W side and a landing place. This area is occupied by the military and approach within 300 metres is discouraged.

Cabo de Palos lighthouse

Mar Menor

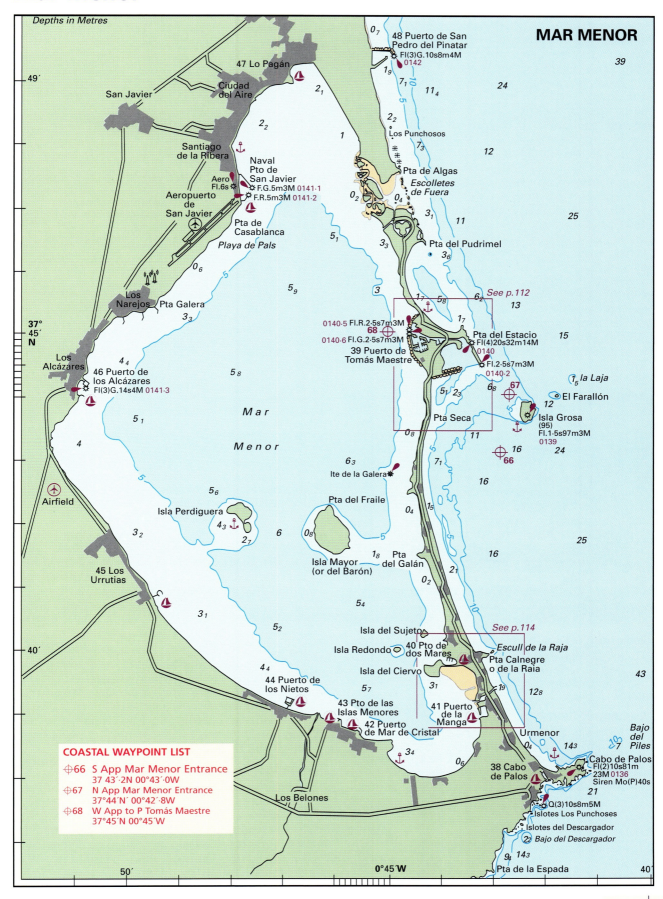

Depths in Metres

MAR MENOR

47 Lo Pagán

San Javier

Ciudad del Aire

Santiago de la Ribera

Naval Pto de San Javier

Aero Fl.6s ✲ ✲ F.G.5m3M 0141·1
✲ F.R.5m3M 0141·2

Aeropuerto de San Javier

Pta de Casablanca

Playa de Pals

Los Narejos Pta Galera

37° 45′ N

Los Alcázares

46 Puerto de los Alcázares
✲ Fl(3)G.14s4M 0141·3

M a r

M e n o r

Airfield

Isla Perdiguera

45 Los Urrutias

44 Puerto de los Nietos

43 Pto de las Islas Menores

42 Puerto de Mar de Cristal

Los Belones

48 Puerto de San Pedro del Pinatar
Fl(3)G.10s8m4M 0142

Los Punchosos

Pta de Algas

Escolletes de Fuera

Pta del Pudrimel

See p.112

0140·5 Fl.R.2·5s7m3M
68
0140·6 Fl.G.2·5s7m3M

39 Puerto de Tomás Maestre

Pta del Estacio
Fl(4)20s32m14M
0140

Fl.2·5s7m3M
0140·2

la Laja

El Farallón

67

Isla Grosa (95)
Fl.1·5s97m3M
0139

16
66

Pta Seca

Ite de la Galera

Pta del Fraile

Isla Mayor (or del Barón)

Pta del Galán

Isla del Sujeto

Isla Redondo

40 Pto de dos Mares

Escull de la Raja

Pta Calnegre o de la Raia

Isla del Ciervo

41 Puerto de la Manga

See p.114

Urmenor

Bajo del Piles

Cabo de Palos
Fl(2)10s81m
23M 0136
Siren Mo(P)40s

38 Cabo de Palos

Q(3)10s8m5M
Islotes Los Punchoses

Islotes del Descargador
Bajo del Descargador

Pta de la Espada

See p.112 · See p.114

COASTAL WAYPOINT LIST

⊕66 S App Mar Menor Entrance
       37 43′·2N 00°43′·0W
⊕67 N App Mar Menor Entrance
       37°44′N 00°42′·8W
⊕68 W App to P Tomás Maestre
       37°45′N 00°45′W

III.i COSTA BLANCA

Mar Menor – An inland sea

An extraordinary inland sea some 12M long and 6M wide separated from the Mediterranean by a narrow band of sand, La Manga, from which a line of mini sky-scrapers rise. In addition to the intensive encouragement of tourists on land, yacht harbours are being built around the shores of the inland sea. The towns themselves are generally dull and the ports small and shallow but in terms of pottering around, anchoring off, small boating and so forth the Mar has its attractions.

Of the three entrances, one is deep and two very shallow. The major entrance is through Puerto de Tomás Maestre, which is the largest harbour of the Mar Menor and is supposedly dredged to 4m though 3m may be nearer the mark. Details of the approach and entrance are given later; the other two entrances are not described. The second largest harbour, San Javier in the NW, is a naval air force harbour and part of the air academy. It is not open to visitors. Seven small harbours are built around the Mar. A number of moorings have been laid but they are generally private.

The five islands are Isla Mayor or del Barón (102m), Perdiguera (45m), del Ciervo (46m) which is actually joined to La Manga by a causeway, Rondella or Redonda and del Sujeto. The first two are large and steep-to. The passage between Isla Mayor and La Manga has uncertain depths, generally less than 1m, and the passage between Isla del Sujeto and La Manga has even less water.

There are depths of five to 6m over the greater part of Mar Menor with gently shallowing sides and the bottom is sand or mud with weed. This makes anchoring possible almost anywhere, according to draught, but a strong wind can quickly kick up a nasty sea with marked currents. The north part is shallower than the south and though the Mar Menor is not tidal, the water level can vary by as much as 50cm or more over a period of weeks, driven by winds or changed by rain. In general terms, do not get on the shoreward side of any harbour entrance.

Beware floating nets; They may be set in a circle about 100m in diameter around a central buoy and supported by small floats which are difficult to see.

Facilities

The better shops of the area are along La Manga and at Los Belones. Shopping elsewhere is basic. There are banks on La Manga (see Puerto de la Manga) Los Nietos and at La Union.

Communications

San Javier airfield, besides holding the Air Force Academy, handles charter flights during the summer. A light railway runs between Los Nietos, La Union and Cartagena (where the station is fairly close to the Continente hypermarket).

39. Puerto de Tomás Maestre

Entrance from the Mediterranean 37°44′.3N 00°43′.4W (between beacons of Los Escolletes).
Entrance from the Mar Menor 37°44′.5N 00°43′.8W

Charts

British Admiralty *1700*. Imray *M12*
French *4719, 7295*. Spanish *4710, 471*

⊕66 32°43′.2N 00°43′0W
⊕67 37°44′N 00°42′.8W
⊕68 37°45′N 00°45′W

Lights

Entrance from seawards
To the south
0136 **Cabo de Palos** Fl(2)10s81m23M Siren Mo(P)40s Grey round tower 51m
0139 **Isla Grosa** Fl.3s97m5M Red round tower 2m
0138 **Islote La Hormiga** Fl(3)14s24m8M White tower 12m
Entrance from seaward
0140 **Punta del Estacio** Fl(4)20s32m14M White tower, black bands 29m
0140.2 **Los Escolletes** Fl.2.5s7m3M Concrete tower 5m
Canal del Estacio
23954(S) **Buoy No.1** Fl.G.5s5M Green spar
23956(S) **Buoy No.1** Fl.R.5s5M Red spar
23956.1(S) **Buoy No.2** Fl(2)G.7s3M Green spar
23956.2(S) **Buoy No.2** Fl(2)R.7s3M Red spar
23956.3(S) **Buoy No.3** Fl(3)G.9s1M Green spar
23956.4(S) **Buoy No.3** Fl(3)R.9s1M Red spar
23956.5(S) **Buoy No.4** Fl(4)G.11s1M Green spar
23956.6(S) **Buoy No.4** Fl(4)R.11s1M Red spar
23956.7(S) **Buoy No.5** Fl.R.5s1M Red cylinder
23956.8(S) **Buoy No.6** Fl(2)R.7s1M Red cylinder
Mar Menor entrance
0140.5 **Dique N** Fl.R.5s7m3M Concrete tower 4m
0140.6 **Dique S** Fl.G.5s7m3M Concrete tower 4m.
Note that the entrance channel may be marked with small buoys in high season

Port communications

VHF Ch 9. *Capitanía* ☎ 968 14 08 16 *Fax* 968 33 70 89
Email puertomaestre@puertomaestre.com
www.puertomaestre.com

Tomás Maestre – canal, harbour, marinas

A modern marina has been built into the 1½ M long canal which connects the sea with the Mar Menor. In normal conditions approach and entrance are easy but because the area is shallow, entry should not be attempted in strong E or SE winds which kick up heavy seas. Facilities are good except that provision shops are limited. It forms a useful base for the exploration of the Mar Menor and as a staging point between the port of Cartagena and the harbours further N. Golf course and swimming pool nearby.

The entrance is now marked with pillar buoys and the entrance to the Mar Menor may be marked from June to October with red and green light buoys joined with floating ropes.

Approach from seaward

From the south Round the prominent and conspicuous Cabo de Palos at 200m off and follow the low-lying coast in a NNW direction at 1¼M. The narrow sand spit has wall-to-wall high-rise buildings along it with a small gap just before the approach to Tomas Maestre. The canal approach is 1M to NW of the off-shore Isla Grosa (95m).

From the north Cabo Roig is prominent and reddish in colour. It has a tower and some buildings above a small yacht harbour which lies on the S side of the cape. Two other small yacht harbours, which may be recognised, lie 1½M and 3M further S. Puerto de San Pedro del Pinatar is easily recognised by its high breakwater.

Follow the coast, which sprouts high rise buildings as Punta de Estacio is approached, in a SSE direction and at least ¼M offshore. Isla Grosa (95m) which is peaked should be easily recognised. Pass about half way between the island and Los Escolletes and then head N/NW for the entrance beacons. NE of Isla Grosa is the rock El Farallón and further out, a shoal of 1.3m – see charts. A shallow rocky spit sticks out a short distance south of Los Escolletes.

GPS approach

From the south steer to ⊕66 and from the north steer to ⊕67 and then steer to pass between the port and starboard buoys marking the canal entrance.

Anchorages in the approach

From the south Anchor to the west of Isla Grosa (see page 95).
From the north Anchor off Playa del Pudrimel (see page 109).
Outer harbour Anchorage (see note plan 34).

Canal Entrance

From seawards Having passed about halfway between Los Escolletes and Isla Grosa (coming from the north) or keeping Isla Grosa well to starboard (coming from the south) identify the two port and starboard buoys marking the entrance to the canal. Proceed on a west of north course to pass between the buoys and on through the outer harbour passing between a series of posts marking the narrow canal entrance. Passing the posts the channel bends round to a west-northwesterly course towards the swing bridge. Note that a falling barometer or an E sector winds can cause a two knot or more inflowing current; a rising barometer with W sector winds an outflowing current. The new lift bridge opens Monday to Friday at 1100 and 1700 and at 1100, 1400 and 1700 at weekends. The headroom is 7.5m when closed. Clients of the marina may call VHF Ch 9 or ☎ 968 14 07 25 at any time to have it opened. The canal continues for a further ½ mile past Tomás Maestre marina into the Mar Menor itself. In high season the channel into and out of the Mar Menor itself may be marked with two green and two red lightbuoys joined by floating ropes with small white floats attached.

From Mar Menor Straightforward between the pier heads but beware traffic.

Tomás Maestre marina from south

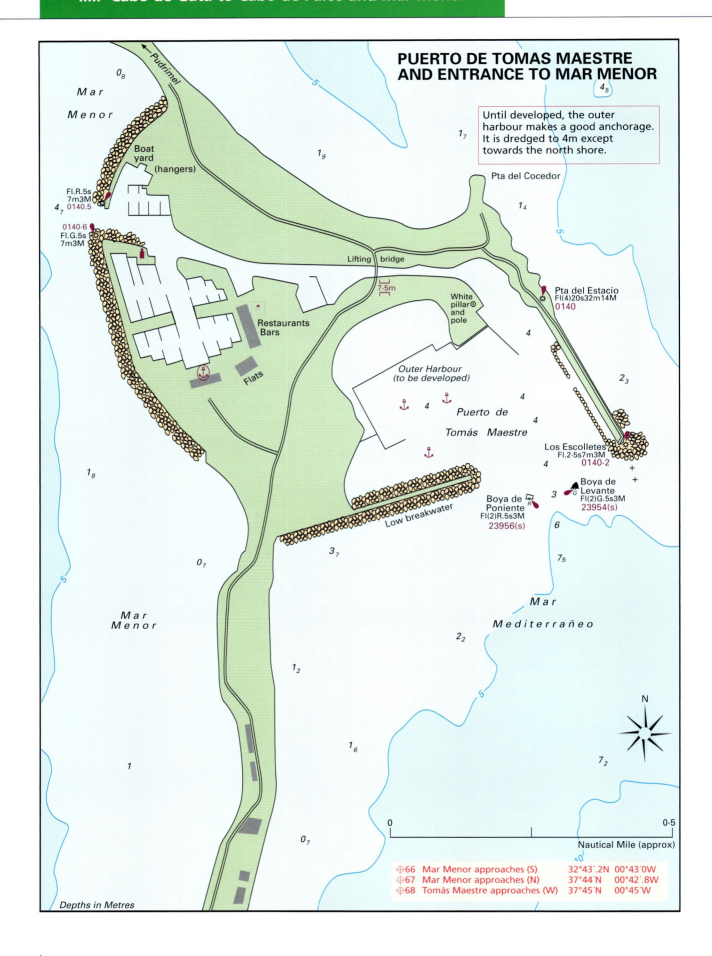

PUERTO DE TOMAS MAESTRE AND ENTRANCE TO MAR MENOR

Mar Menor

0·8

Pudrimel

4·5

1·7

Until developed, the outer harbour makes a good anchorage. It is dredged to 4m except towards the north shore.

Boat yard (hangers)

1·9

Pta del Cocedor

1·4

Fl.R.5s 7m3M
4·7 0140·5

0140·6
Fl.G.5s 7m3M

Lifting   bridge

7·5m

White pillar⊙ and pole

Pta del Estacio
Fl(4)20s32m14M
0140

Restaurants Bars

Flats

Outer Harbour (to be developed)

Puerto de

Tomás   Maestre

4

4

4

4

4

4

2·3

Los Escolletes
Fl.2·5s7m3M
0140·2

+
+

Boya de Levante
Fl(2)G.5s3M
23954(s)

3

Boya de Poniente
Fl(2)R.5s3M
23956(s)

6

Low breakwater

3·7

7·5

1·8

0·7

Mar Menor

Mar
Mediterraneo

2·2

1·2

1·6

N

7·2

1

0·7

0   0·5
Nautical Mile (approx)

⊕66 Mar Menor approaches (S)   32°43′.2N 00°43′0W
⊕67 Mar Menor approaches (N)   37°44′N   00°42′.8W
⊕68 Tomás Maestre approaches (W)   37°45′N   00°45′W

10

Depths in Metres

Tomás Maestre from the east

Marina Entrance

The yacht harbour is on the south side of the canal, opposite the workshop area which has conspicuous working hangars.

Berths

Normal stern-to berths are available. Usually someone is around to tell you where to go. Otherwise, make up where you can and if nobody moves you, go to the *capitanía* under the entrance archway (a long way from most of the marina) to confirm your location.

Charges

High in Summer, medium in winter.

Facilities

Maximum length overall: 22m.
Facilities for most types of repairs (the boatyard is expensive).
100-tonnes slipway.
50 and 15-tonne travel-hoists.
5-tonnes crane.
Chandlers (also provide gas and one which repairs sails).
Water on quays and pontoons.
Shower block on pontoon.
220 and 380V AC on pontoons and quays.
Ice on fuel quay or from office.
Gasoleo A and petrol (the fuelling jetty is at the entrance and may be an awkward lie if there is a current running in the canal).

Communications

☎ Area code 968. Taxis ☎ 56 30 39. There may be an hourly bus to La Manga for shopping.

40. Puerto de Dos Mares

37°40′N 00°44′.5W

Port communications
Club ☎/Fax 968 14 01 17

Shopping stop off
May be useful for shopping along La Manga. Limiting factors are a depth of about 1·9m and maximum length overall length of about 12m. It may pay to investigate by dinghy before entering.

Approach
There is no channel between Isla Sujeto and La Manga. Enter between the red and green buoys on the north side of the entrance, with 1.9m in the channel.

Berth
Bows to floating pontoons.

41. Puerto de la Manga

37°38′.8N 00°43′.6W

Lights
0140.7 **Breakwater head** Fl.R.6s5m Grey mast
0140.72 **Right bank** Fl.G.6s Grey mast

Port communications
Club Náutico la Isleta ☎/Fax 968 14 53 39
Email admin@nauticolaisleta.net

A private club
A private club where visitors are made welcome though not particularly encouraged. If in doubt about depths, a visit by dinghy would pay off.

The south and east sides of the harbour are beaches used for bathing.

Approach
The passage east of Isla Mayor should only be taken with local knowledge and there is no passage east of Isla del Sujeto. It is best to keep west of those two and of Redonda as well.

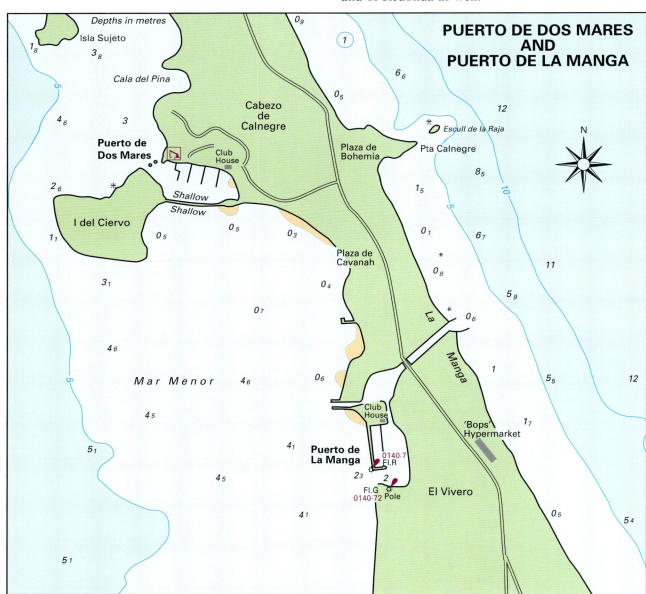

Puerto de la Manga

Entrance

Said to be 1·8m. Come in from the west. The harbour wall is marked 'Club Náutico La Isleta' and the entrance is at the southern end. Keep between the line of buoys, if placed (they are all likely to be small, red and spherical).

Berth

Bows-to piers.

Facilities

Maximum length overall: 12m.
Water and electricity at the berths.
The shops of La Manga: Bop's hypermarket, shops, banks at Plazas Cavanah and Bohemia.
Club Náutico La Isleta has a bar, showers and a part-time restaurant.
Do not pump ship in harbour.

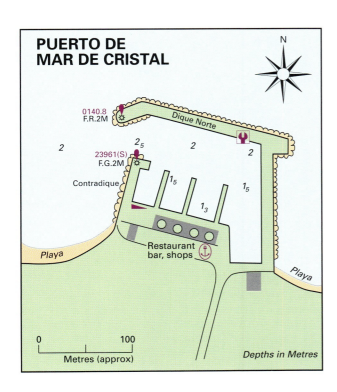

PUERTO DE MAR DE CRISTAL

0140.8 F.R.2M
Dique Norte
2
2 5
2
2
23961(S) F.G.2M
Contradique
1 5
1 5
1 3
Restaurant bar, shops
Playa
Playa
0   100
Metres (approx)
Depths in Metres

Puerto de Mar de Cristal

42. Puerto de Mar de Cristal

37°38′.7N 00°45′.7W

Lights

0140.8 **Breakwater head** F.R.4m Red and white round tower 5m
0140.75 **Contradique** F.G.4m White tower, green bands

Port communications

VHF Ch 9. ☎ 968 13 34 28 *Fax* 968 56 91 07

Small and shallow harbour

A small artificial harbour built as a part of a housing development and located on the SE corner of the Mar Menor. Easy to approach and enter. The facilities are limited.

Approach

In the NW, from the hill El Carmole (112m) and the tower of Los Urrutias the coast is almost straight, low and flat, and most is under cultivation. The village of Los Nietos, the harbours of Los Nietos and Islas Menores may be seen. In the SE, Punta de Plomo is low and has a lone house on it.

Entrance

When entering keep as far off-shore as is consistant with entering as the water shoals sharply near the shore.

Berths

The arrivals berth is alongside the North Wall, immediately to port on entering. If no room there, go alongside another boat and ask ashore.

Facilities

Maximum length overall: 10m.
Slipway in SW corner of the harbour.
Water on quays and pontoons.
220V AC points on quays and pontoons.
Club Náutico de Mar de Cristal.
Some shops in housing development.

III.i COSTA BLANCA

43. Puerto de las Islas Menores

37°38´.9N 00°46´.1W

Lights

0140.85 **Outer breakwater** F.G White tower, green bands
0140.851 **Breakwater head** F.R White tower, red bands

Port communications

Puerto ☎ 968 13 33 44
Email info@clubnauticoislasmenores.com

Small, shallow, private harbour

A small shallow private harbour suitable for dinghies, runabouts and small yachts. Easy to approach and enter. It has a palatial yacht club with associated facilities, but other facilities are limited. It is not a place for cruising yachts.

Approach

From the SE Punta de Plomo with a single large house can be identified as can the Puerto de Mar de Cristal ¾M further E. The harbour projects into the Mar Menor and its large clubhouse is conspicuous.

From the NW The low, flat and almost straight coast is relatively featureless with the exception of El Carmoli (112m) and the town of Los Urrutias, until the large yacht harbour Puerto de Los Nietos, which is conspicuous, is reached. ¾M beyond it lies the low Punta Lengua de Vaca and ½M beyond lies the Punta de Los Barrancones with the harbour on the point.

Anchorage in the approach

Anchor to suit draught to N of this harbour in sand and weed.

Puerto de las Islas Menores

Entrance

Straightforward but harbour shoals to 1m.

Berths

Secure to the inside of Dique del Norte and ask at yacht club for allocation of a berth.

Facilities

Maximum length overall: 8m.
Slipway at yacht club.
Small davit-type crane at head of Dique del Norte.
Water from yacht club.
Small shops near harbour.
The Club Náutico des Islas Menores has bar, restaurant and showers.

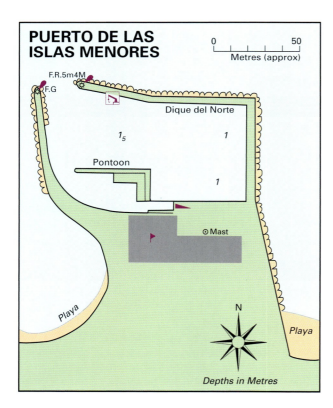

44. Puerto de los Nietos

37°39´.2N 00°47´W

Lights

0140.9 **Muelle Norte NW head** LFl.R.5s5m White tower, red bands 3m
0140.92 **Muelle Norte E corner** F.R.4m Grey post 4m
0140.95 **Contradique head** Iso.G.8s5m White tower, green bands 3m

Port communications

VHF Ch 4 or 9. *Capitanía* ☎ and *Fax* 968 56 07 37
Club Náutico de Los Nietos ☎ 968 13 33 00
Fax 968 13 36 40 *Email* puerto@cnlosnietos.com
www.cnlosnietos.com

Large yacht harbour

A large artificial yacht harbour. Yachts can winter ashore or afloat.

Approach

Pass between Islas Perdiguera and Mayor and head south. El Carmoli hill to the west will identify Los Urrutias. To the south, there is a small, dark wood, just east of the Rambla del Beal. Los Nietos is just east of the wood. The breakwater and masts will be seen as the coast is approached.

PUERTO DE LOS NIETOS

0 100 200
Metres (approx)

0140.9
LFl.R.5s 3
0140.95
Oc.G.3·5s

Shallow

Contradique

Muelle Norte

0140.92
F.R

Control

2_5

1_5

1_5

1_5

1_5

0_5

0_5

0_5

0_5

Muelle Este

Nets

Works

Shallow

Bridge

Shallow

N

Depths in Metres
Sketch plan

Anchorage in the approach

Anchorage is possible in sand and weed anywhere to N of this harbour to suit draught.

Entrance

Approach the head of the Muelle Norte on a S heading. There may be a line of multi-coloured buoys to leave to starboard. Do not go inshore of the harbour entrance as the water shoals quickly.

Berths

Secure alongside the Muelle de Espera, immediately to port on entry (go alongside another if necessary) and ask at the office. Alternatively, call on Ch 9 or 4 before entering.

Charges

Low.

Facilities

Maximum length overall: 15m.
Slipway at the NE side of yacht club.
An 8-tonne crane at NE corner of the harbour.
A 28-tonne mobile crane.
Hardstanding for winter lay-ups.
Water taps on quays and pontoons (but tastes funny).
220V AC points on quays and pontoons.
Club Náutico de Los Nietos, ☎ 968 13 33 00, has a restaurant open at weekends, bar, showers and washing machine.
Supermarkets, ferretarías with gas, Post Office, butcher, baker, bank etc. at Los Belones, 2½km SE.
Bank without a cash point.

Communications

Light railway to Cartagena (where the station is close to the hypermarket Continente). ☎ Area code 968.

Puerto de los Nietos

45. Puerto de los Urrutias

37°40′.6N 00°49′.3W

Lights
0140.97 **Dique de Levante head** F.G
0140.972 **Breakwater head** F.R

Port communications
VHF Ch 9. Club de Regatas Mar Menor
☎/Fax 968 13 44 38
Email informacion@clubregatasmarmenor.com
www.clubregatasmarmenor.com

Easy approach but shallow

The harbour lies at the SE end of the village of Urrutias which is underneath the odd-shaped El Carmoli hill. Easy to approach and enter. Spanish holiday village with a good beach to the N of the harbour.

PUERTO DE LOS URRUTIAS

N

2

2

2

2

Bn
WG

0140·972
F.R

2

F.G
0140·97

3

R

Depths in metres

Sketch plan

III.i COSTA BLANCA

Puerto de los Urrutias

Approach

From the north Past the airport and Los Alcázares. There is a conspicuous hangar-type building before the village and the yacht club is the last major building.

From the south Urrutias lies 2.5M NW of Puerto de los Nietos.

Anchorage

N or S of entrance to suit draught in sand and weed.

Berths

Secure to east wall and ask at the club secretary's office.

Charges

High.

Facilities

Maximum length overall: 15m.
Slipway by crane.
10-tonne crane.
Water taps on pontoons and quays.
220V AC on pontoons and quays.
A few shops in the village, street-market every Thursday.
Club de Regatas Mar Menor has a restaurant, bar, showers and washroom.
Dinghy sailing school.

Communications

☎ Area code 968.

⚓ ISLA PERDIGUERA

Anchor to the SW in 4m sand and mud. Beach bars ashore at weekends.

46. Puerto de los Alcázares

37°44′N 00°50′.9W

Lights

0141.3 **Dique Este head** Fl(3)G.16.5s4M White tower, green top
0141.4 **Dique Oeste** Fl(2)R.14s4M White tower, red top

Port communications

Club Náutico los Alcazares VHF Ch 9 ☎ 968 57 51 29
Fax 968 57 43 16 *Email* cnautico@cnmarmenor.es
www.cnmarmenor.es

Shallow harbour

A shoal (2m or less), artificial yacht harbour alongside an attractive old Victorian-type seaside resort, least touched by mass tourism. Easy to approach and enter. The coast is lined with many piers and shelters of various sizes to enable the inhabitants to fish and bathe. The nearby Aeropuerto de San Javier, its associated harbour and a large amount of land around are part of the Spanish Naval Air Academy and should not be entered.

Approach

From the SE Follow the low flat coast in a NE–N direction. The town of Los Urrutias and El Carmoli (112m), a conical hill, will be recognised. Further E a light aircraft field and a camp site may be seen. Just S of this harbour is a long pier and some large old hangars. The houses of the town of Los Alcázares will be seen from afar.

Puerto de los Alcázares

From the NE The large town of Santiago de la Ribera and the Aeropuerto de San Javier, which has a large shallow harbour alongside (entrance forbidden), will be easily recognised. Punta Galera and Punta de las Olas are not easily identified. The town of Los Alcázares can be seen from afar.

Anchorage in the approach

Anchor off the harbour in suitable depth to suit draught in sand and weed.

Entrance

Approach the head of Dique Este on a course between W and NNW. A line of white buoys parallel to the military espigón marks the boundary of the no-go area; leave them to port.

Berths

Go alongside the pier immediately opposite the entrance and ask at the office.

Facilities

Maximum length overall: 15m.
Simple repairs possible.
Two slipways and a crane at E corner of the harbour.
Water taps on quays and pontoons.
220V AC points on quays and pontoons.
Many shops in the town including supermarket and a large market.
The Club Náutico de Mar Menor at N corner of harbour has limited facilities but they include open-air showers and a bar.

Communications

Excellent and regular buses to Alicante, Cartagena. Coaches to Bilbao, Madrid, Barcelona. ☎ Area code 968.

⚓ PUERTO SANTIAGO DE RIBERA

An open anchorage off a large town serving the air base and the air port and with tourist interests. The *club náutico* has a pier for small boats.

47. Puerto de Lo Pagan

37°49′N 00°47′W

Lights

24016.4(S) **Entrance buoy** Fl(2)G.7s Lateral starboard
24016.5(S) **Entrance buoy** Fl(2)R.7s Lateral port
0141.45 **Dique head** Fl(4)G.9.5s Green mast
0141.455 **Contradique head** F.R. Red post

Port Communications

Club náutico ☎ 968 18 69 69 *Fax* 968 18 69 58
Email info@clubnauticolopagan.com
www.clubnauticolopagan.com

New marina but shallow

A new marina has been developed over the last few years off Lo Pagan at the north end of the Mar Menor. It has berths for about 350 craft and has reasonable shore side facilities of fuel, cranage and a slip. The water is very shallow at the north end of the Mar Menor and there are buoys to indicate the 'deep' entrance channel which is understood to be 1.8 metres, but great care should be exercised in the approach with constant attention paid to the echo-sounder.

Berths

It is essential to call ahead to enquire whether there is a berth available for your vessel, as there are only 20 berths allocated for visitors and these are mostly taken in the high season.

Facilities

All facilities are available for the yachtsman and there is reasonable shopping in the nearby town of Lo Pagan. Close by is the 'Parque Regional de las Salinas' which is an important wetlands area which is of great interest to birdwatchers. Note however, that if one does not wish to enter the Mar Menor, Puerto de San Pedro del Pinatar (see below) is but three kilometres to the east and is also close to this park.

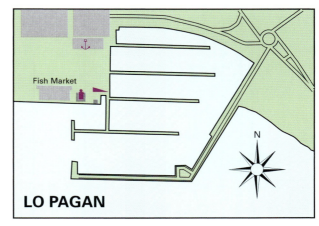

Club Nautico Lo Pagan

III.ii Puerto de San Pedro del Pinatar to Dénia

C. de San Antonio
101 Dénia ●
0180
See p.158 Fl(4)20s175m26M
94
100 Jávea ●
92 Cabo de la Nao
See p.151 0176
69 Moraira ● Fl.5s122m23M
91
0175·2
67 Calpe ●
65 Marina Greenwich Fl(4)R.10s8m3M
See p.145 89
62 Altea ● Pta Ifach
64 Mary Montaña
Pta del Albir
See p.142 Fl(3)27s112m15M
Benidorm 0173·6
60 Villajoyosa ●
Islote Benidorm
Fl.5s60m6M 0172
30
30′
59 Campello ●
Pta del Río
Fl.G.3s8m4M
0167
58 Pto de
San Juan C de la Huerta
57 ALICANTE
0166 80
Fl(5)19s38m14M
See p.137
55 Pto Espato ●
C de Santa Pola
FFl(2+1)20s152m
F11/Fl16M 0152
54 Santa Pola I.de Tabarca Q(3)10s
Oc(2)10s
29m15M BYB
0148 78
53 Pto de Guardamar ●
(105) Oc.R.1·5s443m15M
Radio mast & 7F.R(vert)
0147
38° 52 Torrevieja ●
N C. Cervera
Fl.G.4s15m7M
0146
51 Pto de Cabo Roig
50 Campoamor ●
74
49 La Horadada
48 San Pedro
del Pinatár *See p.109*
30
Fl(4)G.12s13m4M 0141·5
Mar
Menor Pta del Estacio
Fl(4)20s32m14M 0140
FL(3)14s24m8M 0138
Islas Hormigas
Fl(5)Y.20s
65

COASTAL WAYPOINT LIST

⊕			
⊕65	ENE of Islas Hormigas	37°40′N	00°35′.5W
⊕74	Cabo Roig	37°55′N	00°41′W
⊕78	Off Islas de Tarbarca	38°09′N	00°25′W
⊕80	Cabo de las Huertas	38°21′N	00°22′.5W
⊕89	Peñon de Ifach	38°37′N	00°06′·5E
⊕91	Pta de Moraira	38°39′.5N	00°11′.5E
⊕100	Cabo de la Nao	38°44′N	00°16′E
⊕102	Cabo de San Antonio	38°48′N	00°13′E

40′ 20′ 0°W

N

PORTS

48. Puerto de San Pedro del Pinatar

37°49´.2N 00°45´.3W

Charts

British Admiralty *1700*. Imray *M12*
French *7295, 4719*. Spanish *471, 4710*

⊕70 37°49´.2N 00°44´.9W

Lights

0141.5 **Dique Norte** Fl(4)G.12s13m4M Green post 3m
0141.6 **Dique Sur** Fl(4)R.12s6m3M Grey mast 3m
0141.8 **C.N. San Pedro Dique head** Fl.G.2s4m1M Green post 3m
0141.9 **C.N. San Pedro contradique** Fl.R.2s4m3M Red post 3m

Port communications

C.N. Villa San Pedro ☎ 968 18 26 78 *Fax* 968 18 25 00
Email info@clubnauticovillasanpedro.com
www.clubnauticovillasanpedro.com
Marina de las Salinas ☎ 619 274 932 or 676 388 790

Two modern marinas

A 400-berth marina at San Pedro del Pinatar, which was built in the inner part of the harbour in 2001/2, has now been fully completed. There are four pontoons extending from the Dique Norte and a new quay has been built to virtually enclose the inner harbour. At the entrance to the new marina there is a 2.5m green post F.G to starboard and a 2·5m red post F.R to port. The visitors' berth is

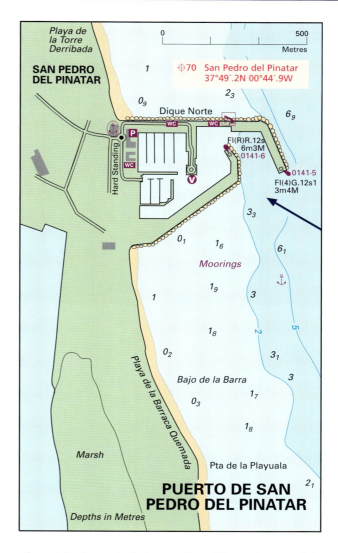

PUERTO DE SAN PEDRO DEL PINATAR

alongside the end of the starboard-hand jetty and is reported to have a depth of at least 1.5m. The 2004 visit saw all shoreside facilities completed and San Pedro is now a fully working marina with all the usual facilities. There is a nice club, a small restaurant, a subaqua school, tennis and small shops all on site. However, out of season stores would probably have to be obtained in either the village or Lo Pagan which is some way away from the marina.

There is now a brand new marina, Marina de las Salinas, in the SW part of the harbour. There are all the usual buildings but mostly empty in early 2008 as clearly this is not yet a fully operational marina although about 60% of the berths are sold and occupied. The maximum length appears to be about 25m. A smart Capitania is built on the south wall while restaurant and shops will be sited on the west wall.

Note that this marina should not be confused with the Marina Salinas in Torreviejo some nine miles up the coast!

Approach

The high breakwater of Puerto de San Pedro del Pinatar can be seen from afar (and is a useful coastal mark).

III.ii **COSTA BLANCA**

San Pedro del Pinatar looking W and note there is a new marina constructed in the SW darsena

From the south Follow the coast up from Punta del Estacio. Development along the sand strip bordering the Mar Menor dies away before the harbour is reached.

From the north Pass Punta de la Torre de la Horadada which has a tower on the point with buildings at its base and yacht harbour on its S side. There is a rocky reef off this head; keep at least 200m off. From there on, keep half a mile off-shore to avoid small rocky islets.

GPS approach

Steer to ⊕70 from the eastern sector and steer for the end of the breakwater (approximately 0.13M).

Entrance

Approach the end of the Dique Norte on a westerly heading rounding the head at 30m, keeping a close watch for fishing vessels leaving the harbour. Steer west of north and round the head of the Dique Sur keeping reasonably close to the Dique Norte. Steer south through the outer harbour, turning to starboard at the end of the internal quay.

Berths

Having entered the harbour moor to the end of the internal quay and enquire at the fuel berth or at the *capitanía* in the NW corner of the marina for berth availability. It is not possible to say anything about the berthing in the new Marina de las Salinas at the time of going to press but updates will be issued as soon as details become clearer.

Facilities

Maximum length 15 metres.
30-ton travel-hoist and crane.
Electricity and water at all berths.
Fuel.
Showers, WC and rubbish bins.
Club náutico
Bar and small shops for essentials.

49. Puerto de la Horadada

37°52′N 00°45′.5W

Charts

British Admiralty *1700*. Imray *M12*
French *7295, 4719*. Spanish *471*
⊕71 37°51′·8N 00°45′·3W

Lights

0142 **Dique de Levante head** Fl(3)G.10s8m4M Green and white column 6m
0143 **Inner spur head** Fl(3)G.10s9m4M Green and white column 6m
0143.5 **Contradique head** Fl(2)R.7s9m4M Red and white column 6m
24090(S) **Channel outer buoy** Fl.G.2s1M Green conical buoy
24091(S) **Channel outer buoy** Fl.R.2s1M Red cylindrical buoy

Port communications

Club Nautico ☎ 966 76 90 87 *Fax* 966 76 96 69
Email cnth@clubnauticotorrehoradada.com
www.clubnauticotorrehoradada.com

Shallow approaches to yacht harbour

A yacht harbour established in an old fishing anchorage to S of Punta de la Horadada. It is well-protected from all directions except S. Swell between W and S can make the approach dangerous as the water is shallow but otherwise it is easy to approach and enter. Facilities are limited.

Approach

The approach to this harbour is shallow and strangers should sound their way in.

From the south The long, low 10M-long sand strip that separates the Mar Menor from the sea is unmistakable as is Isla Grosa (95m) and the breakwater of the harbour of San Pedro del Pinatar. Between Pinatar and Horadada, 3M north, give the coast a ½M berth to avoid rocky islets. The Torre de la Horadada on a low promontory has buildings at its foot and is conspicuous. It has a rocky reef with exposed heads extending 150m off it. In the approach, the harbour walls will be seen.

From the north Between the large harbour of Torrevieja and Punta de la Horadada the coast is only moderately high with rocky cliffs in places. The small promontory of Punta Primo (or Delgada) lies between Torrevieja and Cabo Roig. Cabo Roig is of reddish sandstone and is prominent with a white tower and buildings on its summit. A small yacht harbour lies on the S side of Cabo Roig and another lies to the S of Punta El Cuervo which is to S of Cabo Roig. There are a number of small rocks and islets offshore along this section of coast and a berth of ½ M is advised. The Torre de la Horadada is conspicuous from the north and has a reef extending some 150m to the NNE.

GPS approach

Steer to ⊕71 from the eastern sector and steer for the end of the breakwater (approximately 0.15M).

Entrance

From a position 200m to S of the harbour entrance, approach sounding continuously. Red and green channel buoys to the SW of the entrance now define the beginning of the entrance channel. About 50m from the entrance change to a NW course. Give the inner spur head at least 25m berth as rocks extend 10m west of it. Note the entrance frequently silts up, especially after SW winds and the depth is often less than the 2.5m shown on the plan. Great care must be exercised with constant sounding on entry.

Berths

Secure to the first pontoon and ask at the *capitanía*.

Charges

Low.

Facilities

Maximum length overall: 12m.
Small slipway in the NW corner of the harbour with 1m off it.
5-tonne crane to starboard side of the entrance and a large mobile crane.
Engine mechanics – Volvo agency.
Water taps on quays and pontoons.
Showers and WC.
220V AC points on quays and pontoons.
Some shops in the village.
Gasoleo A and petrol.

Communications

Coastal bus service on main road. ☎ Area code 96.

⊕71 Puerto de la Horadada
37°51´.85N 00°45´.3W

Puerto de la Horadada

III.ii **COSTA BLANCA**

50. Puerto de Campoamor (Dehesa de Campoamor)

37°53´.9N 00°45´.9W

Charts

British Admiralty *1700*. Imray *M12*
French *4719*. Spanish *471*

⊕72 37°53´.8N 00°44´.7W

Lights

0144 **Espigón Este** Iso.G.4s8m4M Green metal mast,
    white bands 6m
0144.2 **Contradique head** Iso.R.4s8m3M Red metal mast,
    white bands 6m

Buoys

Two small green conical buoys mark submerged rocks
    200m off the root of the *contradique*

Port communications

VHF Ch 9. Club Náutico de Campoamor ☎ 965 32 03 86
Fax 965 32 03 88
Email cncampoamor@cncampoamor.com
www.cncampoamor.com

⊕72 Puerto de Campoamor 37°53´.8N 00°44´.7W

Harbour mainly for motor boats

A yacht harbour built primarily for motor boaters
on the site of an old anchorage. It is organised as a
residential club; there are a few berths for transit
yachts but visitors who stay for any length of time
may be expected to join the club, if found
acceptable. Approach and entrance are not difficult
but care must be taken as it is shallow. Facilities in
the harbour and village cater for normal requests.
Swell from S–SW tends to enter the harbour. Fine
sandy beaches.

Approach

From the south The high breakwater of Puerto de
San Pedro del Pinatar is conspicuous. The low coast,
which should be given a berth of ½M or more to
avoid isolated patches of rocks and rocky islets,
stretches as far as the Punta de la Horadada which
has a *torre* with a building at its foot. The coast
further N has low cliffs. Punta El Cuervo, which has
a shoal 50m off its eastern edge, is inconspicuous
unlike the high-rise apartment blocks behind Puerto
de Campoamor.

From the north The large Puerto de Torrevieja is
easily recognised. The coast to the S should be given
a ½M berth due to off-lying dangers; this coastline
has low rocky sandstone cliffs. Cabo Roig which is
of a reddish colour has a tower on its summit and a
small yacht harbour lies on its S side. Puerto de
Campoamor lies just under 2M to S. There is a
shallow river valley just to N of the harbour.

GPS approach

Steer to ⊕72 from the southeastern quadrant and
steer for the end of the breakwater (approximately
0.15M).

Entrance

Keep well away from the harbour walls until the
heads of the two *diques* are in line on approximately
320° and then approach, sounding. There is a shoal
patch (0.3m) 500m SSE of the harbour, on a line

with the entrance of approximately 157°–337°.
When 50m away, divert to port and then round the
head of Dique de Levante.

Berths

Secure to the outer pontoon and ask at the control
office in a hut on the centre pontoon or at the yacht
club if no one is in the office.

Facilities

Maximum length overall: 20m.
Small hardstanding.
Slipway in the W corner of the harbour.
3-tonne crane also in the W corner of the harbour.
Water taps on the quays and pontoons.
220V AC points on quays and pontoons.
Gasoleo A and petrol.
Supermarket in the village.
Club Náutico de Campoamor on the W side of the
    harbour has a bar, showers etc.

Communications

Bus service on the main road. ☎ Area code 96.

Campoamor

51. Puerto de Cabo Roig

37°54′N 00°43′W

Charts

British Admiralty *1700*. Imray *M12*
French *4719*. Spanish *471*

⊕73 37°54′.6N 00°43′.7W

Lights

0145 **Dique de Levante head** Fl(2)G.5.5s9m4M Green and white pole 6m
0145.5 **Contradique head** Fl(2)R.7s8m4M Red and white pole
Inland to the North
0147 **Guardamar del Segura** 38°04′.4N 00°39′.7W, Aero, Oc.R.1.5s443m15M and 7F.R(vert).

Port communications

VHF Ch 9. *Capitanía* ☎/*Fax* 966 76 01 76
Email info@marinacaboroig.com
www.marinacaboroig.com

⊕73   Puerto de Cabo Roig
      37°54′.6N 00°43′.7W

Pleasant small yacht harbour

A small, attractive yacht harbour at a well-established anchorage, only open to the SW. It is tucked away on the W side of Cabo Roig which is entirely given over to low-rise, detached buildings and gardens. The beach to the N is buoyed-off for swimmers. Inshore there is a small village at some distance which has everyday supplies. There is a castle nearby, sand and pebble beaches either side of the harbour and a golf course at Villamartin, 5M.

Approach

From the south From Puerto de San Pedro del Pinatar the coast northwards should be given a ½M berth as there are islets and submerged rocks. Puerto de Torre de la Horadada can be recognised by the tower and buildings on the top of the point of the same name. From here low rocky cliffs stretch 2M to Punta El Cuervo where there is another yacht harbour, Puerto de Campoamor, backed by a group of high-rise apartment buildings. 1½M further along the coast to N is the reddish sandstone Cabo Roig with a large white tower surrounded by trees and villas. The harbour is to SW of the point below the tower.

From the north The Bahía de Santa Pola is 14M wide. The coast is low in the N half and has low rocky cliffs in the S. Sierra de Callosa (547m), 11½M to WNW of Guardarmar, a town on the coast 5M to N of Cabo Cervera, is a good landmark as is the radio mast at Guardamar del Segura. The breakwaters of Puerto de Torrevieja and the town of the same name are conspicuous. 2M to S of this harbour is Punta Prima (or Delgada) which has rocky cliffs and 2M further on is the prominent Cabo Roig which has a white tower on its summit. The harbour lies SW of the tower.

GPS approach

Steer to ⊕73 from the southern sector and steer for the end of the breakwater, sounding carefully (approximately 0.1M).

Entrance

Sand often builds up off the head of the Dique de Levante and it is wise to give it a good 30 metre berth. There may be a small green buoy near the end of the dique, which signals the extent of the accumulated sand. Care must be exercised on entry with constant sounding recommended.

Puerto de Cabo Roig during reconstruction

III.ii **COSTA BLANCA**

Berths

Secure to a pontoon T-piece and ask at the *capitanía* or the *club náutico*.

Facilities

Maximum length overall: 12m.
Slipway on NE side of the harbour – 1.5m of water off it.
1-tonne crane beside the slipway.
Water taps on quays and pontoons.
220V AC points on quays and pontoons.
Supermarket in village.
Club Náutico de Cabo Roig has all normal facilities.

Communications

Bus service on main road 1M inland to Torrevieja.
☎ Area code 96.

52. Puerto de Torrevieja

37°58′.3N 00°41′.2W

Charts

British Admiralty *1544, 1700.* Imray *M12*
French *4719, 6515.* Spanish *4710*

⊕75 37°57′.5N 00°41′.1W

Lights

0146 **Dique de Levante head** Fl.G.4s15m7M Octagonal
    tower 10m
0146.2 **Muelle de la Sal** Fl(3)R.11.5s11m2M Metal
    framework tower 6m
0146.3 **Pontoon head** F.R
0146.4 **Dársena Pesquera breakwater NW head**
    Fl(2)G.7s4m2M Green structure 3m
0146.6 **Club Náutico jetty E head** Fl(4)R.11s4m2M Red
    column 3m
To the north
0148 **Isla de Tabarca** Oc(2)10s29m15M White tower 14m
Inland to the north
0147 **Guardamar del Segura**, Aero Oc.R.1.5s 443m15M
    and 7F.R(vert)
24170a(s) 37°58′.3N 0°41′.4W Buoy Fl.R.6s Red (This buoy
    signals the construction work going on to build a new
    jetty for the fishing fleet)

Port communications

VHF Ch 06, 11, 14.
Real Club Nautico de Torrevieja ☎ 965 71 01 12
Fax 965 71 08 82 *Email* info@rcnt.com www.rcnt.com
Marina Internacional de Torrevieja SA, ☎ 965 71 36 50
Fax 965 71 42 66 *Email* info@rcnt.com
Marina Salinas ☎/*Fax* 965 709 701
Email info@marinasalinas.com www.marinasalinas.com

Useful major harbour

A nice clean harbour with some good yacht berths on pontoons, a good yacht club and an excellent anchorage west of the marina (rare along the coast), but where yachts have sometimes been banned by the harbourmaster. This has been challenged by the local yachtsmen but it seems to be a general feature all along this stretch of coast which comes under the jurisdiction of Valencia. The yacht harbour, Marina Internacional de Torrevieja SA is on the northwest side of the harbour. The commercial quay, Muelle de la Sal, handles large quantities of salt. The approach and entrance are simple and there is good shelter from winds except those from S to SW which make parts of the harbour uncomfortable. There is now a new marina, Marina Salinas, in the SE corner of the harbour which should be fully operational in the 2008 season. It has 700-odd berths and should be a great benefit to yachtsmen on this crowded coast.

The town is of no great interest but it has several restaurants and there are shops quite close to the harbour. A visit to the saltworks, the 'Salt Cellar of the World', is of interest. Good beaches on either side of the harbour.

Approach

From the south Isla Grosa (95m), off the breakwater of Puerto de Tomás Maestre and near the centre of the 10M building strip separating Mar Menor from the sea, is unmistakable as is the high breakwater of

Torrevieja new marina Capitania

Capitania at Marina Torrevieja

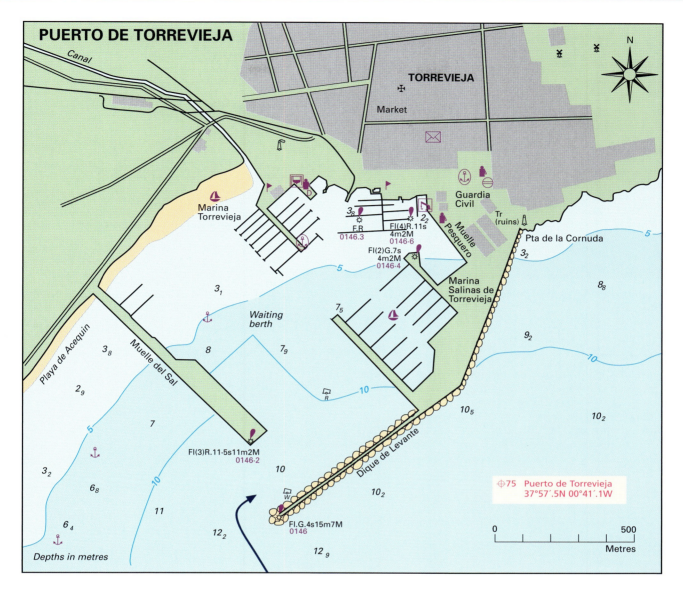

PUERTO DE TORREVIEJA

Canal

TORREVIEJA

Market

Marina
Torrevieja

Guardia
Civil

F.R
0146.3

Fl(4)R.11s
4m2M
0146·6

Fl(2)G.7s
4m2M
0146·4

Muelle
Pesquero

Tr
(ruins)

Pta de la Cornuda

Marina
Salinas de
Torrevieja

Waiting
berth

Playa de Acequin

Muelle del Sal

Fl(3)R.11·5s11m2M
0146·2

Dique de Levante

⊕75 Puerto de Torrevieja
37°57′.5N 00°41′.1W

Fl.G.4s15m7M
0146

0   500

Metres

Depths in metres

Puerto San Pedro del Pinatar. The following three promontories all have yacht harbours on their S sides: Punta de la Torre de la Horadada with a tower on the point and buildings around its base; Punta El Cuervo which has a group of high-rise buildings; and the reddish-coloured Cabo Roig which has a white tower. Keep at least ½M off the coast. From Punta Prima (or Delgada) the rocky cliffs fall away to a low, flat coast near Torrevieja. The breakwaters and town of Torrevieja are visible from afar though quite well inset from Cabo Cervera.

From the north Cross the wide Bahía de Santa Pola which has cliffs in its S part. The Sierra de Callosa (547m) 11½M to WNW of the town of Guardamar and the radio mast at Guardamar del Segura are useful marks. Cabo Cervera is prominent but low; to S of it are several smaller rocky points with coves between. The harbour breakwaters appear when these points have been rounded.

GPS approach

Steer to ⊕75 from the southeastern quadrant and steer for the end of the breakwater (approximately 0.4M).

Anchorage in the approach

Anchor just west of the Muelle Sal to suit draught but keeping out of the way of the harbour entrance.

Entrance

Straightforward but fishing boats move at speed and, at night, often without lights. Their wash can make the outer berths at the marina uncomfortable.

Berths

Go the Marina Torrevieja Marina Salinas or The Réal Club Náutico de Torrevieja on the north side of the fishing harbour. The pontoons at the root of the Muelle de Sal are for small craft only as they are in very shallow water.

III.ii COSTA BLANCA

Club Nautico (on right of photo) and marina Torrevieja moorings

Anchoring

It is hoped that anchoring will remain available between the Muelle de Sal and the marina but it is essential to keep well clear of the salt ships' manoeuvring area and expect to pay a small charge for anchoring. As of 2007 it was stated that anchoring is now prohibited west of the Marina International but several large yachts were anchored there during a 2007 visit.

Facilities

Maximum length overall: 40m.
Repairs and technical service area, contact yacht club for advice.
Slipway alongside the yacht club and a large one near root of Dique de Levante.
80-tonne travel-lift.
Cranes up to 12 tonnes.
Chandlery – Network Yacht & Rigging Services (run by an English couple) have a well stocked shop between the International Marina and the Club Nautico Marina. There is another chandler in the town and also one outside of town on the road to Cartagena.
Water taps on the pontoon and on the quay.
220V AC points on pontoons.
Gasoleo A and petrol.
Ice from factory near customs office or from club.
The Réal Club Náutico de Torrevieja has good facilities including bar, restaurants, lounges, terraces and showers. Visitors are made welcome.
Good shops and small market in the town.
Supermarket in street behind the garage on the N side of the main road in town.
Launderette in the marina or two streets back from the *club náutico*.

Communications

Rail and bus services. ☎ Area code 96.
Taxi ☎ 571 22 77.

53. Marina de las Dunas (Puerto Guardamar)

38°06′.5N 00°38′.6W

Charts

British Admiralty *1700*. Imray *M12*
French *4719*. Spanish *472, 4721*

⊕76 38°06′·7N 00°38′·0E

Lights

0147 **Guardamar del Segura** , Aero, Oc.R.1.5s443m15M and 7F.R(vert). Antenna white and red bands 440m (light is 2.5M S and 0.5M inland of marina)
0147.5 **S Breakwater head** Fl(3)R.9s8m5M Red tower 5m
0147.2 **Interior elbow** Fl(4)R.11s4m1M Red column 3m
0147.51 **N Breakwater head** Fl(3)G.9s5m3M Green tower 5m
0147.52 **Middle breakwater head** Fl(4)G.11s5m1M Green tower on white base 5m
0147.53 **Centre** Fl.G.5s4m1M Green column 3m
0147.54 **W of Fish Wharf** QG.4m1M Green column 3m
0147.55 **Fish Wharf W head** QG.4m1M Green column 3m
0147.7 **Starboard hand entrance** Fl(2+1)G.21s6m1M Green tower, red band, white base 4m
0147.72 **Port hand entrance** Fl.R.5s6m1M Red tower on white base 4m
Buoys A number of small yellow and white buoys mark the 3m channel into the marina.

Port communications

VHF Ch 9. *Capitanía* ☎ 966 72 65 49 *Fax* 966 72 67 41
Email info@marinadelasdunas.com

Quiet sheltered marina

The mouth of the Río Segura has been widened and a channel dug to the south of the old river mouth to give access to a 500-berth marina. The land approach is to the NW corner where a new road leads to the town of Guardamar – about 1km away.

The marina is fully operational with a café and some small shops.

Approach

From the south The large harbour and town of Torrevieja is easily recognised. To N of this harbour are a series of points with small *calas* between, the coast being rocky cliffs. The coast from Cabo Cervera to N is low and sandy. The town of Guardamar, which has a ruined castle, lies 1M to S of the mouth of the Río Segura which has rocky breakwaters. The radio mast Guardamar del Segura is 4½M to NNW of Cabo Cervera.

From the north Cross the Bahía de Santa Pola from Cabo de Santa Pola on a SW course leaving Isla de Tabarca to port and Puerto de Santa Pola to starboard, both of which are easily identified. 2½M to N of Río Segura is the Torre del Pinet off which at 2M ESE lies a fish farm. The coast is low and sandy.

GPS approach

Steer to ⊕76 from the eastern sector and steer for between the breakwaters (approximately 0.21M).

Entrance

Although the entrance has been dredged to 6m between the breakwaters it is liable to silting. Approach the mouth of the river, half way between